TREATING
COMPASSION
FATIGUE

BRUNNER-ROUTLEDGE PSYCHOSOCIAL STRESS SERIES
Charles R. Figley, Ph.D., Series Editor

1. *Stress Disorders among Vietnam Veterans*, Edited by Charles R. Figley, Ph.D.
2. *Stress and the Family Vol. 1: Coping with Normative Transitions*, Edited by Hamilton I. McCubbin, Ph.D., and Charles R. Figley, Ph.D.
3. *Stress and the Family Vol. 2: Coping with Catastrophe*, Edited by Charles R. Figley, Ph.D., and Hamilton I. McCubbin, Ph.D.
4. *Trauma and Its Wake: The Study and Treatment of Post-Traumatic Stress Disorder*, Edited by Charles R. Figley, Ph.D.
5. *Post-Traumatic Stress Disorder and the War Veteran Patient*, Edited by William E. Kelly, M.D.
6. *The Crime Victim's Book, Second Edition*, By Morton Bard, Ph.D., and Dawn Sangrey.
7. *Stress and Coping in Time of War: Generalizations from the Israeli Experience*, Edited by Norman A. Milgram, Ph.D.
8. *Trauma and Its Wake Vol. 2: Traumatic Stress Theory, Research, and Intervention*, Edited by Charles R. Figley, Ph.D.
9. *Stress and Addiction*, Edited by Edward Gottheil, M.D., Ph.D., Keith A. Druley, Ph.D., Steven Pashko, Ph.D., and Stephen P. Weinsteinn, Ph.D.
10. *Vietnam: A Casebook*, By Jacob D. Lindy, M.D., in collaboration with Bonnie L. Green, Ph.D., Mary C. Grace, M.Ed., M.S., John A. MacLeod, M.D., and Louis Spitz, M.D.
11. *Post-Traumatic Therapy and Victims of Violence*, Edited by Frank M. Ochberg, M.D.
12. *Mental Health Response to Mass Emergencies: Theory and Practice*, Edited by Mary Lystad, Ph.D.
13. *Treating Stress in Families*, Edited by Charles R. Figley, Ph.D.
14. *Trauma, Transformation, and Healing: An Integrative Approach to Theory, Research, and Post-Traumatic Therapy*, By John P. Wilson, Ph.D.
15. *Systemic Treatment of Incest: A Therapeutic Handbook*, By Terry Trepper, Ph.D., and Mary Jo Barrett, M.S.W.
16. *The Crisis of Competence: Transitional Stress and the Displaced Worker*, Edited by Carl A. Maida, Ph.D., Norma S. Gordon, M.A., and Norman L. Farberow, Ph.D.
17. *Stress Management: An Integrated Approach to Therapy*, By Dorothy H. G. Cotton, Ph.D.
18. *Trauma and the Vietnam War Generation: Report of the Findings from the National Vietnam Veterans Readjustment Study*, By Richard A. Kulka, Ph.D., William E. Schlenger, Ph.D., John A. Fairbank, Ph.D., Richard L. Hough, Ph.D., B. Kathleen Jordan, Ph.D., Charles R. Marmar, M.D., Daniel S. Weiss, Ph.D., and David A. Grady, Psy.D.
19. *Strangers at Home: Vietnam Veterans Since the War*, Edited by Charles R. Figley, Ph.D., and Seymour Leventman, Ph.D.
20. *The National Vietnam Veterans Readjustment Study: Tables of Findings and Technical Appendices*, By Richard A. Kulka, Ph.D., Kathleen Jordan, Ph.D., Charles R. Marmar, M.D., and Daniel S. Weiss, Ph.D.
21. *Psychological Trauma and the Adult Survivor: Theory, Therapy, and Tranformation*, By I. Lisa MCann, Ph.D., and Laurie Anne Pearlman, Ph.D.
22. *Coping with Infant or Fetal Loss: The Couple's Healing Process*, By Kathleen R. Gilbert, Ph.D., and Laura S. Smart, Ph.D.
23. *Compassion Fatigue: Coping with Secondary Traumatic Stress Disorder in Those Who Treat the Traumatized*, Edited by Charles R. Figley, Ph.D.

TREATING COMPASSION FATIGUE

Edited by
Charles R. Figley

Routledge
Taylor & Francis Group
New York   London

Published in 2002 by
Routledge
29 West 35th Street
New York, NY 10001

Published in Great Britain by
Routledge
27 Church Rd.
Hove, East Sussex, BN3 2FA

10 9 8 7 6 5 4

Library of Congress Cataloging-in-Publication Data
Treating compassion fatigue / [edited] by Charles R. Figley.
     p. ; cm. — (Psychosocial stress series ; no. 24)
     Includes bibliographical references and index.
     ISBN 1–58391–053–0
     1. Medical personnel—Job stress. 2. Burn out (Psychology)—Treatment. 3. Compassion.
I. Figley, Charles R., 1944– II. Brunner-Routledge psychosocial stress series ; no. 24.
[DNLM: 1. Health Personnel—psychology. 2. Stress, Psychological—therapy. 3. Burnout, Professional. 4. Empathy. WM 172 T7837 2002]
RC451.4.M44 T74 2002
616.89—dc21   2002018281

Contents

PART II: TREATMENT AND PREVENTION INNOVATIONS

Contributors

Anna B. Baranowsky, Ph.D.
> The University of Ottawa (Canada)

Thomas A. Cornille, Ph.D.
> The Department of Child and Family Sciences
> Florida State Univeristy (USA)

Kathleen Dunning, MA
> University of Tasmania (Australia)

J. Eric Gentry, MS, CTS
> Traumatology Institute, Florida State University (USA)

Robert King, Ph.D.
> The University of Queensland (Australia)

Lenore Meldrum, B.Ed-B.Psych.
> The Valley Integrated Adult Mental Health Services
> Queensland (Australia)

Carmen C. Moran, Ph.D.
> The University of New South Wales (Australia)

Diane Myers, RN, MSN
> Private Practice, Watsonville, California (USA)

Darren Spooner, B.A.
> The University of Queensland (Australia)

B. Hudnall Stamm, Ph.D.
Idaho State University
and Dartmouth Medical School (USA)

Paul Valent, M.D.
Private Practice, Melbourne (Australia)

David F. Wee, MSSW
University of California, Berkeley
City of Berkeley Mental Health, Berkeley, California (USA)

Geoffry D. White, Ph.D.
Private Practice, Los Angeles (USA)

Tracy Woodard Meyers, Ph.D.
Valdosta State University (USA)

Introduction

CHARLES R. FIGLEY

I have already been horrified by the glaring lack of emphasis in the curriculum on the social and psychological aspects of medicine or the emotional stress of being a physician. None of our professors is willing to discuss the feelings that the phenomenon of disease elicits in both patient and doctor. (Hilfiker, 1985, p. 205)

We all feel or have felt the distress and the isolation. Ultimately, I believe, there is no solution to the problem. All of us who attempt to heal the wounds of others will ourselves be wounded; it is, after all, inherent in the relationship. (Hilfiker, 1985, p. 207)

David Hilfiker (1985) cited these among the hundreds of letters from Harvard-trained physicians as examples of compassion fatigue. They are all too familiar, not just to physicians but to all those who are in the role of healer, helper, or rescuer. And, of course, the burden of tending to the suffering is one of a plethora of stressors. This volume suggests, however, that we are now beginning to sufficiently understand compassion fatigue so that we can do something about it.

The concept has been around only since 1992, when Joinson used the term in a nursing magazine. It fit the description of nurses who were worn down by daily hospital emergencies. That same year, Jeffrey Kottler (1992), in his book *Compassionate Therapy*, emphasized the importance of compassion in dealing with extremely difficult and resistant patients. However, neither work adequately defined *compassionate*. Indeed, the term is not listed in the index of Kottler's book. It was mentioned only once in the final chapter, on "Rules

1

of Engagement."[1] Both authors, however, noted how and why practitioners lose their compassion as a result of their work with the suffering.

The dictionary meaning of *compassion* is a "feeling of deep sympathy and sorrow for another who is stricken by suffering or misfortune, accompanied by a strong desire to alleviate the pain or remove its cause" (*Webster's*, 1989, p. 229). Some would argue it is wrong for a practitioner to have deep feelings of sympathy and sorrow for a client's suffering. And certainly practitioners must understand their limitations in helping to alleviate the pain suffered by their clients.

Yet most systematic studies of the effectiveness of therapy point to the therapeutic alliance between client and clinician, the ability to empathize, to understand, and to help clients (Figley & Nelson, 1989). If that is not present, it is highly unlikely that therapeutic change will take place. The most important ingredient in building a therapeutic alliance is the client liking and trusting her or his therapist. And these feelings are directly related to the degree to which the therapist utilizes and expresses empathy and compassion.

This book builds on the volume *Compassion Fatigue: Coping with Secondary Traumatic Stress Disorder in Those Who Treat the Traumatized* (Figley, 1995). In the years since that book's publication, an impressive number of books, chapters, and articles have been published. This book is an effort to further clarify the concept of compassion fatigue through theory, research, and treatment. The chapters are organized into sections consistent with these elements. This book will attempt to advance our knowledge and applications of compassion fatigue assessment, prevention, research, and treatment.

CONTRASTS BETWEEN COMPASSION FATIGUE AND RELATED CONCEPTS

Compassion fatigue is the latest in an evolving concept that is known in the field of traumatology as secondary traumatic stress. Most often this phenomenon is associated with the "cost of caring" for others in emotional pain (Figley, 1982).

There are a number of terms that describe this phenomenon. It has been described as secondary victimization (Figley, 1982), secondary traumatic stress (Figley, 1983, 1985, 1990; Stamm, 1995, 1997), vicarious traumatization (McCann & Pearlman, 1990; Pearlman & Saakvitne, 1995), and secondary survivor (Remer & Elliott, 1988). A similar concept, "emotional contagion," is defined as an affective process in which "an individual observing another person experiences emotional responses parallel to that person's actual or

---

1. "Yet, in whatever setting a helper practices, he will encounter rude and demanding consumers who require even more than the usual dose of kindness, compassion, and understudying in order to feel cared for" (Kottler, 1992, p. 226).

anticipated emotions" (Miller, Stiff, & Ellis, 1988, p. 254). Also, rape-related family crisis (Erikson, 1989; White & Rollins, 1981) and "proximity" effects on female partners of war veterans (Verbosky & Ryan, 1988) are related concepts. The generational effects of trauma (Danieli, 1985; McCubbin, Dahl, Lester, & Ross, 1977) and the need for family "detoxification" from war-related traumatic stress (Rosenheck & Thomson, 1986) also have been noted.

Finally, some view difficulties with client problems as one of simple countertransference, which has been discussed within the context of PTSD treatment (Danieli, 1988; Herman, 1992; Wilson & Lindy, 1994). However, the concept is encased in an elaborate theoretical context that is difficult to measure and to distinguish from all others in the client–therapist transactions.

The American Psychiatric Association's diagnostic disorders manual (*DSM–IV*, APA, 1994) noted that posttraumatic stress disorder (PTSD) is possible only when one is traumatized either directly (in harm's way) or indirectly (as for a parent). Both may experience trauma, although through different social pathways. The latter pathway is called secondary traumatic stress (compassion fatigue). There are few reports of the incidence and prevalence of this type of stress reaction. However, based on secondary data and theory analysis, burnout, countertransference, worker dissatisfaction, and other related concepts may have masked this common problem (Figley, 1995). Vicarious traumatization, for example, "refers to a transformation in the therapist's (or other trauma worker's) inner experience resulting from empathetic engagement with clients' trauma material." It is also being vulnerable to the emotional and spiritual effects of vicarious traumatization. These effects are cumulative and permanent, and evident in both a therapist's professional and personal life (Pearlman & Saakvitne, 1995, p. 151).

Compassion fatigue is a more user-friendly term for secondary traumatic stress disorder, which is nearly identical to PTSD, except that it applies to those emotionally affected by the trauma of another (usually a client or family member). Compassion fatigue is related to the cognitive schema of the therapist (social and interpersonal perceptions or morale).

Table I.1 provides a useful contrast between the symptom criteria for PTSD and compassion fatigue. It is obvious that we can be traumatized by helping suffering people in harm's way as well as by being in harm's way ourselves.

We have suspected for some time that the mechanism operating within families that accounts for this "spread" of the "virus" of PTSD is the same mechanism that accounts for vicarious traumatization experienced by professionals.

A recent book focused on both the secondary traumatic stress and burnout found among modern families (Figley, 1997). Among the conclusions were these: that families both breed and destroy stress among their members and that PTSD spreads in families like a virus unless they have ways to cope. This finding is consistent with those of others (Figley, 1989a, 1989b, 1995; Figley & McCubbin, 1983; Solomon, 1995). Thus, if stress is linked to a wide variety of

TABLE I.1
Traumatic Symptoms of Primary and Secondary Traumatic Stress Disorder Symptoms

(Primary) PTSD Stressors	(Secondary) Compassion Fatigue Stressors
A. Experienced an event outside the range of usual human experiences that would be markedly distressing to almost anyone, an event such as a rape, the September 11 terrorist attack, family violence, combat, and other terrifying experiences.	Experienced indirectly the primary traumatic stressors through helping those who had experienced these traumas: helping in such roles as a nurse, social worker, rape counselor, or other roles and activities.

B. Traumatic event is persistently reexperienced in one (or more) of the following ways:

(1) Recurrent and intrusive distressing recollections of the event, including images, thoughts, or perceptions	Recurrent and intrusive distressing recollections of the **client**/event, including images, thoughts, or perceptions
(2) Recurrent distressing dreams of the event	Recurrent distressing dreams of the **client**/event
(3) Acting or feeling as if the traumatic event were recurring (includes a sense of reliving the experience, illusions, hallucinations, and dissociative flashback episodes, including those that occur on awakening or when intoxicated)	Acting or feeling as if the traumatic event were recurring (includes a sense of reliving contact with the client and the client's story in order to solve the puzzle and help the client)
(4) Intense psychological distress at exposure to internal or external cues that symbolize or resemble an aspect of the traumatic event	Intense psychological distress at exposure to internal or external cues that symbolize or resemble the aspect of *the work of helping others*
(5) Physiological reactivity on exposure to trauma cues	Physiological reactivity on exposure to *trauma cues that are associated with the role of helper*

C. Persistent avoidance of stimuli associated with the trauma and numbing of general responsiveness (not present before the trauma), as indicated by three or more of the following:

(1) Efforts to avoid thoughts, feelings, or conversations associated with the trauma	Efforts to avoid thoughts, feelings, or conversations associated with *the client's* trauma
(2) Efforts to avoid activities, places, or people that arouse recollections of the trauma	Efforts to avoid activities, places, or people that arouse recollections of *the client's* traumas
(3) Inability to recall an important aspect of the trauma	*Errors in judgment about conceptualizing and treating the trauma case*
(4) Markedly diminished interest or participation in significant activities	Markedly diminished interest or participation in significant activities
(5) Feeling of detachment or estrangement from others	Feeling of detachment or estrangement from others
(6) Restricted range of affect (e.g., unable to have loving feelings)	Restricted range of affect (e.g., unable to know the client personally or savior-oriented)
(7) Sense of foreshortened future (e.g., does not expect to have a career, marriage, children, or a normal life span)	Sense of foreshortened future (e.g., *does not expect or want to have a long career*)

(Continued)

TABLE I.1   *Continued*

(Primary) PTSD Stressors	(Secondary) Compassion Fatigue Stressors
D. Persistent symptoms of increased arousal (not present before the trauma), as indicated by two or more of the following:	
(1) Difficulty falling or staying asleep	Difficulty falling or staying asleep
(2) Irritability or outbursts of anger	Irritability or outbursts of anger
(3) Difficulty concentrating	Difficulty concentrating
(4) Hypervigilance	Hypervigilance
(5) Exaggerated startle response	Exaggerated startle response
E. 30 days' duration	30 days' duration
F. *Disturbance causes clinically significant distress or impairment in social, occupational, or other important areas of functioning:* Evidenced by increase family conflict, sexual dysfunction, poor interpersonal communication, less loving, more dependent, reduced social support, poor stress-coping methods.	*Disturbance causes clinically significant distress or impairment in social, occupational, or other important areas of functioning:* Evidenced by increased work conflict, missed work, insensitivity to clients, lingering distress caused by trauma material, reduced social support, poor stress-coping methods.

medical and psychological ills (cf., Lazarus & Folkman, 1984), it is important to help families manage their stress—especially PTSD and other byproducts of catastrophe. Compassion fatigue is one form of burnout. Family burnout is its interpersonal equivalent (Figley, 1997).

A recent study of emergency medical personnel, for example, found that parents are traumatized by caring for their injured child (Barnes, 1997). The consensus among these experts: Families need more attention to heal both themselves and the member most physically injured. Indeed, the trend in the 1990s has been toward greater support for the American family to cure many social ills.

EXTENT OF THE PROBLEM OF COMPASSION FATIGUE

This volume reports on five research projects that investigated the incidence and prevalence of compassion fatigue among professionals working with the suffering. The picture that emerges is clear: Those who work with the suffering suffer themselves because of the work. A recent study is illustrative.

In a doctoral dissertation based on the data analysis of 132 marriage and family therapists (MFTs), drawn from those listed in their national association's directory, Lee (1995) found a statistically significant relationship ($r = .20$) between compassion fatigue (CF) scores and caseload dissatisfaction. The results indicate that CF was significantly correlated with compassion fatigue. The results also indicated that MFT professionals experienced compassion fatigue that was higher than that of medical students but lower than that of

PTSD clients. MFT professionals in the sample reported that an average of 63% of their client load was traumatized. However, MFT professionals as a group experience only a moderate level of compassion fatigue, as measured by the Impact of Events Scale (IES; Horowitz, Wilner, Kaltreider, & Alvarez, 1980).

The study predicted and found a strong relationship between compassion fatigue and various cognitions associated with general morale in one's personal and professional life (cognitive schema). The usual limitations of survey-based studies requiring retrospective self-analysis apply to this study (Winston, 1974).

The results show that a measure of cognitive schema was significantly correlated ($r = .34$) with a measure of compassion fatigue. These results support the relationship and perhaps overlap between these two variables. Future research should use additional measures of compassion fatigue (e.g., Self-Test for Psychotherapists; Figley, 1995) and additional measures of cognitive schemas (Stamm, 1995). Further speculations about the implications of these findings are risky until other studies confirm the relationship. However, there is growing, indirect evidence that perceptions about self-worth (personally and professionally) and the value of family, friends, community, and other social resources are closely related to general morale.

Another recent report of an unpublished study (Pelkowitz, 1997) noted that nurses working with prisoners in a trauma unit in South Africa were especially vulnerable to compassion fatigue. Pelkowitz offered a useful table on the impact of compassion fatigue. Table I.2 draws from her original conceptualization and many of the symptoms.

In an exhaustive review of the professional literature, Beaton and Murphy (1995) asserted that emergency or first responders and crisis workers absorb the traumatic stress of those they help. By doing so, they put themselves at risk for experiencing compassion fatigue. Among the negative consequences not often linked to their work are substance abuse and relationship conflicts. This is consistent with the finding of McCammon and Jackson (1995), who reviewed emergency medical professionals.

Two central questions in future studies should be these: Who is most vulnerable to compassion fatigue in what type of work setting and under what types of conditions? Once developed, how can we treat it and return the worker back to good morale? These questions are addressed in this volume.

Moreover, as research suggests, there is a significant overlap in effectiveness of treatment methods found useful for clients suffering from PTSD and those found useful for professionals suffering from compassion fatigue. This is the basic thesis of the volume.

In the years since the publication of *Compassion Fatigue: Coping with Secondary Traumatic Stress Disorder in Those Who Treat the Traumatized* (Figley, 1995), an impressive number of books, chapters, and articles have been published. Here we make an effort to further clarify the concept of compassion

TABLE I.2
Examples of Compassion Fatigue Burnout Symptoms

Cognitive	Emotional	Behavioral	Spiritual	Personal Relations	Somatic	Work Performance
Lowered concentration	Powerlessness	Inpatient	Questioning the meaning of life	Withdrawal	Shock	Low morale
Decreased self-esteem	Anxiety	Irritable	Loss of purpose	Decreased interest in intimacy or sex	Sweating	Low motivation
Apathy	Guilt	Withdrawn	Lack of self-satisfaction	Mistrust	Rapid heartbeat	Avoiding tasks
Rigidity	Anger/rage	Moody	Pervasive hopelessness	Isolation from others	Breathing difficulties	Obsession about details
Disorientation	Survivor guilt	Regression	Anger at God	Overprotection as a parent	Aches and pains	Apathy
Perfectionism	Shutdown	Sleep disturbance	Questioning of prior religious beliefs	Projection of anger or blame	Dizziness	Negativity
Minimization	Numbness	Nightmares	Loss of faith in a higher power	Intolerance	Increased number and intensity of medical maladies	Lack of appreciation
Preoccupation with trauma	Fear	Appetite changes	Greater skepticism about religion	Loneliness	Other somatic complaints	Detachment
Thoughts of self-harm or harm to others	Helplessness	Hypervigilance		Increased interpersonal conflicts	Impaired immune system	Poor work commitments
	Sadness	Elevated startle response				Staff conflicts
	Depression	Accident proneness				Absenteeism
	Emotional roller coaster	Losing things				Exhaustion
	Depleted					Irritability
	Overly sensitive					Withdrawal from colleagues

fatigue by reviewing contemporary theory and research. However, the primary focus is on action: the assessment and treatment of compassion fatigue.

CONTENTS OF THE CURRENT VOLUME

The book is divided into two sections. "Section I: Contemporary Views and Findings" brings together six chapters. The purpose of the chapters is to help the reader appreciate the conceptual complexity of compassion fatigue.

Chapter 1 was written by Australian psychiatrist Paul Valent. The aim of this chapter is to conceptualize compassion fatigue through a new "wholist perspective." Valent introduced this perspective in his two recently published books, which focus on survival strategies of traumatized people. Here he notes that a wide variety of helper responses and treatments provide a framework for the stress experienced by helpers and the related health, emotional, and interpersonal problems. The model suggests useful tools to enrich as well as tailor helper treatments. In the process, terms such as countertransference, secondary stress, secondary stress disorder, compassion fatigue, and burnout are given meaningful places in a new coherent web. Clinical examples of application of the new perspective are provided.

In Chapter 2, family therapy professors Tracy Woodard Meyers and Tom Cornille discuss their findings of a study of child protection workers in southern Georgia. The purpose of their study was to assess the prevalence of secondary traumatic stress (STS) symptoms among south Georgia child protective services (CPS) workers and to explore factors that contributed to the severity of those symptoms. A survey research design was employed to investigate the hypotheses related to this study. The results indicated that STS symptoms were common among the CPS workers surveyed. Specifically, 77% of these CPS workers reported having been assaulted or threatened while on the job. CPS workers who reported they had witnessed the death of another person reported they experienced more nightmares, intrusive thoughts, images, distress, anxiety, and anger than those who had never witnessed a death. They also reported experiencing more suspiciousness, fear of loss of autonomy, delusions, projective thoughts, withdrawal from others, isolation, and schizoid lifestyles than those workers who had not witnessed a death. Workers who reported experiencing a serious injury prior to working with child abuse victims related that they suffered from more muscular pain, discomfort, and cardiovascular, gastrointestinal, and respiratory complaints than workers who had not suffered a serious injury. Workers who disclosed that they had experienced other types of trauma reported being more symptomatic than those who had not suffered from another type of trauma. These workers reported being more depressed, anxious, somatic, withdrawn, isolated, and distressed than workers who had not experienced another type of trauma. Intervention and prevention strategies are suggested.

David Wee and Diane Myers, who wrote Chapter 3, are two well-known traumatologists who have helped communities recover from most of the major national disasters in the last decade. Their chapter summarizes a recently completed study that focuses on a population different from that of Chapter 2, but their findings are similar. They studied the disaster mental-health workers involved in long-term mental health recovery activities, providing crisis-counseling services to victims of the Oklahoma City bombing disaster. Of special interest were the disaster experiences, postdisaster stress responses, perceptions of social support, and reactions of the workers assigned to Project Heartland (the Federally-funded Crisis Counseling Program for Oklahoma City Bombing Survivors). Each received the Alfred P. Murrah Federal Building Bombing Reaction Questionnaire packet nine months after the bombing. The packet included the Compassion Fatigue Self-Test for Helpers (Figley, 1995), the Frederick Reaction Index–A (Frederick, 1985, 1987), and the Symptom Checklist 90–Revised (Derogatis, 1994). The most significant psychological feature of this bombing disaster for these disaster mental-health workers was that someone they knew might have died in the bombing. However, most of the disaster mental-health workers reported some degree of severity for stress disorder. More than half the workers studied indicated that the work was more stressful than other jobs. However, only a small percentage of the sample had levels of distress that were within the clinical range of symptoms. Apparently, the factors most associated with increased severity of stress disorder are the type of job (e.g., administrator) and larger number of months providing disaster mental health services to bombing survivors. Scores indicated that the entire sample was at risk of developing both compassion fatigue and burnout. The risks increased with the number of months worked with bombing survivors. The disaster mental health workers' distress levels were higher than those found in almost all other groups of emergency and rescue workers studied in the last 14 years. Implications for future research and practice are discussed, although most of the implications for training and preparation are discussed in their other chapter (Chapter 10).

In Chapter 4, Australian psychologists Lenore Meldrum, Robert King, and Darren Spooner report on the results and implications of a study initiated by the Department of Psychiatry, University of Queensland. The study investigated the psychosocial and emotional consequences of work on experienced case managers in mental health services in Australia. The results, derived from 300 survey documents, showed that a significant proportion of these workers not only experienced the symptoms of secondary traumatic stress, but approximately 18% reported experiencing compassion fatigue at levels equivalent to those experienced by people who meet criteria for a diagnosis of posttraumatic stress disorder. The authors were unable to conclude exactly why so many were debilitated. However, they report a significant statistical relationship between the severity of the symptoms and secondary exposure to specific stressors. This is consistent with the findings of other studies of compassion fatigue. The authors conclude that their data suggest the possibility of significant occupational health and safety risks associated with the mental health case manager role, and that there is a clear public interest and duty to help these workers through various prevention and treatment programs.

In Chapter 5, Dr. Stamm emphasizes the importance of compassion satisfaction in work with the suffering. She also reports on a study to establish the psychometric properties of a new measure of compassion fatigue that incorporates the self-test published in Figley (1995), with an addition of a subsection on compassion satisfaction. Dr. Stamm notes that about half the people in the United States have been exposed to at least one event that would qualify as a precursor to posttraumatic stress disorder, yet only about 8% develop the disorder. Being exposed to others' traumatic material compounds helpers' risks and, although some providers do experience negative effects of secondary traumatic stress, many do not. Thus, the question was raised: Is there some protective factor, perhaps compassion satisfaction? In response, Dr. Stamm developed a compassion satisfaction scale as a companion to the burnout and compassion fatigue scales. This scale helps identify the positive effects of caregiving and may lead toward a clearer understanding of the relationship between the positive and negative aspects of compassion.

In Chapter 6, the first of six treatment and prevention chapters, Eric Gentry, Anna Baranowsky, and Kathleen Dunning present one of the first treatments specifically designed for compassion fatigue. It is an "accelerated" program, in that it is designed to work quickly with professionals with varying degrees of compassion fatigue. This program was developed for and with the assistance of the Green Cross Projects to help members traumatized in the line of duty. The Accelerated Recovery Program (ARP) for compassion fatigue is a multimodal brief (five-session) treatment protocol for professional caregivers who suffer the combined effects of burnout and secondary traumatic stress. The program is designed to assist caregivers in reducing the intensity, frequency, and duration of compassion fatigue *symptoms*. The five-session treatment protocol is standardized and directed toward the completion of the following major objectives.

1. ARP helps practitioners identify, understand, and develop a hierarchy of the events, situations, people, and internal experiences that trigger symptoms of compassion fatigue in their lives.
2. ARP helps practitioners review present personal methodologies of addressing these difficulties and begin developing self-treatment plans in *four pathways to healing:* skills acquisition, self-care, connection with others, and internal conflicts.
3. ARP helps to identify resources (external and internal) available to professionals that can be used to combat compassion fatigue.
4. ARP teaches extremely effective self-soothing techniques.

5. ARP teaches mastery of state-of-the-art grounding and containment skills.
6. ARP engages practitioners in self-care, boundary-setting, and skills acquisition and highlights any impediments to full clinical potency.
7. ARP teaches mastery of the video-dialogue, a technique for internal conflict resolution and self-supervision.
8. And ARP facilitates the development of a self-administered after-care plan.

In Chapter 7, psychologist and professor of social work Carmen Moran emphasizes the place and vital importance of humor in preventing and treating compassion fatigue. Professor Moran reports on the role of humor in extreme environments, particularly those involving emergency rescue workers and people in related helping professions. The chapter notes that emergency workers are those who are called upon to respond to emergency incidents such as major accidents, melees, and conflicts, as well as those who deal with the physical and psychological aftermath of these incidents. The chapter reviews the scholarly and professional literature on the role of humor in coping with life stressors. Among other things, the chapter notes that humor is not readily defined, as it has many manifestations. Dr. Moran notes that it is reasonable to assume that different aspects of humor will serve different functions, some of which will be more beneficial than others. She also argues that humor can contribute to physical well-being and may help people cognitively reframe stressful events. In cases of trauma, reframing with humor may be contraindicated by a need to find meaning in past events. In such cases, humor can still be valuable in coping with the here and now. Emergency workers' discussions of humor in the emergency environment support the notion that humor helps coping and performance in potentially traumatic scenarios. Not everyone regards humor as healthy. On balance, however, humor in extreme and traumatic environments appears to have an important role in assisting performance and coping. The challenge may be to give us permission to laugh in these contexts.

In Chapter 8, clinical psychologist Anna Baranowsky notes that one psychological consequence of exposure to trauma for the caregiver is the "silencing response." Dr. Baranowsky defines the silencing response as "based on a series of assumptions, which guide the clinician to redirect, shutdown, minimize, or neglect the traumatic or other relevant material brought by the client to the therapeutic session." The response can be either an indication of compassion fatigue or an effort on the part of the practitioner to avoid it. The author reports, based on preliminary research, that there is a strong correlation between compassion fatigue and the silencing response (e.g., $r = .43$, $p = .002$). Thus, either they are part of the same syndrome or the former is a response to the latter. Because of the risk of misdiagnosis and ineffective clinical services, Baranowsky suggests that practitioners should monitor themselves and their colleagues for signs of the silencing response. She also suggests some steps to take if there is any indication. A copy of the Silencing Response Scale is included in the chapter, along with scoring instructions.

In Chapter 9, clinical psychologist Geoffry White focuses attention on those working in the war-torn former Yugoslavia in the late 1990s. He and others conducted trauma treatment training in eye movement desensitization and reprocessing (EMDR) for mental health workers. This chapter describes the training program and a cost-effective system of international supervision and consultation. This program, developed specifically for those living and working in combat zones, provides a way of monitoring and maintaining the training and treatment program following initial training. Most of the chapter discusses a special facet of the ongoing program. It is a way of measuring and evaluating compassion fatigue and burnout among trainees. Monthly group meetings were held wherein the trainees could discuss and practice what they had learned during the initial workshops. During these meetings trainees completed a compassion fatigue self-inventory, which allowed group leaders to identify participants who were at risk for compassion fatigue. The latter part of the chapter discusses plans for development of this system to support future training and consultation programs in Bosnia and other war-torn areas.

In Chapter 10, Diane Myers and David Wee turn their attention to the broader implications of disaster work. They base their observations on what they have learned from the Oklahoma City bombing disaster, but they go beyond it as well. They report that the literature, including their own research, confirms that first responders, disaster workers, and trauma counselors working in disasters are at greater risk for developing PTSD, compassion fatigue, burnout, and secondary traumatic stress, compared to those not exposed to trauma work. Their chapter is a report of a recent study on the counselors from Project Heartland. These research participants provided treatment and supportive mental health services to the victims of the Oklahoma City bombing. Myers and Wee report that counselors were psychologically affected by their work whether or not they had personally experienced the bomb blast, and a large proportion of counselors were at moderate to extremely high risk for compassion fatigue, as measured by the Compassion Fatigue Self-Test for Psychotherapists. They report that multiple stressors face counselors exposed to disasters. Among other things, these factors are related to the *individual, interpersonal factors, community factors,* and factors related to the *disaster* itself. Based on their research, Myers and Wee suggest some helpful strategies and interventions to help traumatologists before, during, and after disaster assignments. Such help will maintain the psychological health and well-being of these trauma counselors. Among other things, they describe various stress management protocols, educational materials, and training programs. These recommendations are based on what the authors have learned from more than a dozen major U.S. disasters.

Consistent with the purpose of the previous volume on compassion fatigue in this book series, this volume is a call to arms. We challenge our colleagues to meet the challenges of professional burnout caused by caring for the suffering. Collectively, the authors of this volume believe that helping others effectively starts with effectively helping ourselves.

REFERENCES

American Psychiatric Association. (1994). *Diagnostic and statistical manual of mental disorders* (4th ed.). Washington, DC: Author.

Barnes, M. F. (1997). Understanding the secondary traumatic stress of parents. In C. R. Figley (Ed.), *Burnout in families: The systematic costs of caring* (pp. 75–90). Boca Raton, FL: CRC Press.

Beaton, R. D., & Murphy, S. A. (1995). Working with people in crisis: Research implications. In C. R. Figley (Ed.), *Compassion fatigue: Coping with secondary traumatic stress disorder in those who treat the traumatized* (pp. 51–81). New York: Brunner/Mazel.

Danieli, Y. (1985). The treatment and prevention of long-term effects and intergenerational transmission of victimization: A lesson from Holocaust survivors and their children. In C. R. Figley (Ed.), *Trauma and its wake* (pp. 295–313). New York: Brunner/Mazel.

Danieli, Y. (1988). Treating survivors and children of survivors of the Nazi Holocaust. In F. Ochberg (Ed.), *Post-traumatic therapy and victims of violence* (pp. 278–294). New York: Brunner/Mazel.

Derogatis, L. (1994). *SCL-90-R Symptom Checklist-90-R: Administration, coding, and procedures manual*. Minneapolis, MN: National Computer Systems.

Erickson, C. A. (1989). Rape and the family. In C. R. Figley (Ed.), *Treating stress in families* (pp. 257–290). New York: Brunner/Mazel.

Feinauer, L. (1982). Rape: A family crisis. *American Journal of Family Therapy, 10*(4), 35–39.

Figley, C. R. (1982). *Traumatization and comfort: Close relationships may be hazardous to your health.* Keynote presentation at the Conference on Families and Close Relationships: Individuals in Social Interaction. Texas Tech University, Lubbock, TX.

Figley, C. R. (1983). Catastrophes: An overview of family reactions. In C. R. Figley & H. I. McCubbin (Eds.), *Stress and the family, vol. II: Coping with catastrophe* (pp. 3–20). New York: Brunner/Mazel.

Figley, C. R. (1985). The family as victim: Mental health implications. *Psychiatry, 6*, 283–291.

Figley, C. R. (1989a). *Helping traumatized families*. San Francisco: Jossey-Bass.

Figley, C. R. (Ed.). (1989b). *Treating stress in families*. New York: Brunner/Mazel.

Figley, C. R. (Ed.). (1995). *Compassion fatigue: Coping with secondary traumatic stress disorder in those who treat the traumatized*. New York: Brunner/Mazel.

Figley, C. R. (Ed.). (1997). *Burnout in families: The systematic costs of caring*. New York: CRC Press.

Figley, C. R., & McCubbin, H. I. (Eds.). (1983). *Stress and the family, vol. II: Coping with catastrophe*. New York: Brunner/Mazel.

Figley, C. R., & Nelson, T. (1989). Basic family therapy skills, I: Conceptualization and initial findings. *Journal of Marital and Family Therapy, 15*(4), 211–130.

Frederick, C. J. (1985). Children traumatized by catastrophic situations. In S. Eth & R. S. Pynoos (Eds.), *Post-traumatic stress disorders in children* (pp. 71–100). Washington, DC: American Psychiatric Press.

Frederick, C. J. (1987). Psychic trauma in victims of crime and terrorism. In G. R. Vandenbos & B. K. Bryant (Eds.), *Cataclysms, crises and catastrophes: Psychology in action master lecture series*. Washington, DC: American Psychological Association.

Herman, J. L. (1992). *Trauma and recovery: The aftermath of violence–from domestic abuse to political terror.* New York: Basic Books.

Hilfiker, D. (1985). *Healing the wounds: A physician looks at his work.* New York: Pantheon Books.

Horowitz, M. J., Wilner, N., Kaltreider, N., & Alvarez, W. (1980). Signs and symptoms of post-traumatic stress disorder. *Archives of General Psychiatry, 37,* 85–92.

Kottler, J. A. (1992). *Compassionate therapy: Working with difficult clients.* San Francisco: Jossey-Bass.

Joinson, C. (1992). Coping with compassion fatigue. *Nursing, 22*(4), 16–122.

Lazarus, R. S., & Folkman, S. (1984). *Stress, appraisal, and coping.* New York: Springer.

MaCammon, S. L., & Allison, E. J. (1995). Debriefing and treating emergency workers. In C. R. Figley (Ed.), *Compassion fatigue: Coping with secondary traumatic stress disorders in those who treat the traumatized* (pp. 115–130). New York: Brunner/Mazel.

Miller, K. I., Stiff, J. B., & Ellis, B. H. (1988). Communication and empathy as precursors to burnout among human service workers. *Communication Monographs, 55*(9), 336–341.

McCubbin, H. I., Dahl, B. B., & Ross, B. (1977). The returned prisoner of war and his children: Evidence for the origin of second generational effects of captivity. *International Journal of Sociology of the Family, 7,* 25–36.

Pearlman, L. A., & Saakvitne, K. W. (1995). Treating therapists with vicarious traumatization and secondary traumatic stress disorders. In C. R. Figley (Ed.), *Compassion fatigue: Coping with secondary traumatic stress disorders in those who treat the traumatized* (pp. 150–177). New York: Brunner/Mazel.

Remer, R., & Elliot, J. (1988). Characteristics of secondary victims of sexual assault. *International Journal of Family Psychiatry, 9*(4), 373–387.

Rosenheck, R., & Thomson, J. (1986). "Detoxification" of Vietnam war trauma: A combined family–individial approach. *Family Process, 25*(4), 559–570.

Solomon, Z., Waysman, M., Avitzur, E., & Enoch, D. (1991). Psychiatric symptomatology among wives of soldiers following combat stress reaction: The role of the social network and marital relations. *Anxiety Research, 4,* 213–223.

Solomon, Z., Waysman, M., Belkin, R., Levy, G., Mikulincer, M., & Enoch, D. (1992). Marital relations and combat stress reaction: The wives' perspective. *Journal of Marriage and the Family, 54,* 316–326.

Solomon, Z., Waysman, M., Levy, G., Fried, B., Mikulincer, M., Benbeneshty, R., Florian, V., & Bleich, A. (1992). From the front line to home front: A study of secondary traumatization. *Family Process, 31,* 280–302.

Stamm, B. H. (Ed.). (1995). *Secondary traumatic stress: Self-care issues for clinicians, researchers, and educators.* Lutherville, MD: Sidran Press.

Stamm, B. H. (1997). Work-related secondary traumatic stress. *PTSD Research Quarterly, 8*(2). Available on-line at http://www.dartmouth.edu/dms/ptsd/RQSpring1997.html

Verbosky, S. J., & Ryan, D. A. (1988). Studied the female partners of Vietnam veterans: Stress by proximity. *Issues in Mental Health Nursing, 9*(1), 95–104.

White, P. N., & Rollins, J. C. (1981). Rape: A family crisis. *Family Relations, 30*(1), 103–109.

Wilson, J. P., & Lindy, J. D. (1994). *Countertransference in the treatment of PTSD.* New York: Guilford.

Part I

CONTEMPORARY VIEWS AND FINDINGS

Introduction to Part I: Contemporary Views and Findings

The five chapters in this section help from the empirical, theoretical, and assessment basis for the volume. The first chapter promotes the wholist perspective. This perspective promotes the importance of viewing the traumatized as attempting to use all of the various systems to survive. In contrast to his previous books, here Valent attends to the special circumstances of being traumatized through our work. The next three chapters, although focusing on three different contexts, report similar results of their studies: that helping the traumatized is hard work and exacts an emotional toll. The final chapter of the section is the beginning of doing something about the problem of compassion fatigue. Here, Stamm emphasizes the importance of using a new self-test that measures not only the degree to which the respondent is at risk of burnout and compassion fatigue, but also satisfaction: how satisfied respondents are in their work with the suffering. It is the sense of work satisfaction that is the antidote to both burnout and compassion fatigue and makes the rest of the book especially important.

1

Diagnosis and Treatment of Helper Stresses, Traumas, and Illnesses*

PAUL VALENT

In the last two decades it has become accepted that people can be secondarily affected by the sufferings of others. The attunement and effort needed to help others in trouble may provide great rewards for helpers when they meet with success. But when they are strained, or worse, when they fail, helpers may be the next dominoes who follow primary victims in suffering themselves.

Although secondary stress and trauma have become widely recognized in traumatology, efforts to conceptualize them have taken place only recently. The purpose of this chapter is to overview these efforts and to extend some of my own recent conceptualizations of (primary) stress and trauma disorders (Valent, 1995, 1998a, 1998b) to secondary ones.

BACKGROUND

Soon after the recognition of traumatization and the need for early help for victims in the late 1970s and early 1980s, it became clear that helpers became

---

*I want to acknowledge Brunner-Routledge for allowing reproduction of Table 1.1 and Figures 1.1 and 1.2 from previous publications.

secondarily affected. For instance, Berah, Jones, and Valent (1984) noted that helpers in a disaster outreach team suffered shock, depression, sadness, fatigue, sleep disturbance, and dreams about helpers being victims in the disaster. They also suffered reminders of past traumas and a variety of physical symptoms, colds and flus, as well as minor accidents.

The Scope of the Problem: A Wide Variety of Symptoms

A great variety of symptoms was described over the years, and one may say came to parallel the similar great variety of symptoms in victims. For instance, a selection from the previous volume of *Compassion Fatigue* (Figley, 1995a) described a heterogeneity of physiological and physical symptoms, some extending to serious illnesses, and ultimately a higher mortality rate among helper professionals than among controls (Beaton & Murphy, 1995). A similar heterogeneity of psychological symptoms included sadness, grief, depression, anxiety, dread, horror, fear, rage, and shame; intrusive imagery in nightmares, flashbacks, and images; numbing and avoidance phenomena; cognitive shifts in viewing the world and oneself, such as suspiciousness, cynicism, and poor self-esteem; and guilt for survival and enjoying oneself (Dutton & Rubinstein, 1995). Social problems included drug abuse and relational problems (Beaton & Murphy, 1995). Figley (1988) noted early that families also become secondary victims.

To add to the complexity of symptoms, it has been pointed out that they appear differently in different disaster phases (Beaton & Murphy, 1995; Valent, 1984), and they range from reflex responses to moral and philosophical dilemmas (Herman, 1992), existential meanings, and spirituality (Lahad, 2000; Pearlman & Saakvitne, 1995a, 1995b).

A Wide Variety of Helper Treatments

In parallel to the wide variety of helper symptoms, a wide variety of treatments has been advocated for helpers. Yassen (1995) suggested that the following provide resistance against helper stress and trauma: management of vital functions, such as sleep, food, exercise, rest, and recreation; contact with nature; maintaining structures of work; and limiting exposure to traumatic situations. Others have suggested peer, institutional, and personal help and support (Dutton & Rubinstein, 1995), whereas Munroe et al. (1995) suggested a special team that provides outside perspective and mediates helpers' roles in the community. A number of workers emphasize the advantages of proper training, including helpers' ability to read and care for their own stress responses.

For helpers who have been involved in traumatic situations, a variety of programs has been advocated. In order of proximity to the traumatic situation, they have included decompression, defusion, and a variety of debriefing programs ranging from single sessions to relatively ongoing care with peer support or professionals (McCammon & Allison, 1995). These programs vary in their educative, cognitive, emotional, and existential approaches.

Finally, some workers recommend supervision and personal therapy, especially for helpers who are involved in deep psychotherapy with clients with multiple early life traumas (e.g., Pearlman & Saakvitne, 1995a, 1995b).

Helper Stress and Trauma Conceptualizations

In order to make sense of the wide variety of symptoms and methods of treatment, some researchers have postulated phenomenological categorizations and mechanisms of symptom formation.

Regarding phenomenological categorizations, Figley (1995b) suggested that PTSD should be called *primary posttraumatic stress disorder,* whereas the same symptoms appearing secondarily to victim care in helpers should be called *secondary traumatic stress disorder* (STSD). The only difference between PTSD and STSD was that, in the latter, exposure was to the traumatized person(s) rather than to the traumatic event itself, and intrusion and avoidance symptoms related to the primary victim's experience, not to one's own. Figley (1995c) gave a special name, *compassion fatigue,* to the specific STSD resulting from deep involvement with a primarily traumatized person. Next, in parallel to the concept of (primary) stress, Figley delineated compassion stress (secondary traumatic stress, or STS). Here, helpers knew about, and were affected by, traumatizing events, but this did not reach traumatic STSD proportions.

However, just as for primary victims PTSD was insufficient to delineate and make sense of the wide variety of symptoms, so STSD did not heuristically delineate and make sense of the variety of symptoms described above. Figley (1995b) therefore distinguished two other commonly used terms that captured the significance of certain symptoms.

Burnout is a result of frustration, powerlessness, and inability to achieve work goals. It is characterized by some psychophysiological arousal symptoms, including sleep disturbance, headaches, irritability, and aggression, yet also physical and mental exhaustion. Other symptoms included callousness, pessimism, cynicism, problems in work relationships, and falling off of work performance. Burnout can result from the noxious nature of work stressors themselves or from hierarchical pressures, constraints, and lack of understanding.

Countertransference explains the mechanism of producing helper symptoms. It is described as the unconscious attunement to and absorption of victims' stresses and traumas. The latter are often expressed nonverbally, such as through gestures and enactments. These are vehicles of transferring especially emotional information not readily expressible in words. Such transferring of information is called *transference*. On the receiving side, empathy is the vehicle whereby helpers make themselves open to absorption of traumatic information. The absorption and subsequent impulse to respond may be life-saving in ongoing traumatic events. After the events, countertransference reads the relived transference information. This is done through one's own affective reactions, cognitive unfoldings, and impulses to action (Wilson & Lindy, 1994) and helps helpers to understand their clients' relived experiences and needs.

Such permeability to clients' traumatic events of necessity leads to stress, called *empathic strain* by Wilson, Lindy, and Raphael (1994), or to trauma, called *vicarious traumatization* by Pearlman and Saakvitne (1995a, 1995b).

Wilson et al. (1994) divided empathic strain into two categories approximately corresponding to intrusive and avoidance features of PTSD. Intrusive-type countertransference strain includes loss of boundaries, overinvolvement, reciprocal dependency, and pathological bonding. Avoidance-type counter-transference strain includes withdrawal, numbness, intellectualization, and denial. On the other hand, vicarious traumatization includes disruptions of self-capacities, beliefs, relationships, world view, and spirituality (Black & Weinreich, 2000; Pearlman & Saakvitne, 1995a).

Finally, a number of workers have recognized that the intimate relationship between helpers and victims is a two-way affair. Helpers also bring unconscious current and past stresses and traumas into their interactions with clients (Figley, 1995b). For example, helpers may be attracted to clients who suffer similar traumas to the helpers' repressed ones. Helpers' unconscious transference of their problems onto clients may evoke countertransference in the latter, which may compound their traumas.

Current Dilemmas

STSD and compassion fatigue were diagnoses waiting to happen, and they provided meaningful and respectful labels for affected trauma workers. However, like PTSD, they do not categorize or heuristically make sense of the wide variety of manifestations and symptoms (e.g., Blair & Ramones, 1996) that are relived or avoided, or explain why they should be suffered. Although counter-transference responses explain the means of transmission and reason for suffering, countertransference responses do not classify or provide reasons why particular symptoms should be transmitted at any particular time. Burnout seems to go some way toward providing a reason for a particular cluster of symptoms, but it does not explain why they should occur and not others and it does not explain symptoms outside its cluster.

Often implied reasons for the nature of symptoms lie in survival strategies such as fight and flight. However, these two strategies are insufficient to explain the variety of symptoms.

In the last volume, I suggested that eight survival strategies provide a more extensive framework for diagnosing, classifying, and making sense of the wide variety of STS phenomena. Which particular ones were experienced at any one time depended on specific identifications with, or responding in complementary fashions to, victims' needs and survival strategies (Valent, 1995).

In this chapter I intend to explain in greater detail how survival strategies provide a framework for the wide variety of STS and STSD manifestations and countertransference responses. It also will be suggested that two specific survival strategies (Rescue–Caretaking and Assertiveness–Goal Achievement) can heuristically delineate compassion fatigue and burnout, respectively.

A further tool, the triaxial framework, will be used to indicate how symptoms derived from survival strategies spread across the extensive field of traumatology, and how different treatments fit into its coordinates. Finally, treatment implications of the combined view of survival strategies and the triaxial framework (called the wholist perspective) will be examined.

SURVIVAL STRATEGIES AND CONCEPTUALIZATION OF SECONDARY STRESS AND TRAUMA RESPONSES

In this section survival strategies will be summarized and applied to STS and STSD, compassion strain and fatigue, burnout, and countertransference responses.

Survival Strategies

Survival strategies such as fight and flight are biopsychosocial templates that have evolved to enhance maximum survival within evolutionary social units. Their level of operation is in the "old mammalian" brain (MacLean, 1973), functionally between instincts and abstract functioning. In traumatic situations, they correspond to acute stress responses.

Although the arousal symptoms in PTSD imply that only fight and flight acute stress responses are relived and avoided, I suggest that they and six further such survival strategies contribute to reliving and avoidance responses. The eight survival strategies are Rescuing (Caretaking), Attaching, Asserting (Goal Achievement), Adapting (Goal Surrender), Fighting, Fleeing, Competing, and Cooperating. Further, it is their adaptive and maladaptive, biological, psychological, and social components that contribute to the wide variety of manifestations in traumatic stress. The survival strategies and their acute stress response manifestations are depicted in Table 1.1.

Survival strategies and their components are parts of a dynamic process (Figure 1.1). They are evoked by appraisals of stressors with which they are to

TABLE 1.1
Survival Strategy Components

APPRAISAL OF MEANS OF SURVIVAL	SURVIVAL STRATEGIES	SUCCESSFUL / ADAPTIVE RESPONSES		
		BIOLOGICAL	PSYCHOLOGICAL	SOCIAL
MUST SAVE OTHERS	**RESCUING** PROTECT PROVIDE	↑ ESTROGEN ↑ OXYTOCIN ↑ OPIOIDS	CARE EMPATHY **DEVOTION**	RESPONSIBILITY NURTURE **PRESERVATION**
MUST BE SAVED BY OTHERS	**ATTACHING** PROTECTED PROVIDED	? ↑ OPIOIDS	HELD, CARED FOR NURTURED **LOOKED AFTER**	CLOSE SECURE CONTENT **UNION**
MUST ACHIEVE GOAL	**ASSERTING** COMBAT WORK	↑E, NE ↓ CORTISOL ↑ IMMUNOCOMP	STRENGTH CONTROL **POTENCY**	WILL HIGH MORALE **SUCCESS**
MUST SURRENDER GOAL	**ADAPTING** ACCEPT GRIEVE	PARASYMP AROUSAL ↑ CORTISOL	ACCEPTANCE SADNESS GRIEF **HOPE**	YIELDING MOURNING **TURN TO NEW**
MUST REMOVE DANGER	**FIGHTING** DEFEND RID	SYMP. AROUSAL ↑N, NE ↑BP	THREAT REVENGE **FRIGHTEN**	DETERRENCE WOUNDING **RIDDANCE**
MUST REMOVE ONSELF FROM DANGER	**FLEEING** RUN, HIDE SAVE ONESELF	SYMPATHETIC & PARASYMP AROUSAL	FEAR TERROR **DELIVERANCE**	RETREAT FLIGHT **ESCAPE**
MUST OBTAIN SCARCE ESSENTIALS	**COMPETING** POWER ACQUISITION	↑TESTOSTERONE SYMP. AROUSAL	WINNING STATUS **DOMINANCE**	CONTEST HIERARCHY **POSSESSION**
MUST CREATE MORE ESSENTIALS	COOPERATING TRUST MUTUAL GAIN	↑ OPIATES ↓BP, E, NE	MUTUALITY GENEROSITY LOVE	INTEGRATION RECIPROCITY CREATAIVITY

Notes for Table 1.1. E = epinephrine. NE = norepinephrine. Immunocomp = immunocompetence. Parasymp = parasympathetic (nervous system). Symp = sympathetic

UNSUCCESSFUL / MALADAPTIVE RESPONSES

BIOLOGICAL	PSYCHOLOGICAL	SOCIAL	TRAUMA RESPONSES
SYMPATHETIC & PARASYMP. AROUSAL	BURDEN DEPLETION **SELF-CONCERN**	RESENTMENT NEGLECT **REJECTION**	ANGUISH COMPASS FATIGUE CAUSED DEATH
↑ OPIOIDS	· YEARNING NEED CRAVE **ABANDONMENT**	CRY INSECURE DEPRIVED **SEPARATION**	HELPLESSNESS CAST OUT LEFT TO DIE
↑↑ E, NE DEPLETION E, NE ↑ BP, ?CHD	FRUSTRATION LOSS OF CONTROL **IMPOTENCE**	WILLFULNESS LOW MORALE **FAILURE**	EXHAUSTION "BURN-OUT" POWERLESSNESS
↑ CORTISOL ↓ IMMUNOCOMP ↑ INFECTION, ?↑ CA	OVERWHELMED DEPRESSION **DESPAIR**	COLLAPSED WITHDRAWAL **GIVING UP**	DAMAGED GIVEN IN SUCCUMBING
↑↑ SYMP AROUSAL ↓ CORTISOL	HATRED PERSECUTION **KILLING**	ATTACK ERADICATION **DESTRUCTION**	HORROR EVIL MURDER
NE DEPLETION ↑ E & CORTISOL	PHOBIA PARANOIA **ENGULFMENT**	AVOIDANCE PANIC **ANNIHILATION**	"INESCAPABLE SHOCK", BEING HUNTED, KILLED
↓ TESTOSTERONE ↓ FEMALE HORMS ↑ CORTISOL	DEFEATE GREED, ENVY **EXPLOITATION**	OPPRESSION STRUGGLE **PLUNDER**	TERRORIZATION MARGINALIZATION ELIMINATION
↓ OPIATES ?↑ PARASYMP AROUSAL	BETRAYAL SELFISHNESS **ABUSE**	DISCONNECTION CHEATING **DISINTEGRATION**	FRAGMENTATION ALIENATION DECAY

(nervous system). BP = blood pressure. CHD = coronary heart disease.
CA = cancer. Compass = compassion.   ©Paul Valent

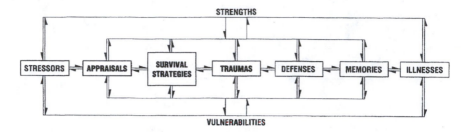

FIGURE 1.1. The place of Survival Strategies on the process axis.

deal. If they fail to do so, trauma and illnesses may result, although they may be mitigated by defenses and lack of memory for traumatic events. This process forms one axis of the triaxial framework (Figure 1.2), described below.

The reader is referred to more detailed descriptions of survival strategies and the triaxial framework, and clinical application of the wholist perspective to treatment in Valent (1998a and 1998b, respectively).

Application of Survival Strategies to Conceptualizing Helper Stresses and Traumas

In this part it will be shown that secondary traumatic stress and secondary traumatic stress disorder are the results of countertransference identification

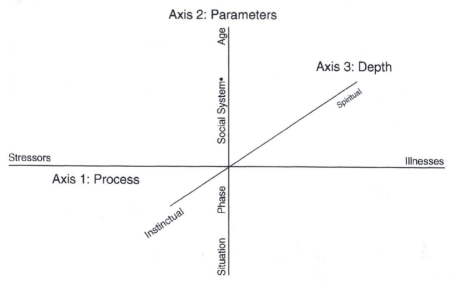

FIGURE 1.2. Triaxial view of traumatic stress.

with victims' maladaptive and traumatic aspects of helpers' survival strategies, respectively, and/or one's own complementary survival strategies being insufficient to various degrees. It will be shown that compassion fatigue and burnout are specific failed Rescue–Caretaking and Assertiveness–Goal Achievement survival strategy responses. They are salient in helpers because they are commonly complementary to victim needs.

Secondary Traumatic Stress and Countertransference Responses

Secondary traumatic stress responses are the maladaptive (stress) responses in Table 1.1. As mentioned above, they may be evoked in helpers through identification with victim survival strategies and/or complementing victim survival strategies with their own. In identification, the helper is in attunement and reverberates with client signals and needs. By reading the reverberations in themselves, helpers understand client experiences better. This is called countertransference.

The purpose of such reverberation in helpers is to evoke in them adaptive survival strategies that fortify insufficient victims. For instance, a person in panic (maladaptive Flight) may be offered escape and deliverance (adaptive Flight); defeated people (maladaptive Competition) may be empowered and offered status (adaptive Competition); abandoned, needy people (maladaptive Attachment) may be offered care and nurture (adaptive Rescue–Caretaking); inability to grieve (Adaptation–Goal Surrender) may be helped by hope and a shoulder to cry on. Helpers' survival strategies often are the adaptive equivalents of victims' maladaptive ones, or the adaptive equivalents of adjacent reciprocal survival strategies (the other of the pair delineated by double lines in Table 1.1), or adaptive aspects of wider ranging survival strategies.

A number of points follow from the above:

- Although countertransference usually is recognized in long-term psychotherapy, its mechanisms can be intense in acute situations, as well.
- When helpers' survival strategies are insufficient to resolve victim stresses, helpers become secondarily stressed by carrying both maladaptive victim survival strategies with which they identify and their own maladaptive complementary survival strategies, which become insufficient.
- Because in traumatic situations all survival strategies may be attempted, helper reverberations and evocation of complementary survival strategies (even if not acted on) may mean that all survival strategies are experienced to some degree.
- Both victims and (more so) helpers experience adaptive survival strategies as well as maladaptive ones. In other words, helpers are not only stressed but also fulfilled.

Secondary Traumatic Stress Disorder

Secondary traumatic stress disorder in this schema arises in parallel to secondary traumatic stress. In other words, helpers may identify with the trauma responses of victims (see Table 1.1), or their own failed complementary efforts may reach traumatic proportions. For instance, a rescuer may respond to a trapped woman's cries but not be able to save her. The rescuer's STSD may include both the identification with inescapable shock and terror of imminent annihilation (trauma of Flight) of the victim, and his own compassion fatigue (trauma of Rescue).

Compassion Strain and Fatigue

Appreciation of the survival strategy Rescue–Caretaking allows a heuristic separation of compassion stress and compassion fatigue from the more generic STS and STSD.

Referral to Table 1.1 shows that the appraisal in helpers that they must save or help others evokes adaptive Rescue–Caretaking responses. The psychological and social components of these responses are care; empathy and devotion; and responsibility, nurture, and preservation, respectively. Together, these responses are the components of compassion.

Compassion stress can be seen in the unsuccessful, maladaptive psychological and social stress responses of Rescue–Caretaking. They are a sense of burden; depletion and self-concern; and resentment, neglect, and rejection, respectively. In helpers these feelings gather into strain, stress, and distress.

Compassion stress can be aggravated by specific negative psychosocial feedback judgments (such as "irresponsible" in the Judgments column of Table 1.1) and by nascent meanings about one's poor role, failed expectations, and existential shortcoming.

In the traumatic situation where victims could not be saved or properly cared for, compassion strain reaches traumatic proportions and may be called compassion fatigue. It includes maladaptive compassion strain, but in addition includes severe anguish and intense guilt associated with the meaning of not having prevented, or even having caused, harm or death. The distress and trauma of not having done enough to avert suffering or death is a common secondary stress and secondary trauma response in helpers.

The word *compassion* also could be applied to deep sympathy and sorrow for those afflicted by suffering and misfortune (Figley, 1995c). However, it may be better to use the words *sympathy* and *sorrow* as specific responses to those in grief (Adaptation–Goal Surrender). Other specific words that fall under a generic term of compassion can also be honed as specific survival strategy responses. Examples are *pity* for refugees (Flight), *support* for the helpless (Attachment), and *tenderness* for the abused (Cooperation).

Burnout

Burnout relates to the survival strategy of Assertiveness–Goal Achievement. Like the hunters and warriors for whose goals this survival strategy evolved in particular, helpers also have life and death goals that may contain hazards, whose execution requires training and effort and often requires group coordination.

When goals are being attained, helpers feel that they are executing their will, they feel strong, in control, and potent. They have high morale, and feel successful (see Table 1.1).

Inability to achieve goals is accompanied by frustration, a sense of loss of control and impotence, increased willful efforts, diminishing morale, and failure to achieve goals. Many symptoms described for burnout—such as poor work performance, irritability, and inability to concentrate—are secondary to the stress symptoms listed above. As well, work effort and frustration elevate sympathetic nervous system arousal, which then produces common burnout symptoms such as sleep difficulties, muscle tensions and pains, and may contribute to hypertension, coronary heart disease, and stroke (Valent, 1998a). These are the illnesses that were seen to contribute to higher helper mortality rates.

Traumatic intensities of Assertiveness contain earlier burnout stress symptoms as well as intense exhaustion and powerlessness. Burnout exhaustion may be the civilian equivalent of combat exhaustion, which was the definitive military trauma diagnosis of World War II (Bartemeier, Kubie, Menninger, Romano, & Whitehorn, 1946). The exhaustion may be severe, but it is not associated with ability to rest and sleep. Rather, it is accompanied by sleeplessness, anger, and rumination about one's ineffectiveness. The sense of powerlessness is one in which one senses that no amount of one's exertions and efforts can achieve important life goals.

Associated negative judgments include being weak, incompetent, inadequate, a failure, and associated meanings include not being able to make it, not being a man, and being a weakling in life.

In summary, maladaptive and traumatic survival strategy responses account for and explain the wide variety of helper stress and trauma responses to victims. Compassion stress and fatigue, and burnout stress and fatigue are stress and trauma responses in two specific survival strategies: Rescue–Caretaking and Assertiveness–Goal Achievement.

DIAGNOSIS OF HELPER DYSFUNCTIONS

Helper dysfunctions appear in different forms at different points in the process between stressors and illnesses, as depicted in Figure 1.1. Thus insufficient, overdetermined, or inappropriate survival strategies may stem from faulty appraisals. Symptoms of stress stem from unsuccessful or maladaptive survival strategies, whereas traumas stem from failed survival strategies (see Table 1.1). In each case, stress and trauma symptoms may be classified or diagnosed as biological, psychological, and social aspects of specific survival strategies. They in turn may be traced to identificatory or complementary survival strategies in specific victim–helper interactions.

Case 1. A nurse who had intensively looked after a severely ill young man who eventually died felt extreme exhaustion, irritability with other patients, headaches, tremors, and an unexplained chest pain. She had an inordinate fear that she would die of a heart attack.

In this nurse's case, the initial STS group of symptoms was traced to incipient burnout due to the extensive effort that failed to achieve its goal (Assertiveness stress). The latter symptom was an identification of being annihilated (Flight) by the same enemy as the young man, who died of a heart problem.

In parallel with the reliving and avoiding features of PTSD, helpers may experience intrusive STS and STSD symptoms, or they may manifest defenses to avoid and mitigate traumatic states, judgments of guilt and shame, and shattered meanings. In such cases their memories of the original helping situations may be incomplete or absent. Symptoms and illnesses are a vector result of relived and avoided biological, psychological, and social secondary stress and trauma symptoms. Survival strategies add the content, the flesh and blood to what is relived and avoided, and the sense of why. Their specific features facilitate tracing a wide variety of symptom and illness fragments and clusters back to their sources and contexts in traumatic events and victim relationships.

Enrichment of Diagnoses Through the Triaxial Framework

The triaxial framework (Valent, 1998a) sees the stressor → illness process as one of three axes: the process axis (Figure 1.1), the parameter axis, and the depth axis (Figure 1.2).

The parameter axis takes into account the nature of the stressor, the phase of disasters, social systems of helpers, and their maturity, knowledge, and experience. The nature of stressors includes their severity (such as whether they include deaths and mutilations), duration, identification with victims through relationship or similar age, and place of the event in relation to other traumatic events. For instance, it is possible that a traumatic event reverberates with past or subsequent traumatic events, evoking untoward major symptoms or defenses and blind spots.

The phase of disasters includes time in relation to the event. Social system includes the helper's peers, institutions, family, and community. Sometimes institutional, career, and family conflicts are as stressful as the helping itself.

The depth axis takes into account external and internal judgments, morality, meanings, principles, ideals, ethics, status, dignity, identity, beliefs, spiritual aspirations, and life's purpose. All of these may be stressed and traumatized through reverberations with victims and through one's own perceived failures to respond.

I believe that each survival strategy manifests itself in all three axes. This extends and enriches both victim and helper diagnoses. For instance, in the case of the nurse, her stresses influenced her behavior with her family, fiancee, subsequent patients, and colleagues, and had negative influence on her self-views, identity as a nurse, and sense of purpose in saving lives.

Influence of Secondary Stresses and Traumas on Clients

One specific social parameter interaction deserves special examination—the helper–client social system. This is because client–helper relationships are two-way, and helper stresses and traumas have at least as large secondary effects on clients as client stresses and traumas have on helpers.

Whether through current stresses with victims or through blind spots from previous traumas, helpers themselves emit survival strategy signals with which clients reverberate and to which they respond countertransferentially. Detrimental interactions may be diagnosed in helpers, clients, and their interactions.

Helper stresses and traumas may be reflected in nonrecognition, denial of client traumas, fragmented attention, lack of empathy, intellectualization, dehumanization of victims as cases or research subjects, and partial and foreclosed diagnoses and treatments. Occasionally helpers may manifest a paradoxically overenthusiastic (even if short-lived) involvement with client traumas.

Reciprocally, clients may see their helpers as naive, ignorant, limited, patronizing, denigratory, unsympathetic, lacking understanding and compassion, and at worst more traumatic than the original trauma. Often clients and patients of necessity deny helper problems and accommodate to them.

Negative interactions may manifest as patient distress, acting out, intensification of symptoms, decompensation, and premature termination of treatment. Excessive accommodations can lead to treatment enmeshments, such as ever-grateful patients who gratify insecure therapists. In extreme cases, enmeshments may lead to clients absorbing helper problems, such as their depressions. They may act them out, even through suicidal acts. The following case is mild by comparison, though more common.

Case 2. The daughter of a traumatized and depressed mother became a psychologist. She felt compelled to "reach out" to those bereaved in a local calamity. However, talking to bereaved victims evoked depression in her, and she left the scene after some days. The only help she had been able to offer was intellectual explanations of responses and conventional wisdoms, which seemed to distress victims.

Diagnosis of helper symptoms and blind spots can be enriched in extent and accuracy using the triaxial framework and survival strategies. In this case, the helper was blind to grief (Adaptation), which was transmitted to her by her mother. Her career was a transference of her role of being mother's caregiver (Rescue–Caretaking).

TREATMENT OF HELPER DYSFUNCTIONS

Just as the wide variety of helper symptoms can be orientated and speci-fied with the help of the wholist perspective (that is, the triaxial framework and survival strategies), so can the wholist perspective orientate and specify a wide variety of helper treatments. In addition, the wholist perspective can add to the enrichment, rationalization, and tailoring of treatment of helper stresses and traumas.

Orientation and Specifications of Current Treatments

Although most treatments span various axes and survival strategies, it may help conceptualization of treatments to see where they mainly fit in the wholist perspective.

Thus, on the *process axis* a variety of treatments are aimed at ameliorating stresses—that is, maladaptive survival strategies. Some programs are mainly educational (e.g., Zimmerman & Weber, 2000). Others include stress man-agement treatments, which limit the intensity of exposure to stressors through rest, recreation, meditation, and communion with nature (Yassen, 1995). De-compressions, defusings, and debriefings emphasize understanding stress symptoms as normal survival strategy responses to abnormal situations. Dif-ferent types of debriefings emphasize understanding different combinations of biological, cognitive, emotional, and social stress symptoms. Entrenched traumas and illnesses require more extensive help, such as through cognitive behavior or psychodynamic psychotherapy. Many workers emphasize train-ing as preparation to enhance adaptive and diminish maladaptive responses.

Treatment *parameters* may include different times of initiation and frequency and duration of different treatments. They include individual, group, or insti-tutional treatment targets. Further, therapists of helpers may also be individu-als, cotherapists, or treatment teams.

Depth axis involvement may involve deeper debriefings over longer times. They take into account emotions, moralities, meanings, and existential issues (e.g., Lahad, 2000). Deeper vicarious traumatization or role-, identity-, spiri-tual-, and existential-level disruptions as well as helper blind spots and earlier traumas (Black & Weinreich, 2000) may require long-term supervision and treatment (Pearlman & Saakvitne, 1995a, 1995b).

Sometimes specific helper survival strategies are targets for treatment. For instance, helpers may be facilitated to grieve their losses (Adaptation) or manage anger and work frustrations (Assertiveness) or their helper anguish (Rescue–Caretaking).

Thus, the wholist perspective can help to orient the different foci of various treatments and to provide a view of the strengths and boundaries of those treatments.

Ubiquitous Treatment Principles

Trauma therapies include one or more of four ubiquitous principles (Valent, 1998b): recognition, nonspecific, symptomatic, and specific treatment approaches. *Recognition* here includes helper stresses and traumas and their wholist diagnoses. *Nonspecific treatment* includes countertrauma environments in which helpers are intuitively provided with adaptive antidotes to their maladaptive survival strategies. *Symptomatic treatment* deals with specific biological, psychological, or social survival strategies at particular triaxial framework points.

Specific therapy includes remembering and specifying symptoms and understanding them according to their traumatic sources. Through dual focus of attention on the traumatic source and current perspectives of that situation in the present, stressful and traumatic responses and significances are readjusted to a nonstressful meaningful story, which subsumes past and current realities.

Application of the Wholist Perspective to Treatment Principles in Helpers

In order to provide as wide and rich yet specific treatment to helpers, the aim of wholist therapy is to apply the wholist perspective to each treatment principle. The following general approach will be applied specifically to compassion fatigue and burnout. Finally, a unified yet potentially specific tailored approach across disaster phases will be presented.

Recognition

According to the first treatment principle, it is recognized that helpers are living or reliving stress and trauma survival strategy responses. Their specific biological, psychological, and social features give clues to the specific survival strategy involved and the type of appraisal that evoked it in the traumatic event. Recognition thus includes specific reconstruction of traumatic events and helpers' responses to them. This includes recognition of responses as reverberations in unison with victims, responding to victims' needs, or survival strategies of one's own, irrespective of victims.

This recognition is fed back to helpers. It includes the understanding that their responses were normal reactions in abnormal situations, but it also specifies the evolutionary and specific contexts of a wide range of survival strategies in which victims and helpers participated in the situations.

Nonspecific Therapy

The intuitive placing of boundaries between helpers and victims allows the latter to safely concentrate on and express solely their own survival strategy responses.

Further, each adaptive survival strategy is intuitively enhanced. The bounded place of therapy away from demanding situations provides a sanctuary (Flight). The respect accorded ensures status and dignity (Competition). The goal of therapy is greater control in one's work (Assertiveness) and gaining weapons to defeat trauma in the future (Fight). A safe place to cry for losses facilitates grief and hope (Adaptation). The therapeutic relationship encourages a sense of support and being cared for (Attachment), and identification with the care and empathy of the therapists facilitates Rescue–Caretaking. Mutuality of sharing enhances a sense of love and creativity (Cooperation).

Symptomatic Therapy

As mentioned, symptomatic therapy alleviates specific biological, psychological, or social symptoms at specific triaxial points. For instance, headaches are managed with analgesics, anxiety with anxiety management, powerlessness with empowerment, and so on.

Specific Therapy

In this case, helpers' specific stress and trauma survival strategy responses, whose sense and sources have already been recognized, are contrasted with past and present realities. This may need to be done for each component of each survival strategy. Compassion fatigue and burnout will be used as examples.

Compassion fatigue. Helpers may present with any of the stress and trauma symptoms of Rescue–Caretaking (Table 1.1), such as feeling burdened, rejecting victims, anguish for not having prevented damage or death, not having done enough, having neglected their responsibilities, and so on. Helpers may also complain of reverberating still with the cries of the helpless, those they abandoned—that is, the maladaptive and trauma symptoms of Attachment of those they were to help.

In a sympathetic environment each of these and related symptoms is traced back through adaptive Rescue–Caretaking responses that helpers also had but which were insufficient for the situation, to the situation itself. It may become clear that the causes of the damage were the insurmountable situations, impossible choices, and too few resources—not the helpers themselves. Each stress and trauma response may need to be reworked in terms of those realities and current and future possibilities. What was done, could be done and may be done, better in the future become part of a coherent and meaningful story of caring.

Burnout. In this case helpers may suffer a range of Assertiveness stress and trauma responses such as exhaustion, impotence, sense of failure, tension, arousal, and so on. They may also reverberate with victims' losses, which they failed to avert.

Helpers may be given rest, recreation, exercises to manage anger, and tasks in which they succeed. In addition, it is necessary once again for the symptoms to be recognized and traced back via adaptive efforts that were insufficient to specific traumatic stressor contexts. It may be understood how strength, morale, and all the will in the world were insufficient to achieve success in the situation. It may be realized that the task was too great for the resources, that institutions and community provided too little support, or that one was thrown into situations with too little training. This may be contrasted with realistic expectations and current and future resources and possibilities. The event then becomes part of a learning process of experience, knowing what is possible and what could be improved.

Extension of Treatment Across the Triaxial Framework

Principles of treatment for survival strategy stress and trauma responses apply for their ramifications across the triaxial framework. For instance, on the depth axis each survival strategy may be associated with specific anxieties and strained or shattered moral judgments, meanings, principles, ideals, and existential beliefs. Each of these may require application of all treatment ingredients.

Similarly, each principle of treatment for each survival strategy is adapted to disaster phases, social system levels, type of disaster, helper experience, and previous traumas.

A Rationale for Tailored Application of Wholist Helper Treatment

Ideally all maladaptive and traumatic survival strategy responses are treated with all treatment ingredients across the whole triaxial framework. While this is seldom possible, education, planning, and checking throughout treatments highlights what is being treated and what is not.

Each lack in wholist treatment carries potential costs. For instance, biological, psychological, or social responses may be unattended; one or another survival strategy may be ignored; treatment possibilities in different disaster phases may not be utilized; individuals, teams, or institutions may be forgotten; and humanist treatment potentials may be ignored.

The following takes disaster phases as a pragmatic central point for checking and tailoring helper treatments. In different circumstances other points may be taken as central. For instance, one may check that all survival strategies are covered in a debriefing. Alternately, a single survival strategy, such as Assertiveness, may be taken as the focus in order to make sure that burnout is prevented or treated in all circumstances.

Preimpact

At different social levels, education and training includes preemption of stressors. Failing that, preparation is made to facilitate all adaptive survival strategies and to prevent maladaptive ones. Helpers are educated in the wholist framework, especially compassion fatigue and burnout. Structures are put in place to prepare for helping helpers in each subsequent disaster phase. Helpers are given tasks within their capacities and available resources.

During Traumatic Events

All is done to facilitate adaptive survival strategies at all social system levels. Helpers have themselves access to helpers who understand and support them (Rescue–Caretaking); provide resources and coordinate services and hierarchies (Assertiveness); help through cutting of losses (Adaptation); are allies (Fight); maintain authority (Competition); provide relief (Flight), tea, and sympathy (Attachment); and provide trust and generosity, and facilitate creativity (Cooperation). They preempt burnout and compassion fatigue by tailoring tasks, providing rosters, relieving burdens, and taking responsibility for prioritizations and necessary choices. They explain expected survival strategy responses and place them quickly in context. Helper ethics, values, ideals, and self-views are protected. Negative client–helper relationships are identified and treated, or alternate helpers are provided.

After Traumatic Events

In decompressions and defusions, especially problematic survival strategies are given space for expression and put in current realistic perspective. In debriefings in a safe countertrauma environment, all survival strategy responses are covered, including all their adaptive and maladaptive, biological, psychological, and social components. Each response is explained, understood in context, and readjusted to realistic perspectives. The same is done for negative judgments and meanings, as well as for shattered principles, self-views, and deeper meanings. This is done for individuals, groups, and institutions. New adaptive ways of dealing with future events are facilitated at all levels.

Over the next period, defensive responses and emerging illnesses are identified. Vulnerabilities and blind spots associated with other current or past traumas are identified or treated. The same treatment principles are applied, perhaps over a longer period, to clear multiple defenses and maladaptive survival strategy ramifications.

Long-Term Problems

Involvement in traumatic events may reverberate with and uncover long-term traumatic events and their sequelae. Helpers may require long-term supervision and therapy, in which entrenched and defended maladaptive and traumatic survival strategy responses and their ramifications are readjusted across the triaxial framework.

This chapter does not evaluate specific treatments, but points to where research may be fruitfully directed. For instance, particular treatments may be most efficacious at particular paramater axis points, such as of time (e.g., Campfield & Hills, 2001). Treatments must also be judged according to what they measure and what they do not (e.g., Deahl, Srinivasan, Joness, Neblett, & Jolly, 2001).

SUMMARY

In summary, the wholist perspective, with its concepts of survival strategies and the triaxial framework, may help conceptualization of the wide variety of helper symptoms and treatments.

Eight survival strategies and their components are the basis for explaining the great variety of lived and relived stress and trauma symptoms in helpers. The mechanism for evoking survival strategies in helpers is through reverberation with victims' survival strategies in an attempt to understand their needs and/or responding to them with complementary helper survival strategies in order to execute the needs. These early countertransference phenomena were the basis of subsequent sequelae, which formed the wide range of helper stress and trauma phenomena.

This wide range of maladaptive survival strategy manifestations forms what has been called STS. In the same vein, secondary traumatic survival strategy responses account for a variety of STSDs. Two commonly used helper survival strategies, Rescue–Caretaking and Assertiveness–Goal Achievement, account for two common specifically delineated syndromes: compassion fatigue and burnout, respectively. Although the term compassion fatigue has been used generically for helper traumas, the current suggestion limits it to Rescue–Caretaking trauma, while the general term remains STSD.

Survival strategies are represented triaxially on the process, parameter, and depth axes of traumatic stress. Using them as coordinates for survival strategies allowed a wholist perspective that is both a unifying and a specifying view of helper symptoms, diagnoses, and treatments.

Finally, the wholist perspective can be usefully applied to recognition, nonspecific, symptomatic, and specific components of trauma therapy. An example was given of its application to helper treatment across disaster phases.

This view needs verification, working through, and adjusting. However, it may have applications in other secondarily affected populations, such as in families, including across generations.

REFERENCES

Bartemeier, L. H., Kubie, L. S., Menninger, K. A., Romano, J., & Whitehorn, J. C. (1946). Combat exhaustion. *Journal of Nervous and Mental Disease, 104,* 358–389.

Beaton, R. D., & Murphy, S. A. (1995). Working with people in crisis: Research implications. In C. R. Figley (Ed.), *Compassion fatigue: Secondary traumatic stress disorder in helpers* (pp. 51–81). New York: Brunner/Mazel.

Berah, E., Jones, H. J., & Valent, P. (1984). The experience of a mental health team involved in the early phase of a disaster. *Australian and New Zealand Journal of Psychiatry, 18,* 354–358.

Black, S., & Weinreich, P. (2000). An exploration of counselling identity in counsellors who deal with trauma. *Traumatology, 6,* 25–40.

Blair, D. T., & Ramones, V. A. (1996). Understanding vicarious traumatization. *Psychosocial Nursing Mental Health Serv, 34,* 24–30.

Campfield, K. M., & Hills, A. M. (2001). Effect of timing of critical incidence stress debriefing (CISD) on post-traumatic symptoms. *Journal of Traumatic Stress, 14,* 327–340.

Deahl, M. P., Srinivasan, M., Joness, N., Neblett, C., & Jolly, A. (2001). Evaluating psychological debriefing: Are we measuring the right outcomes? *Journal of Traumatic Stress, 14,* 527–529.

Dutton, M. A., & Rubinstein, F. L. (1995). Working with people with PTSD: Research implications. In C. R. Figley (Ed.), *Compassion fatigue: Secondary traumatic stress disorder in helpers* (pp. 82–100). New York: Brunner/Mazel.

Figley, C. R. (Ed.). (1995a). *Compassion fatigue: Secondary traumatic stress disorder in helpers.* New York: Brunner/Mazel.

Figley, C. R. (1995b). Compassion fatigue as secondary traumatic stress disorder: An overview. In C. R. Figley (Ed.), *Compassion fatigue: Secondary traumatic stress disorder in helpers* (pp. 1–20). New York: Brunner/Mazel.

Figley, C. R. (1995c). Introduction. In C. R. Figley (Ed.), *Compassion fatigue: Secondary traumatic stress disorder in helpers* (pp. xiii–xxii). New York: Brunner/Mazel.

Herman, J. L. (1992). *Trauma and recovery.* New York: Basic Books.

Lahad, M. (2000). Darkness over the abyss: Supervising crisis intervention teams following disaster. *Traumatology, 6,* 273–293.

MacLean, P. D. (1973). *A triune concept of the brain and behaviour.* Toronto, Canada: Toronto University Press.

McCammon, S. L., & Allison, E. J. (1995). Debriefing and treating emergency workers. In C. R. Figley (Ed.), *Compassion fatigue: Secondary traumatic stress disorder in helpers* (pp. 115–130). New York: Brunner/Mazel.

Munroe, J. F., Shay, J., Fisher, L., Makary, C., Rapperport, K., & Zimering, R. (1995). Preventing compassion fatigue: A team treatment model. In C. R. Figley (Ed.), *Compassion fatigue: Secondary traumatic stress disorder in helpers* (pp. 209–231). New York: Brunner/Mazel.

Pearlman L. A., & Saakvitne, K. W. (1995a). *Trauma and the therapist.* New York: Norton.

Pearlman, L. A., & Saakvitne, K. W. (1995b). Treating therapists with vicarious traumatization and secondary traumatic stress disorder. In C. R. Figley (Ed.), *Compassion fatigue: Secondary traumatic stress disorder in helpers* (pp. 150–177). New York: Brunner/Mazel.

Valent, P. (1984). The Ash Wednesday bushfires in Victoria. *Medical Journal of Australia, 141,* 291–300.

Valent, P. (1995). Survival strategies: A framework for understanding secondary traumatic stress and coping in helpers. In Figley, C. R. (Ed.), *Compassion fatigue: Secondary traumatic stress disorder in helpers* (pp. 21–50). New York: Brunner/Mazel.

Valent, P. (1998a). *From survival to fulfillment: A framework for the life-trauma dialectic.* Philadelphia: Brunner/Mazel.

Valent, P. (1998b). *Trauma and fulfillment therapy.* Philadelphia: Brunner/Mazel.

Wilson, J. P., & Lindy, J. D. (1994). Empathic strain and countertransference. In J. P. Wilson & J. D. Lindy (Eds), *Countertransference in the treatment of PTSD.* New York: Guildford.

Wilson J. P., Lindy, J. D., & Raphael, B. (1994). Empathic strain and therapist defense: Type I and II countertransference reactions. In J. P. Wilson & J. D. Lindy (Eds.), *Countertransference in the treatment of PTSD.* New York: Guilford.

Yassen, J. (1995). Preventing secondary traumatic stress disorder. In C. R. Figley (Ed.), *Compassion fatigue: Secondary traumatic stress disorder in helpers* (pp. 82–100). New York: Brunner/ Mazel.

Zimmerman, G., & Weber W. (2000). Care for caregivers: A program for Canadian military chaplains serving in NATO and United Nations peacekeeping missions. *Military Medicine, 165,* 687–690.

2

The Trauma of Working with Traumatized Children

TRACY WOODARD MEYERS
THOMAS A. CORNILLE

INTRODUCTION

Kendra has been a child protective investigator for the state for the past three years. During that time she has interviewed children who have been hit, burned, neglected, and sexually abused by their caretakers. She has written and read reports that include overwhelming details about these experiences, as well as taken and viewed photographs that document the maltreatment. Her caseload has continued to grow, and as she becomes more experienced, new workers talk to her about their cases because they value her opinion and advice. Although she does not mind helping her coworkers, it has become difficult to do so lately because she has been extremely tired. For the past two months, Kendra has been waking up at 3:00 each morning unable to breathe. She gets out of bed and goes into the living room so she can lay on the couch with the ceiling fan on high. She is hot and sweaty, her heart is racing, and her arms hurt. She cries because she thinks she is having a heart attack and is afraid she is going to die. When she does not die and the symptoms subside, she assumes she is crazy. Finally she falls back to sleep at 5:30, only to have to get up at 6:00 a.m. for work. She also has been having severe pain in her arms and legs, and at times it is difficult for her to walk. Because it is more difficult for her to breathe after she eats, she skips meals and has lost 15 pounds. After her last sleepless night, Kendra promised herself that if she lived until morning she would see her family doctor. After a full battery of medical exams and tests, the doctor was unable to find any physical cause for her symptoms. Although relieved she was not dying, Kendra was upset when the doctor suggested she take an antidepressant to help with the symptoms. Thinking this would validate her biggest fear, that she was, crazy she decided not to take the medicine.

One day, after being on call for five days and up all night answering crisis calls, she was talking to her coworker, Andy. He started working investigations about the same time that she did. When she tried to describe what she had been experiencing, she began to cry. Although he likes Kendra, when Andy saw her crying he felt no empathy for her pain. As a matter of fact, he felt nothing at all. Andy said that he had not been having any of those problems, as he had been quite successful in blocking all of that garbage out of his mind. When he is at home, he sits in front of the television unaware of where the past hours have gone. He is sure that he had supper, bathed his kids, and talked to his wife, but he cannot remember any details. Kendra knows that Andy no longer staffs his cases with the supervisor, and he does not talk to the other workers about his cases. He just wants to be left alone. She has never seen him upset or crying, so she assumes that he is able to handle the job. None of the other workers talk about these kinds of experiences, so Kendra assumes she is the only one who is having such difficulties, which makes her feel more inadequate. Although she loves what she is doing, she is looking for another job. Andy and the other workers are also actively looking for other employment.

What Kendra and Andy do not realize is that, because they do their jobs so well, they are experiencing secondary traumatic stress symptoms. They care about the children with whom they work, and that caring opens them up to becoming victims, much like the children they try to protect. This chapter will be organized to provide the reader with specific information about this condition. First, we will offer a brief, necessarily limited review of the literature to set the stage. Next, we will describe the experiences of one group of child protective service (CPS) professionals who participated in a quantitative and qualitative study that focused on the extent of secondary traumatic stress and the personal and family characteristics that appear to predispose them to or insulate them from these problems. Following a brief summary of this informative research, we will provide some suggestions given both directly and indirectly by the women and men who participated in this study about how agencies, supervisors, and professionals themselves can deal with this risk.

LITERATURE REVIEW

Every day innocent children are physically abused, sexually assaulted, and neglected by their caretakers. In 1999, 50 states reported that 826,000 children were determined to have been victims of abuse and neglect (U.S. Department of Health and Human Services, 1999). At the end of the nineteenth century, special laws were passed and public authorities were hired to provide for the protection of children from such traumatizing events. Unfortunately, state and county social service agencies throughout the country continue to report difficulties in both recruiting and retaining CPS caseworkers. Although attrition is common among human service professionals, the losses are particularly heavy and the costs more substantial in the child protection field. In this crucial group, high turnover leads not only to a higher cost in hiring and training of workers but to a lowered quality of services delivered and a decrease in the agencies' ability to protect children (Balfour & Neff, 1993; Graef & Hill, 2000).

High turnover rates guarantee a constant supply of inexperienced workers. Because of their lack of knowledge and experience, these workers often make poor or delayed decisions that affect the safety and well-being of the children they are charged with protecting. According to McCurdy and Daro (1994), 35% of the child abuse victims who died between 1990 and 1992 had prior or current contact with child protective service agencies. Tens of thousands of other children receive serious injuries while under child protective supervision. CPS workers make decisions about what actions to take in cases of abuse and neglect based on their specialized knowledge. Many agencies report that qualified, competent applicants with CPS backgrounds often are not available (Graef & Hill, 2000). Therefore, newly hired workers must undergo extensive training. The initial training generally lasts several months and is followed by a long period of supervised practice. With a lower retention rate than other social service programs, the need for recruiting and training new caseworkers is an ongoing process. The agencies have to bear the expense of training new employees, which proves to be a costly endeavor.

High turnover rates among CPS workers not only drain the agency's already tight budget but also has a negative impact on the quality of services delivered. When workers resign, their cases have to be reassigned to other CPS workers, who are already overworked. This results in workers being responsible for even larger and less manageable caseloads. Consequently, performance becomes disorganized and worker effectiveness decreases (Graef & Hill, 2000).

While the consequences of a high turnover rate are fairly well understood, the reasons for such turnover are less apparent. Although other professions—such as law enforcement, disaster relief, and psychotherapy—have acknowledged the effects of working with trauma victims, the effects of being exposed to child abuse victims on a regular basis have not received adequate attention in the CPS field. To date, researchers, theorists, and administrators speculate that CPS workers are forsaking their commitment to protect children because they are suffering from burnout (Anderson, 2000; Balfour & Neff, 1993; Savicki & Cooley, 1994; Walden, Gettelman, & Murrin, 1993). Burnout, the feeling of emotional exhaustion (Maslach, 1982), has been thought to be caused by organizational stressors such as ever-increasing caseloads, lack of resources, unrealistic policies, and the possibility of being criminally charged for errors. Some researchers, however, have questioned the connection between burnout and worker turnover rates (Balfour & Neff, 1993; Fryer, Miyoshi, & Thomas,

1989; LeCroy & Rank, 1986). These findings, along with new discoveries in the field of traumatic stress, suggest there may be alternative explanations for CPS professionals abandoning their vocation.

Employees who work with trauma victims, especially traumatized children, may be leaving their jobs because they too have become traumatized and, as a result, suffer from symptoms that affect their ability to function. CPS professionals, those persons who work directly with or have direct exposure to child abuse and neglect victims, put themselves in situations where they are exposed to children's traumatic material on a daily basis. Until recently, it was thought that these workers, because of their training, were immune to traumatic stress reactions. According to Figley's (1995) secondary traumatic stress (STS) theory, persons who work directly with or have direct exposure to trauma victims are just as likely as the primary victims to experience traumatic stress symptoms and disorders. People can be traumatized without actually being physically harmed or threatened with harm. They can be traumatized simply by learning about the traumatic event (Figley, 1995, p.4). Persons are more likely to suffer from secondary traumatic stress disorder (STSD) when exposed to traumata on a regular basis. Furthermore, Figley recognized that persons who are exposed to traumatized children are especially vulnerable to the noxious side effects of STSD. Not only are CPS workers indirectly exposed to a number of children's traumas, they endure this pain on a daily basis throughout their careers. Therefore, CPS workers appear to be just as vulnerable as other types of trauma workers to suffer from STS symptoms (Cornille & Meyers, 1999; Meyers, 1996).

OVERVIEW OF THE STUDY

Method

Sample and Procedure

This study was conducted to assess the prevalence of secondary traumatic stress symptoms in CPS professionals and to identify factors that were associated with STS symptoms. The main thrust of the investigation was to examine the relationships of (a) exposure to child abuse victims' traumatic material, (b) gender, (c) family of origin functioning, and (d) personal trauma history to the STS symptoms of CPS professionals. Letters were sent to department of family and children's services directors in 92 counties in a large southern state requesting permission to survey their CPS workers. CPS workers are those persons who investigate child abuse and neglect reports, provide ongoing services to abused and neglected children, and supervise children in out-of-family placements. Of the 92 directors contacted, 46% ($n = 42$) responded. Forty directors gave permission to survey CPS workers in their counties, and two directors chose not to participate. Directors furnished 360 names and addresses of CPS workers, of whom 84% ($n = 303$) were females and 16% ($n = 57$) were males. Fifty-seven percent (*n* = 205) of the workers completed and returned the questionnaires in a timely fashion. Eighty-three percent (*n* = 170) of the participants were females, and 17% (*n* = 34) were males. Sixty-nine percent (*n* = 141) were Caucasians, and 31% were minorities. The majority (88%) of the workers had completed at least four years of college, and 35% had completed some graduate work or a master's degree.

Dependent Variable

Primary and Secondary Traumatic Stress Symptoms

Two instruments that have been widely used in a variety of clinical and nonclinical samples measured the severity of workers' STS symptoms. The shortened version of the SCL–90–R, the Brief Symptom Inventory (BSI) by Derogatis (1975), was used to assess general psychological symptoms in the CPS workers. The internal consistency of that measure has been reported a number of times and typically has a Chronbach's alpha of about .90. Tests of its internal validity have been examined by Derogatis (1975) and others (Derogatis, Rickels, & Rock, 1976). Consistently, the BSI has been be a respectable measure of general psychological symptoms. The Impact of Event Scale–Revised (IES–R) by Weiss and Marmar (1996) was used to assess specific STS symptoms. This measure has been reported to have internal consistency of approximately .87 for the Intrusion subscale, .85 for the Avoidance subscale, and .79 for the Hyperarousal subscale (Marmar, Weiss, Metzler, Ronfeldt, & Foreman, 1996; Weiss, Marmar, Metzler, & Ronfeldt, 1995). Its ability to provide information related to secondary trauma has been examined both in its original form and subsequently in the process of its revision. In both versions, it provides an excellent approach to acquiring an appreciation of the distress of the respondent. These two instruments were selected primarily because of their extensive use in the measurement of traumatized people and their low-demand characteristics. Both are brief and easily self-administered. The BSI and the IES–R also were selected for this study because, at the time, there were no measures available to assess STS symptoms in persons who become symptomatic after being indirectly exposed to trauma. Since this study was conducted, several other measures have been made available to researchers. However, at that time, the IES–R and SCL–90–R were the most commonly used approaches to tapping either primary or secondary trauma.

Independent Variables

Personal Trauma History

CPS workers were asked to disclose if they had ever experienced, witnessed, or been confronted with a traumatic event prior to or while working in the

CPS field. A list of traumatic events taken from the *DSM-IV* (American Psychiatric Association, 1994) was provided for the workers to check yes or no, according to their experience.

Duration and Intensity of Exposure to Children's Traumatic Material

Respondents were asked a series of questions designed for this study to determine the duration and intensity of exposure to children's trauma. In order to measure the duration of exposure to children's trauma, workers were asked to briefly describe their jobs and to estimate the length of time employed in their current position.

The intensity of exposure to children's trauma was determined by asking participants to estimate the average number of hours they worked per week. Workers were also asked to estimate their average caseload size for the prior month.

Family-Functioning Characteristics

The Structural Family Interaction Scale (SFIS) by Perosa, Hansen, and Perosa (1981) was used to measure CPS workers' family of origin functioning. The SFIS is a self-report, 85-item inventory that measures family interaction patterns defined in accordance with Minuchin's (1974) structural model of family functioning (Perosa et al., 1981).

Summary of Relevant Findings

The Impact of Duration of Exposure

When CPS workers have worked for longer periods of time in the CPS field and thus been exposed to longer duration of traumatic material, they experienced more severe STS symptoms than those persons with fewer years of experience. The ANOVA yielded a significant difference in the severity of obsessive-compulsive symptoms ($F = 3.82$, $p < .05$) experienced by CPS workers. Those CPS workers who were employed for five or more years reported experiencing more severe obsessive-compulsive symptoms, such as irresistible thoughts, impulses, and actions, than those CPS workers who were employed for less than five years. When new CPS workers (employed one year or less) were compared to veteran workers (with more than one year experience), the veteran workers reported experiencing more anxious symptoms ($F = 3.12$, $p < .08$)—including nervous tensions, panic attacks, and feelings of terror—than those workers with less experience. Contrary to the original hypotheses, no other STS symptom severity levels were found to be significantly different in the two CPS groups.

The Impact of Intensity of Exposure

When CPS workers who worked more than 40 hours per week were compared to workers who worked less than 41 hours a week (only one person was part-time, the rest worked 40 hours per week), the 40-plus-hours-a-week group reported experiencing more anger, irritability, jumpiness, exaggerated startle response, trouble concentrating, hypervigilance, nightmares, and intrusive thoughts and images than those who worked fewer hours per week (see Table 2.1). In addition, those working longer hours reported feeling more distressed, depressed, anxious, hostile, suspicious, paranoid, and delusional than those working fewer hours per week.

These findings reinforce what other researchers (Alexander & Klein, 2001; Beaton & Murphy, 1995; Bryant & Harvey, 1996; Hodgins, Creamer, & Bell, 2001) have determined. The amount of exposure to secondary traumatic material has an impact on the severity of symptoms workers experience.

The findings did not support a relationship between the intensity of exposure when determined by average monthly caseload size and STS symptom severity. The lack of findings may indicate that the actual number of cases a worker has is not as important in determining the symptom severity as the actual time spent working on cases. In other words, it may not be how many cases workers have that makes them more likely to experience severe STS symptoms; it is the amount of time they spend working the cases that makes them more distressed.

Sex Differences

A comparison was made of the intensity of symptoms reported by men and women in the study (see Table 2.2). When the responses of female workers were compared to those of male workers in terms of severity of symptoms, female workers reported more symptoms—such as anger, irritability, jumpi-

TABLE 2.1
ANOVA for STS Symptom Scales by Average Number of Hours Worked per Week

	Worked Less than 41 Hours (*n* = 74)	More than 40 Hours (*n* = 129)	
	Mean (*sd*)	Mean (*sd*)	*F*
Avoidance	1.01 (.71)	1.13 (.71)	1.28
Hyperarousal	.83 (.77)	1.18 (.77)	9.96 **
Intrusion	1.31 (.86)	1.70 (.84)	9.63 **
GSI	.54 (.52)	.70 (.51)	4.47 *
Somatization	.38 (.52)	.49 (.56)	1.59
Obsessive-Compulsive	1.07 (.81)	1.23 (.83)	1.76
Interpersonal–Sensitivity	.66 (.83)	.72 (.72)	.35
Depression	.50 (.66)	.71 (.71)	4.22 *
Anxiety	.61 (.60)	.81 (.67)	4.36 *
Hostility	.47 (.53)	.72 (.65)	8.08 **
Phobic Anxiety	.17 (.38)	.21 (.44)	.38
Paranoid Ideation	.62 (.64)	.88 (.76)	6.01 *

Note: Standard deviations are shown in parentheses. $*p < .05$, $**p < .01$.

TABLE 2.2
ANOVA for STS Symptoms by Gender

	Males ($n = 34$)	Females ($n = 169$)	
Avoidance	.81 (.62)	1.14 (.72)	6.17 **
Hyperarousal	.83 (.71)	1.10 (.80)	3.22 *
Intrusion	1.28 (.84)	1.61 (.87)	4.08 **
GSI	.59 (.51)	.66 (.52)	.45
Somatization	.28 (.42)	.49 (.56)	4.26 **
Obsessive-Compulsive	.99 (.71)	1.20 (.84)	1.89
Interpersonal–Sensitivity	.66 (.67)	.70 (.78)	.08
Depression	.62 (.70)	.64 (.70)	.03
Anxiety	.62 (.64)	.76 (.65)	1.31
Hostility	.65 (.75)	.62 (.59)	.06
Phobic Anxiety	.27 (.57)	.17 (.38)	1.28
Paranoid Ideation	.82 (.77)	.78 (.73)	.06

Note: Standard deviations are shown in parentheses. *$p < .05$, **$p < .01$.

ness, exaggerated startle response, trouble concentrating, hypervigilance, nightmares, intrusive thoughts and images, and numbing of responses—than their male counterparts. In addition, women reported experiencing more cardiovascular problems, gastrointestinal problems, respiratory problems, and muscular pain and discomfort than male CPS workers.

These findings are consistent with other studies that took gender into consideration (Brown, Fielding, & Grover, 1999; Gerdenio & Anderson, 1993; Kassam-Adams, 1995; McCarroll, Ursano, & Fullerton, 1993). It should not necessarily conclude, however, that secondary trauma is primarily a risk for women. A plethora of studies have demonstrated that men suffer from traumatic stress symptoms as well (Carlier, Lamberts, & Gersons, 1997; Carlier, Lamberts, Van Uchelen, & Gersons, 1998; Clohessy & Ehlers, 1999; Labbate, Cardena, Dimitreva, Roy, & Engel, 1998; Marmar et al., 1996; Robinson, Sigman, & Wilson, 1997; Ursano, Fullerton, Vance, & Kao, 1999; van Minnen & Keijsers, 2000). A possible explanation for the difference in male and female distress levels could be that, because of sex role socialization, women are more likely than men to disclose their emotions. It may also be that women are socialized so they are more susceptible than men to distress. Additional research needs to be conducted to gain a better understanding of how a person's gender impacts the onset and severity of traumatic stress symptoms.

Impact of Family-of-Origin Functioning

A significant relationship was found between enmeshed family interaction patterns and intrusive symptoms. CPS workers who grew up in families with enmeshed interaction patterns reported more nightmares, intrusive thoughts and images, and feelings than workers who grew up in families with less enmeshed patterns. The findings also revealed a significant relationship between CPS workers who grew up in families with disengaged interaction patterns and higher scores on the Psychoticism scale of the BSI. The Psychoticism scale represents a continuous dimension of human experience and is indicative of a withdrawn, isolated, and schizoid lifestyle (Derogatis, 1993). Therefore, CPS workers who grew up in families with disengaged interaction patterns reported more withdrawn, isolated, and schizoid lifestyles.

A possible interpretation of these findings can be found in Minuchin's (1974) notion of enmeshed and disengaged families. He described enmeshed family members as having a tendency to become intrusively involved with one another. The behavior of one family member immediately and intensely affects the other members, and when a person experiences stress, it is felt by everyone in the family. On the other hand, families in which interaction patterns are extremely disengaged tend to have difficulty communicating, are excessively emotionally distant, and are not supportive of one another when help is needed. Members of disengaged families tend to function autonomously, have a skewed sense of independence, and lack feelings of loyalty and belonging. Minuchin (1974) also described these family members as being emotionally and behaviorally unaffected by events going on around them.

CPS workers who grew up in families with intrusive interaction patterns experience intrusive STS symptoms. Similarly, workers who grew up in families with disengaged interaction patterns (i.e., had trouble communicating, were emotionally distant, and were extremely autonomous) experience withdrawn, isolated, and schizoid lifestyles. These findings suggest that, instead of concentrating only on the severity of symptoms, attention should also be paid to the type of symptoms CPS workers experience. It appears that growing up in enmeshed families may make individuals more vulnerable to traumatic symptoms, whereas growing up in disengaged families appears to be connected to more general mental health symptoms

The Impact of Trauma History

Most of the CPS workers (82%) reported that they had experienced a trauma prior to working in the CPS field, and 77% reported having been assaulted or threatened while on the job. These findings are consistent with Elliot and Briere's (1995) survey, in which 76% of American adults reported having experienced a trauma. CPS workers who reported they had witnessed the death of another person described themselves as experiencing more nightmares; intrusive thoughts, images, and feelings; distress; anxiety; and anger than those who had never witnessed a death (see Table 2.3). They also reported experiencing more suspiciousness; fear of loss of autonomy; delusions; projective thoughts; and withdrawn, isolated, and schizoid lifestyles than those workers who had not witnessed a death.

Workers who reported experiencing a serious injury prior to working with

TABLE 2.3

ANOVA for STS Symptoms if CPS Worker Witnessed the Death
of Another Person or Experienced Other Trauma.

	NO (n = 102) Mean (sd)	Witnessed Death (n = 102) Mean (sd)	F
Avoidance	1.07 (.70)	1.09 (.73)	.00
Hyperarousal	1.01 (.85)	1.08 (.72)	.43
Intrusion	1.43 (.88)	1.67 (.85)	4.05*
GSI	.58 (.46)	.71 (.56)	3.28*
Somatization	.28 (.42)	.49 (.56)	.85
Obsessive-Compulsive	.99 (.71)	1.20 (.84)	1.04
Interpersonal–Sensitivity	.66 (.67)	.70 (.78)	1.51
Depression	.62 (.70)	.64 (.70)	2.29
Anxiety	.62 (.64)	.76 (.65)	3.74*
Hostility	.65 (.75)	.62 (.59)	4.81**
Phobic Anxiety	.27 (.57)	.17 (.38)	.18
Paranoid Ideation	.82 (.77)	.78 (.73)	5.28**
Psychoticism	.41 (.52)	.56 (.61)	3.52*

Note: Standard deviations are shown in parentheses. $*p < .05$, $**p < .01$.

child abuse victims related that they suffered from more muscular pain and discomfort and cardiovascular, gastrointestinal, and respiratory complaints than workers who had not suffered a serious injury. It may be that these individuals were injured and therefore suffered from more discomfort, or it could be that they were symptomatic because of emotional distress. In addition, workers who disclosed that they had experienced a trauma other than those listed also reported being more symptomatic than those who had not suffered another type of trauma. These workers reported being more depressed, anxious, somatic, withdrawn, isolated, and distressed than workers who had not experienced another type of trauma. These results reinforce other findings that suggest that personal trauma histories of trauma workers affect the severity of STS symptoms they suffer (Dougall, Herberman, Delahanty, Inslicht, & Baum, 2000; Follette, Polusny, & Milbeck, 1994; Kassam-Adams, 1995; Moran & Britton, 1994; Pearlman & Saakvitne, 1995; Schauben & Frazier, 1995; Ursano et al., 1999).

Although whether a CPS worker experienced a trauma while on the job was not related to symptom severity, there was a positive relationship between the number of assaults or threats they endured while working and symptom severity. The more ordeals CPS workers encountered while on the job, the more severe symptoms of anxiety, anger, unremitting and irresistible thoughts, suspiciousness, delusions, and overall distress they displayed. These findings may be indicative of the literature that suggests it is not the actual incident that makes an event traumatic, but whether a person perceives it as an extreme traumatic stressor (APA, 1994; van der Kolk & McFarlane, 1996). In many cases, CPS workers are trained and work in a culture that suggests to its employees that trauma is the norm instead of the exception. If workers come to view being assaulted or threatened as part of their job, it might take something out of the ordinary to cause a worker to interpret an event as an extreme stressor.

Summary

In summary, we discovered 12 findings:

1. When examining the overall symptoms of the workers (BSI), we found they were more symptomatic than the general population and less symptomatic than a population of persons in outpatient psychotherapy.
2. When comparing their families of origin, we found they came from families that were more enmeshed and less disengaged than families with children with learning disabilities (Perosa et al., 1981).
3. CPS workers who had been employed for longer periods of time in the CPS field, and thus exposed to longer durations of traumatic material, experienced more severe STS symptoms than those with fewer years of experience.
4. When CPS workers who worked more than 40 hours per week were compared to those who worked fewer than 41 hours a week, the 40-plus-hours-a-week group reported more anger, irritability, jumpiness, exaggerated startle response, trouble concentrating, hypervigilance, nightmares, and intrusive thoughts and images than those who worked fewer hours per week.
5. CPS workers who grew up in families with enmeshed interaction patterns reported more nightmares and intrusive thoughts, images, and feelings than workers who grew up in families with less enmeshed patterns.
6. CPS workers who grew up in families with disengaged interaction patterns reported more withdrawn, isolated, and schizoid lifestyles.
7. Female workers reported more symptoms such as anger, irritability, jumpiness, exaggerated startle response, trouble concentrating, hypervigilance, nightmares, intrusive thoughts and images, and numbering of responses than their male counterparts.
8. Women also reported more cardiovascular problems, gastrointestinal problems, respiratory problems, and muscular pain and discomfort than male CPS workers.
9. The majority of CPS workers (82%) reported that they had experienced a trauma prior to working in the CPS field, and 77% reported having been assaulted or threatened while on the job.
10. CPS workers who reported they had witnessed the death of another

person described themselves as experiencing more nightmares; intrusive thoughts, images, and feelings; distress; anxiety; and anger than those who had never witnessed a death. They also reported more suspiciousness; fear of loss of autonomy; delusions; projective thoughts; and withdrawn isolated, and schizoid lifestyles than those workers who had not witnessed the death of another person

11. Workers who reported experiencing a serious injury prior to working with child abuse victims related that they were suffering from more muscular pain and discomfort and more cardiovascular, gastrointestinal, and respiratory complaints than workers who had not suffered a serious injury.

12. Workers who disclosed that they had experienced a trauma other than those listed also reported being more symptomatic than those who had not suffered another type of trauma. These workers reported being more depressed, anxious, somatic, withdrawn, isolated, and distressed than workers who had not experienced another type of trauma.

IMPLICATIONS FOR INTERVENTION AND PREVENTION SERVICES FOR CHILD PROTECTIVE SERVICES WORKERS

Based on the findings of this study, there are a number of intervention and prevention techniques child protection agencies, supervisors, and direct service professionals themselves can use to reduce the risk of secondary traumatization.

1. Improving Training

When CPS workers are hired, they must undergo a large amount of training to prepare them to do their jobs. During this training, workers are taught agency policies and procedures; how to fill out paperwork, assess for, and identify abuse and neglect symptoms in children; and how to interview victims and perpetrators. CPS workers are not taught about the nuances of working in jobs that indirectly expose them to children's traumatic material, nor are they taught how to take care of themselves "emotionally."

Recognize and Normalize STS Symptoms

In order to help workers stay in their jobs and deal with the stressors to which they are exposed, we must educate them about STS and teach them to identify, anticipate, and prepare for coping with STS symptoms. During training, STS symptoms need to normalized, and workers need to be provided with help in assessing for personal factors that may make them more vulnerable to STS symptoms.

Identify and Recognize the Impact of Family-of-Origin Patterns

Workers need training to recognize the interaction patterns in the families in which they grew up. Workers need to be aware that the type of family patterns they experienced as children has an impact on the way they react to the traumatic material to which they are exposed through their jobs. For example, CPS workers in the study who were raised in families that were overly intrusive were more likely to experience intrusive symptoms (nightmares and intrusive thoughts, images, and feelings) after being exposed to child abuse victims' traumatic material. Workers who were raised in families that were extremely disengaged were most likely to react by withdrawing or isolating themselves after being exposed to children's traumatic material.

Owning Personal Trauma History

Because the vast majority of workers had experienced, witnessed, or been confronted with a trauma prior to employment in the CPS field, training to assist them to recognize that history, is vital to preventing of further trauma. CPS workers who have experienced previous traumas need to be made aware that these previous experiences may make them more vulnerable to STS symptoms. Certain experiences—such as witnessing a death, experiencing a serious injury, or other trauma, such as rape—may make workers more prone to becoming symptomatic. Through training, workers can be made aware of this possibility, recognize when it happens, and learn how to deal with it.

Gender Differences in Response to Traumatic Material

Female CPS workers need to be educated about the vulnerabilities and the types of symptoms they may experience that are different from those of their male counterparts. They also need to be taught how to deal with these symptoms. By recognizing the differences in how men and women react after being exposed to child abuse victims, they can learn to be more supportive of one another.

Coping Strategies

Workers need to receive specific training in strategies effective in preventing and minimizing symptoms after being exposed to traumatic material. For example, the American Red Cross provides training to disaster relief workers about the importance of using active coping strategies to deal with the difficult situations they encounter at disasters. CPS workers would benefit from similar training.

2. Handling On-the-Job Victimization

Because 77% of CPS workers reported that they had been threatened or assaulted while on the job, they need to be provided with mandatory self-defense training. In addition, agencies need to develop safety procedures and a buddy system when workers have to go into dangerous areas and situations. Workers need to be equipped with cellular telephones, so they can remain in contact with supervisors and call for help if needed. When assaults or threats occur, supervisors need to be supportive of their staff and provide them with professional help when it is deemed necessary.

3. Providing a Supportive Work Environment

Supervisors could minimize the adverse effects of working with child abuse victims by providing supportive environments and debriefing workers after traumatic experiences (both primary and secondary). Supervisors need to be trained to recognize and acknowledge the effects of being exposed to trauma on a daily basis. Allowing workers a safe place to release emotions and talk about the specific trauma, their fears, and regrets could help minimize the symptoms they experience. Having peer support groups in place, in which workers can engage in group discussion, exchange information, and provide support, can also help in minimizing the likelihood of severe STS symptoms.

4. Limiting Work Hours

As the results of the study indicate, the number of hours CPS employees work per week is related to their level of distress. An argument can be made for a change in the policies and procedures that mandate employees work more than 40 hours a week. For instance, in some child abuse and neglect investigation units, policy and procedures require that one worker be on-call for one week each month. This means the on-call worker must work his or her normal hours during the day and also be available for after-hours emergencies. Because this study supports a link between more hours worked in one week and the level of distress in CPS workers, it could be argued that these policies need to be altered to allow workers to adjust their hours so no one works more than 40 hours in a week's time. Along these same lines, employees should be assigned an amount of work that can be completed in a 40-hour work week. Supervisors should encourage their workers to take time off and have fun without being afraid they are going to fall behind in their work or put a child's life in danger. A work environment that encourages vacations needs to be created. Directors can use this information to lobby legislators for funding to hire additional workers in order to ensure no one works more than 40 hours per week.

5. Personal Care

CPS workers need to be encouraged to practice healthy lifestyles in order to reduce and eliminate secondary traumatic stress symptoms. Employers should provide seminars to educate workers on the need for proper nutrition and exercise. Gyms equipped with exercise equipment could be provided for workers, along with an hour off each day for their use. In addition, chiropractic care, massage therapy, and psychotherapy—methods that have proven to be excellent in reducing stress and promoting healthy lifestyles—should be covered by the workers' insurance policy to ensure affordable access.

In conclusion, this preliminary study suggests that professionals who work with abused and neglected children are at risk of developing symptoms consistent with secondary trauma. Workers who participated in this project provided invaluable information about both the depth of their distress and potential interventions to reduce or prevent further harm to them and the children they serve. Making the programmatic and personal changes this study calls for will not be easy. However, ignoring this serious situation can only result in further damage to the victims the system is designed to help. In addition, we need further information about the process of some staff developing these symptoms, whereas others appear not to be in distress. It is not clear from this single cross-sectional study whether others have the symptoms and are less open to acknowledging them, or if they somehow have found successful ways to shield themselves from the potential harm of working in this context. We need to understand this process so that we can design more effective and efficient interventions to help these professionals be successful in their life work.

REFERENCES

Alexander, D., & Klein, S. (2001). Ambulance personnel and critical incidents: Impact of accident and emergency work on mental health and emotional well-being. *British Journal of Psychiatry, 178*, 76–81.

American Psychiatric Association. (1994). *Diagnostic and statistical manual of mental disorders* (4th ed.). Washington, DC: Author.

Anderson, D. (2000). Coping strategies and burnout among veteran child protection workers. *Child Abuse and Neglect, 24*(6), 839–848.

Balfour, D., & Neff, D. (1993). Predicting and managing turnover in human service agencies: A case study of an organization in crisis. *Public Personnel Management, 22*(3), 473–486.

Beaton, R., & Murphy, S. (1995). Working with people in crisis: Research implications. In C. Figley (Ed.), *Compassion fatigue: Coping with secondary traumatic stress disorder in those who treat the traumatized* (pp. 51–81). New York: Brunner/Mazel.

Brown, J., Fielding, J., & Grover, J. (1999). Distinguishing traumatic, vicarious and routine operational stressor exposure and attendant adverse consequences in a sample of police officers. *Work and Stress, 13*(4), 312–325.

Bryant, R., & Harvey, A. (1996). Posttraumatic stress reactions in volunteer firefighters. *Journal of Traumatic Stress, 9*(1), 51–63.

Carlier, I., Lamberts, R., & Gersons, B. (1997). Risk factors for posttraumatic stress symptomatology in police officers: A prospective analysis. *Journal of Nervous and Mental Disease, 185*(8), 498–508.

Carlier, I., Lamberts, R., Van Uchelen, A., Gersons, B. (1998). Disaster-related post-traumatic stress in police officers: A field study of the impact of debriefing. *Stress Medicine, 14*(3), 143–148.

Clohessy, S., & Ehlers, A. (1999). PTSD symptoms, response to intrusive memories and coping in ambulance service workers. *British Journal of Clinical Psychology, 38,* 251–265.

Cornille, T., & Meyers, T. (1999). Secondary traumatic stress among child protective service professionals: Prevalence, severity, and predictive factors. *Traumatologye, 5*(1), article 2.

Derogatis, L. (1975). *Brief symptom inventory.* Baltimore: Clinical Psychometric Research.

Derogatis, L. (1993). *BSI–brief symptom inventory. Administration, scoring, and procedures manual.* Minneapolis, MN: National Computer Systems.

Derogatis, L., Rickels, K., & Rock, A. (1976). The SCL–90 and the MMPI: A step in the validation of a new self report scale. *British Journal of Psychiatry, 128,* 280–289.

Dougall, A., Herberman, H., Delahanty, D., Inslicht, S., & Baum, A. (2000). Similarity of prior trauma exposure as a determinant of chronic stress responding to an airline disaster. *Journal of Consulting and Clinical Psychology, 68*(2), 290–295.

Elliot, D., & Briere, J. (1995). Posttraumatic stress associated with delayed recall of sexual abuse: A general population study. *Journal of Traumatic Stress, 8*(4), 629–648.

Figley, C. R. (1995). Compassion fatigue as secondary traumatic stress disorder: An overview. In C. Figley (Ed.), *Compassion fatigue: Coping with secondary traumatic stress disorder in those who treat the traumatized* (pp. 1–20). New York: Brunner/Mazel.

Follette, V., Polusny, M., & Milbeck, K. (1994). Mental health and law enforcement professionals: Trauma history, psychological symptoms, and impact of providing service to child sexual abuse survivors. *Professional Psychology: Research and Practice, 25*(3), 275–282.

Fryer, G., Miyoshi, P., & Thomas, J. (1989). The relationship of child protection worker attitudes to attrition from the field. *Child Abuse and Neglect, 13,* 345–350.

Gerdenio, M., & Anderson, K. (1993). Stress and coping: The Loma Prieta earthquake. *Current Psychology, 12*(2), 130–142.

Graef, M., & Hill, E. (2000). Costing child protective services staff turnover. *Child Welfare, 79*(1), 75–95.

Hodgins, G., Creamer, M., & Bell, R. (2001). Risk factors for posttrauma reactions in police officers: A longitudinal study. *Journal of Nervous and Mental Disease, 189*(8), 541–547.

Kassam-Adams, N. (1995). The risks of treating sexual trauma: Stress and secondary trauma in psychotherapists. In H. Stamm (Ed.), *Secondary traumatic stress: Self care issues for clinicians, researchers, and educators* (pp. 37–48). Lutherville, MD: Sidran Press.

Labbate, L., Cardena, E., Dimitreva, J., Roy, M., & Engel, C. (1998). Psychiatric syndromes in Persian Gulf war veterans: An association of handling dead bodies with somatoform disorders. *Psychotherapy and Psychomatics, 67*(4/5), 275–279.

LeCroy, C., & Rank, M. (1986). Factors associated with burnout in the social services: An exploratory study. *Journal of Social Service Research, 10*(1), 95–105.

Marmar, C., Weiss, D., Metzler, T., Ronfeldt, H., & Foreman, C. (1996). Stress responses of emergency services personnel to the Loma Preita earthquake interstate 880 freeway collapse and control traumatic incidents. *Journal of Traumatic Stress, 9*(1), 63–85.

Maslach, C. (1982). *Burnout: The cost of caring.* Englewood Cliffs, NJ: Prentice Hall.

McCarroll, J., Ursano, R., & Fullerton, C. (1993). Symptoms of post traumatic stress disorder following recovery of war dead. *American Journal of Psychiatry, 150*(12), 1875–1877.

McCurdy, K., & Daro, D. (1994). Child maltreatment. *Journal of Interpersonal Violence, 9*(1), 75–95.

Meyers, T. (1996). *The relationship between family of origin functioning, trauma history, exposure to children's traumatic traumata and secondary traumatic stress symptoms in child protective service workers.* Unpublished doctoral dissertation, Florida State University.

Minuchin, S. (1974). *Families and family therapy.* Boston: Harvard University Press.

Moran, C., & Britton, N. (1994). Emergency work experience and reactions to traumatic incidents. *Journal of Traumatic Stress, 7*(4), 575–585.

Pearlman, L., & Saakvitne, K. (1995). *Trauma and the therapist: Counselor transference and vicarious traumatization in psychotherapy with incest survivors.* New York: Norton.

Perosa, L., Hansen, J., & Perosa, J. (1981). Development of the structural family interaction scale. *Family Therapy, 8*(2), 77–90.

Robinson, H., Sigman, M., & Wilson, J. (1997). Duty related stressors and PTSD symptoms in suburban police officers. *Psychological Reports, 81*(3), 835–845.

Savicki, V., & Cooley, E. (1994). Burnout in child protective service workers: A longitudinal study. *Journal of Organizational Behavior, 15*, 655–666.

Schauben, L., & Frazier, P. (1995). Vicarious trauma: The effects on female counselors of working with sexual violence survivors. *Psychology of Women Quarterly, 19*, 49–64.

Ursano, R., Fullerton, C., Vance, K., & Kao, T. (1999). Posttraumatic stress disorder and identification in disaster workers. *American Journal of Psychiatry, 156*(3), 353–359.

U.S. Department of Health and Human Services. (1999). *Child maltreatment 1999: Reports from the states to the National Child Abuse and Neglect Data System (NCANDS).* Washington, DC: Administration for Children and Families.

van der Kolk, B., & McFarlane, A. (1996). The black hole of trauma. In B. van der Kolk, A. McFarlane, & L. Wisaeth (Eds.), *Traumatic stress: The effects of overwhelming experience on mind, body, and society* (pp. 3–23). New York: Guilford.

van Minnen, A., & Keijsers, G. (2000). A controlled study into the (cognitive) effects of exposure treatment on trauma therapists. *Journal of Behavior Therapy and Experimental Psychiatry, 31*(3/4), 189–200.

Walden, N., Gettelman, T., & Murrin, M. (1993). Understanding occupational stress in child welfare supervisors. *Journal of Applied Social Psychology, 23*(24), 2043–2054.

Weiss, D., & Marmar, C. (1996). Impact of Event Scale-Revised. In J. Wilson & T. Keane (Eds.), *Assessing psychological trauma and PTSD* (pp. 399–411). New York: Guilford.

Weiss, D., Marmar, C., Metzler, T., & Ronfeldt, H. (1995). Predicting symptomatic distress in emergency services personnel. *Journal of Consulting and Clinical Psychology, 63*, 361–368.

3

Stress Response of Mental Health Workers Following Disaster: The Oklahoma City Bombing

DAVID F. WEE
DIANE MYERS

In his research and work on compassion fatigue, or secondary traumatization of persons caring for victims of trauma, Figley (1995) noted that nearly all of the hundreds of reports focusing on traumatized people exclude those who were traumatized indirectly or secondarily, although the *DSM-IV* (American Psychiatric Association, 1994) clearly indicates that mere knowledge of another's traumatic experience can be traumatizing. It would seem evident that mental health counselors listening to the experiences of disaster victims would clearly be at risk for this secondary traumatization. In his earlier work, Figley (1989) noted his dismay at seeing so many colleagues abandon clinical work and research with traumatized people because of their inability to deal with the pain of others. He noted that those most vulnerable to this contagion of trauma were those who "begin to view themselves as saviors, or at least as rescuers" (Figley, 1989, pp. 144–145) as is usually the case with workers who intervene in disaster.

LITERATURE REVIEW

There are three related bodies of literature relevant to this research project. The first concerns the psychological impact of disasters on the *primary victims*, which include people who directly experienced the impact of the event, threat to life and safety, loss of property, and destruction of the immediate environment. The second body of literature addresses the impact of disaster work on *emergency service workers*. This group responds to the disaster and disaster victims, providing services to protect life and property and to recover the dead and injured, consistent with professional roles and responsibilities. This group also may be victims of the disaster, but they have a primary role to respond in a professional capacity. The third body of literature covers *disaster mental health workers* who assist disaster victims and personnel with disaster-related mental health concerns for extended periods of time following the disaster.

The body of literature on the *primary victims* of disasters is extensive. Disasters are overwhelming events that test the capability of the community and individuals to respond and can temporarily lead to massive disruption (Raphael, 1986). Humans have been victims of disasters throughout recorded history (Lystad, 1988). Populations affected by natural disasters show a variety of responses to the event. The responses can range from adaptive restoration of functioning, normal stress response syndromes, resilient recovery, or serious and persisting psychological responses consistent with Post Traumatic Stress Disorder (Horowitz, Stinson, & Field, 1991). Disaster survivors experiencing psychological reactions to disaster are viewed as normal people in abnormal circumstances. Stress responses that would be excessive at other times are now viewed as normal (Myers, 1994b).

Psychological reactions can continue long after the disaster (Green & Gleser, 1983; Linderman, 1944). For example, some individuals who experienced the Loma Prieta Earthquake continued to identify symptoms of distress six months after the earthquake (Wee, 1991). Individuals who lost their homes in the Eastbay Firestorm also showed a persistent and significant stress response fifteen months after the fire (Wee & Mills, 1993).

Families also are affected by a multitude of stressors following natural disasters, including evacuation; changes in roles, relationships, and routines; economic losses; and destruction of home and surrounding environment (Smith, 1983). Children may exhibit psychological and behavioral symptoms, some of which may become long-term (Frederick, 1985). In addition, disaster worker families also can become a source of stress if they feel excluded or deprived by the worker's absence and involvement in the disaster work (Raphael, 1986). But even when struck by catastrophe, the family is a critical support system during and following a traumatic event (Figley, 1983).

Emergency service and disaster workers who experience the intensity of the disaster directly and for prolonged time periods can experience psychological reactions (Lystad, 1988). The psychological impact on disaster workers and emergency service personnel has been examined by a number of investigators (Durham, McCammon, & Allison, 1985; Forman, 1986; Lanning & Fannin, 1988; McFarlane, 1988; Miles, Demi, & Mostyn-Aker, 1984; Mitchell, 1986; Moran & Britton, 1994; Robinson, 1989; Taylor & Frazer, 1982; Wee, 1990). Disasters can cause psychological effects in the workers and influence those closest to them (Hartsough & Myers, 1985; Wee, 1994; Wraith & Gordon, 1988).

The third body of literature is on *disaster mental health workers*. The literature that exists on stresses for long-term recovery workers focuses primarily on stress among American Red Cross and Federal Emergency Management Agency (FEMA) workers. Myers (Hartsough & Myers, 1985) described the typical phases involved in disaster work and the stressors inherent in each phase for the workers, including the letdown involved after long-term disaster assignments. Eby (1984) outlined some sources of stress for Red Cross workers involved in small, local disasters as well as those workers who responded repeatedly to major disasters. The Center for Mental Health Services (CMHS, formerly the National Institute of Mental Health) and FEMA have developed many publications and training materials on management of disaster worker stress (Department of Health and Human Services [DHHS], 1988a; 1988b; FEMA, 1987a, 1987b).

Rosensweig and Vaslow (1992) conducted a study to identify sources of stress among FEMA Disaster Assistance Program employees. Five hundred FEMA employees were surveyed, and the resulting report made specific recommendations for stress reduction for FEMA workers. Myers (1992; 1993; 1994a; 1994b), Myers and Zunin (1993a; 1993b; 1994b), and Zunin, Myers, and Cook (1995) incorporated many of Rosensweig and Vaslow's ideas in the stress management programs they developed and directed for FEMA workers in many disasters, including Hurricane Andrew, the Midwest Floods of 1993, the Northridge earthquake of 1994, and the Oklahoma City bombing. Armstrong, O'Callahan, and Marmer (1991) described stressors experienced by Red Cross relief personnel working in the two-month period following the Loma Prieta earthquake and described a multiple stressor debriefing model they developed for use in exit debriefings for personnel before they returned home.

A small number of studies have examined the impact of disaster recovery work on mental health staff providing postdisaster counseling. These studies recommended that this specialized group of disaster recovery workers pay special attention to their vulnerability to stress and posttrauma sequelae, lest they become "victims-by-proxy" (Bartone, Ursano, Wright, & Ingraham, 1989; Berah, Jones, & Valent, 1984; Frederick, 1977; Hodgkinson & Shepherd, 1994; Raphael, Singh, Bradbury, & Lambert, 1984; Winget & Umbenhauer, 1982).

Hartsough and Myers (1985) described numerous stressors for disaster workers, of which two types are most prominent in the long-term recovery efforts: (a) event stressors and (b) occupational stressors. Event stressors include the type of disaster, personal loss and injury of disaster workers who are primary victims of the disaster, fatigue, exposure to traumatic stimuli, and the sense of mission failure or human error. These stressors will influence the postimpact recovery environment and have influence on worker stress during the long-term recovery phase.

Occupational stressors affecting disaster workers have to do with the work itself and include time and responsibility pressures and emotional demands through contact with survivors. The emotional reactions and behavior of disaster victims change over time. Different phases of disaster recovery have different impacts on disaster workers. Immediate response occurs in what are called the heroic and honeymoon phases, with a high level of energy and a generally optimistic outlook for a swift recovery. The disillusionment phase is the phase in which long-term recovery workers toil. Workers are vulnerable to strong identification with the feelings of the survivors, which in the disillusionment phase include grief, fatigue, irritability, and anger. Workers also are often targets of displaced emotions of the victims, particularly anger.

Symptoms of acute, delayed, and cumulative stress among emergency workers have been extensively covered in the literature (Hartsough & Myers, 1985; Mitchell & Bray, 1990; Mitchell & Everly, 2001; Myers & Zunin, 1994a; Myers, 1995). For the most part, stress reactions experienced by long-term disaster recovery workers fit those of the cumulative stress category. Symptoms commonly observed by stress management consultants and crisis counseling staff working with disaster personnel are fatigue and depression; concentration, memory, and cognitive problems; irritability and interpersonal conflicts; anxiety, especially related to how long the disaster work will continue and obligations at home or in the worker's regular job that are "left undone"; feeling unappreciated; distancing from others and from the job; cynicism and negativity; use of derogatory labels; "sick" or gallows humor; blaming others; poor job performance; absences; physical complaints and illness; accident proneness; and alcohol and substance abuse.

Little empirical research has been done on long-term disaster mental health workers and the effects of their work-related stressors. The research that exists suggests that workers continue to experience significant levels of symptomatology during their entire tenure of disaster support work. In their study of disaster crisis counselors, Hodgkinson and Shepherd (1994) found significant levels of symptomatology 12 months into the disaster recovery work. Symptoms most frequently reported included cognitive difficulties, depression, and feelings of inadequacy and insecurity. Wee and Myers (1997) found that providing mental health services to disaster victims during long-term recovery appears to be associated with increased levels of stress for the workers doing this work. The disaster mental health worker group was significantly more distressed than the nondisaster mental health worker group. Despite current knowledge about the impact of trauma on the primary victims, little has been empirically researched or written about the "cost of caring" (Figley, 1982; 1989). It is vitally important to know how disaster mental health counselors are affected and, in many cases, traumatized as a result of their exposure to victims. By understanding this process not only can we prevent additional, subsequent traumatic stress among this population, but we can increase the quality of care for the victims they help (Figley, 1995). Research can help further fine-tune disaster worker selection procedures, training, development of self-care approaches, mental health education programs, and stress management interventions to help this dedicated and at-risk group of personnel.

DISASTER CRISIS COUNSELING PROGRAM

Alfred P. Murrah Federal Building Bombing

On April 19, 1995, at 9:02 AM the Alfred P. Murrah Federal Building was torn apart by a bomb that killed 168 and injured approximately 700 individuals in the building and nearby areas. The shock waves from the blast traveled at 40,000 feet per second, sending shards of metal and glass through walls and bodies. The 30,000-square-foot, nine-story building with its five-story garage housed 19 federal agencies and 3 private agencies. One of the agencies most directly hit by the blast was the daycare center within the federal building premises.

An estimated 646 people were thought to have been in the building when the bomb exploded. Four of the deaths occurred in the Athena building across the street from the federal building; two deaths occurred in the Oklahoma Water Resources Building, also across the street from the federal building; and one death occurred at the Journal Record Building. Three of the fatalities were dead on arrival at local hospitals, and three died in hospitals following delays of 2 to 23 days (Jordan, 1997). More than 16,744 people work or reside in the area impacted by the bomb, and many of the injured were on the streets in the neighborhood or in nearby buildings. Many of the injured were children in the federal building's childcare center and in the nearby YMCA's daycare center. There were approximately 50 children in the two daycare centers combined, and 13 of them died in the blast.

Several square blocks required search and rescue activities. Over 220 square blocks surrounding the federal building sustained damage; 800 buildings received damage ranging from major structural damage to broken windows. Nine structures, including the federal building, suffered partial collapse (FEMA, 1995; Oklahoma City Public Works Department, 1995). Following the bombing, the federal building and 29 other damaged structures were demolished

(Oklahoma City Fire Department, 1995). The replacement value of the federal building alone was estimated at $30 million.

The emotional devastation was even greater than the physical devastation of the bombing. Although most of the victims were from Oklahoma County, in which Oklahoma City is located, many neighboring towns and counties suffered losses. The town of Guthrie, north of Oklahoma City, lost 11 persons, and there were 7 deaths from the town of Norman, just south of Oklahoma City. Individuals flocked to Oklahoma City from all areas of the nation, searching for news of loved ones who worked in or near the building.

The emotional impact on children extended far beyond the deaths of the 13 killed in the bombing. In all, 271 children lost at least one parent in the blast; 60 of those children were left orphaned; and 80% of the schools within the Oklahoma City School District had children who had immediate family members injured or killed in the bombing.

In addition to those emotionally affected by the injury or death of a loved one, more than 12,000 rescue workers from throughout Oklahoma and the nation participated in the recovery effort. They were exposed to unspeakable hardship and horror as they persevered to recover every body and body fragment. In addition, their own lives were threatened by the unstable condition of the building and its hazardous contents. Firefighters took off their helmets and put them over the heads of nurses who were trying to start intravenous fluids on victims in the rubble (Oklahoma City Fire Department, 1995). One nurse was killed by falling debris, and an additional 26 rescuers were hospitalized with injuries. Work conditions were grueling. For the first eight days, over 100 tons of rubble were dug out by hand every 12 hours, using small military shovels, and removed in increments of five-gallon buckets. Urban search and rescue teams worked 12 hours a day for up to 10 days, averaging about 4 hours of sleep per night (Oklahoma City Fire Department, 1995). When there was no longer hope that live survivors would be found, rescue efforts changed to recovery efforts, and heavy equipment was brought in to remove the debris. On May 4, recovery efforts were halted because of the unstable condition of the building. Three bodies were not recovered until after the implosion of the building on May 23. On May 25, all bodies had been recovered.

Once bodies were recovered, issues of documentation, identification, and determination of cause and manner of death were the responsibility of the chief medical examiner for the state of Oklahoma (Jordan, 1997). The medical examiner's investigators worked 24 hours a day during the recovery operation. They were present at the scene of the disaster, where a temporary morgue was established; at the medical examiner's office and morgue, where processing and identification of bodies took place; at the Oklahoma County Sheriffs' Training Academy, where sifting of debris for body fragments and evidence was carried out; and at the Compassion Center, where families of victims awaited word of their loved ones.

In addition to the search, rescue, recovery, and body identification personnel, dozens of agencies and hundreds of workers provided health care, mental health counseling, pastoral care, social services, and compassion to the survivors and the families of victims. Much of the care was provided at the Compassion Center, established in the first hours of the disaster at the First Christian Church in Oklahoma City. Under the auspices of the medical examiner's office, the Compassion Center was established to provide a safe haven for family members awaiting news of their loved ones. The center was run by the American Red Cross, in cooperation with numerous agencies and organizations. A wide range of supportive services were provided, along with regular, daily briefings by the fire department and Medical Examiner's Office on the status of the recovery activities.

One of the most important tasks to be carried out in the Compassion Center was the collection of antemortem data about possible victims. This entailed interviewing family members for information about their loved ones' characteristics, clothing, personal effects, availability of fingerprints and dental records, and other data that might assist in body identification. This difficult and sensitive interviewing was accomplished by members of the Oklahoma State Funeral Directors' Association, who served as medical examiner representatives. These professionals were chosen for the task because of their experience dealing with issues of death, disaster, and tragedy on a daily basis, and because they are superbly equipped to handle the interviews with sensitivity, to anticipate problems, and to deal with distraught family and friends (Jordon, 1997). When positive identification of a victim was made, formal death notification to family members was conducted by a team consisting of a medical examiner's representative, clergy, a health care professional (usually a registered nurse), and a mental health counselor.

An array of stress management approaches was used to preserve the emotional health of the workers involved in all aspects of the Oklahoma City disaster. Critical incident stress management teams provided opportunity for individuals and groups to defuse and debrief. Chaplains provided emotional and spiritual support to personnel. In addition, food service areas provided a place for rest, recreation, and camaraderie (Jordon, 1997). Massage therapy; aquatherapy in donated hot tubs; personal services such as haircuts; entertainment; interaction with pet "therapists" including dogs, rabbits, and a very spirited monkey; donations; and letters and prayers of support from around the nation sustained the morale and spirits of the dedicated and exhausted workers.

Mental Health Services in a Presidentially Declared Disaster

When it is determined in a large-scale disaster that the needs of the affected community will exceed those resources available locally and at the state level, the governor of the state may request that the president of the United

States declare the situation a major disaster. This disaster declaration makes available to the community a wide range of federal assistance. Section 416 of the Robert T. Stafford Disaster Relief and Emergency Assistance Act (Public Law 93–288, as amended) authorizes funding for mental health services following a presidential declared disaster (FEMA/CMHS, 1992):

> Sec. 416. The President is authorized to provide professional counseling services, including financial assistance to state or local agencies or private mental health organizations to provide such services or training of disaster workers, to victims of major disasters in order to relieve mental health problems caused or aggravated by such major disaster or its aftermath.

The Crisis Counseling Assistance and Training Program for survivors of major disasters provides support for direct services to disaster survivors and to disaster workers. A training component in disaster crisis counseling for direct services staff of the project and other disaster services workers may be included. This program was developed in cooperation with FEMA and the Center for Mental Health Services (CMHS) within the Substance Abuse and Mental Health Services Administration (SAMHSA; Meyers, 1994a).

The law was enacted and the program developed in response to the recognition that disasters produce a variety of emotional and mental disturbances that, if left untreated, may become long-term and debilitating. Such problems as phobias, sleep disturbances, depression, irritability, and family discord occur following a disaster. Programs funded under Section 416 are designed to provide timely relief and prevent long-term problems from developing (Myers, 1994b).

Assistance under this program is limited to presidentially declared major disasters. Moreover, the program is designed to supplement the available resources and services of states and local governments. Thus, support for crisis counseling services to disaster victims may be granted if these services cannot be provided by existing agency programs. The support is not automatically provided, and a grant application with a needs assessment and program plan must be prepared and submitted through the state mental health authority to FEMA (Myers, 1994b). The program must provide plans for outreach to affected populations, crisis counseling, referral, consultation, public education, and training of crisis counselors. The program also must reflect attention to cultural, ethnic, or geographic needs or to other special factors unique to the disaster or indigenous to the area (Myers, 1994b).

Oklahoma Governor Frank Keating named the Oklahoma Department of Mental Health and Substance Abuse Services as the lead agency for coordinating and providing the mental health crisis response in the aftermath of the bombing. On May 8, 1995, the department opened the Project Heartland Center, funded by the FEMA Crisis Counseling Assistance and Training Program. Services that had been provided by a variety of agencies at the Compassion Center began to transition to Project Heartland during the second week after the bombing. Project Heartland provided crisis intervention, crisis counseling, support groups, and outreach to individuals affected by the bombing. Project Heartland and its contract agencies had a total of 74 staff.

Project Heartland crisis counseling staff were exposed regularly to the pain, loss, anger, and anguished stories of the survivors, family members of victims, and disaster response workers. Because of the intensity of the emotional climate in which the crisis counselors worked, the program employed a private consultant to provide stress management services to the crisis counselors. It is this group of crisis counselors who were surveyed for this study.

SURVEY POPULATION

This study was approved by the Oklahoma Department of Mental Health and Substance Abuse Services. The research proposal was reviewed for the protection of human subjects and was approved by the Institutional Review Board, Office of Research Administration, Oklahoma University Health Sciences Center, Oklahoma City. Subjects for this study consisted of volunteers from the Oklahoma Department of Mental Health and Substance Abuse Services working in the Alfred P. Murrah Federal Building Bombing Crisis Counseling Program. Seventy-four mental health personnel provided crisis counseling, outreach, and educational services to persons affected by the bombing. All subjects were over 21 years of age and employed by the Oklahoma Department of Mental Health and Substance Abuse Services or contract agencies. Subjects were provided with a questionnaire packet nine months after the bombing. The Alfred P. Murrah Federal Building Bombing Reaction Questionnaire included an explanatory cover letter that described the general purpose and intent of the study, an informed consent statement, and the questionnaire. The cover letter described the safeguard to confidentiality for the subjects, plus the benefits and nonbenefits to the participants. Consultation was offered for any subject who might experience anxiety aroused in the retelling of his or her experiences. Subjects were informed of the nature and purpose of the study and what use would be made of the information—that is, helping mental health workers providing crisis counseling services following disaster to identify their personal stress responses and to develop effective interventions to mitigate their stress responses during long-term disaster recovery activities.

PROCEDURES

Disaster mental health workers received an Alfred P. Murrah Federal Building Bombing Reaction Questionnaire packet nine months after the bombing.

This is a 179-item self-report questionnaire. The questionnaire has items concerning demographic information, personal experiences with the bombing, experiences with the crisis counseling program, empathy received from people involved or not involved with this incident, involvement in stress management activities, and several open-ended questions. Instrumentation included three standardized measures.

The Compassion Fatigue Self-Test for Helpers (Figley, 1995) was used to identify the presence and degree of severity of experiences associated with secondary traumatic stress and burnout. Secondary traumatic stress (used interchangeably with the term compassion fatigue) is defined as "the natural consequent behaviors and emotions resulting from knowing about a traumatizing event experienced by a significant other stress resulting from helping or wanting to help a traumatized or suffering person" (Figley, 1993). Burnout can be defined as a gradual and progressive process with key features being physical exhaustion, emotional exhaustion, depersonalization, and reduced personal achievement with work-related and interpersonal symptoms. The Compassion Fatigue Self-Test for Helpers is still being developed and is reported to have good psychometric properties (Figley, 1995).

The Frederick Reaction Index–A (FRI–A; Frederick, 1985) was used to examine the presence of symptoms and the degree of severity of posttraumatic stress disorder ranging from doubtful, mild, moderate, severe, and very severe. The scale has been found to have a reliability coefficient that yielded an interrated reliability of 0.77 for a single rater in which 50 cases were given anonymous clinical ratings including levels of severity by three raters. A Greenhouse-Geisser probability of .92 and Huy-Feldt probability of .95 were found when epsilon factors for degrees of freedom adjustment were applied (Frederick, 1985, 1987).

The Symptom Checklist 90–Revised (SCL–90–R; Derogatis, 1994), was used to evaluate the presence and severity of psychological symptoms of distress experienced by the respondents. The SCL–90–R is a 90-item self-report symptom inventory that has nine primary symptoms dimensions and three global indices of distress. The SCL–90–R was designed to reflect psychological symptom patterns in community, medical, and psychiatric respondents and has been used in an extensive number of studies (Derogatis, 1993).

Questionnaires were returned to the researchers for coding, data entry, and analysis. The Statistical Package for the Social Sciences (SPSS, 1993) was used to analyze the data. The analysis included descriptive and inferential statistics using univarate, bivarate, and multivariate procedures including crosstabs, analysis of variance, one-way analysis of variance, *t*-test, chi-square, kappa, and Pearson correlation.

RESULTS

Sample

Thirty-four questionnaires were returned, for a return rate of 45.9%. The workers returning the questionnaire were mostly female, middle-aged, ethnically diverse, had earned master's degrees, and were involved in crisis counseling work. The respondents were largely female (83.4%; $n = 28$), mean age was 41.72 years, 73.5% ($n = 25$) were Caucasian, 8.8% ($n = 3$) were African American, 2.9% ($n = 1$) were Latino, and 8.8% ($n = 3$) were Native American. 55.9% ($n = 19$) had earned master's degrees, and 44.1% ($n = 15$) worked as crisis counselors as opposed to managers, supervisors, community outreach workers, or peer counselors (see Table 3.1).

Disaster Experiences

Respondents' direct exposure to the disaster was measured by the number of persons who directly experienced the bombing, reported injury to self or

TABLE 3.1
Demographics of Disaster Mental Health Workers

Sex	females 83.4%	28
	males 17.6%	6
Age	mean = 41.72	
Ethnicity		
Caucasian	73.5%	25
African American	8.8%	3
Latino	2.9%	1
Native American	8.8%	3
Missing	5.9%	2
Education		
High school	8.8%	3
Junior college	5.9%	2
College degree	23.5%	8
Masters degree	55.9%	19
Other	2.9%	1
Missing	2.9%	
Job Title		
Manager	8.8%	3
Supervisor	2.9%	1
Crisis counselor	44.1%	15
Community worker	17.6%	6
Peer counselor	14.7%	5
Other	5.9%	2
Missing	5.9%	2
Disasters experienced in lifetime	1.66	range: 0–6

family, reported death of a family member, experienced loss or damage to property, or feared they might die. The proportion of persons who directly experienced the bombing of the federal building was 35.3% ($n = 12$), injury to a family member was reported by one person, and death of a family member was reported by one person. One person reported loss or damage to property. One reported a "little fear" he or she would die as a result of the bombing.

The respondents who experienced the disaster ($n = 12$) were examined for stress response using the Frederick Reaction Index–A (FRI–A). Stress response from working with survivors of the bombing was measured by the Compassion Fatigue Self-Test for Helpers, which has a Compassion Fatigue Scale (CFS) and Burnout Scale (BOS). General signs and symptoms of distress were measured by the SCL–90–R and the Global Severity Index (GSI). Respondents who experienced the bomb blast scored higher on the FRI–A, CFS, BOS, and GSI, but none of the differences in mean scores was significant. The group of respondents who experienced the bombing had a mean FRI–A score of 19.41, compared to the mean FRI–A score of 15.9 for the group of respondents who did not experience the bombing. The mean GSI score was 55.42 for respondents who experienced the bombing, compared to a mean GSI score of 53.78 for those who did not. No significant relationship existed between life threat, experience of the bombing, injury to family member, death of family member, or injury to self.

Many of the respondents (61.8%, $n = 21$) reported that they believed someone they knew might die as a result of the bombing. In response to the question, "At the time of the bombing, I believed that someone I knew might die as a result of the bombing," 38.2% ($n = 13$) reported "not at all," 20.6% ($n = 7$) "a little," 14.7% ($n = 5$) "somewhat," 11.8% ($n = 5$) "very much," and 14.7% ($n = 5$) "extremely." Disaster mental health workers who experienced fear for the safety of someone they knew had significantly increased disaster-related stress reactions as measured by the FRI–A ($p = 0.006$; see Table 3.2).

The disaster mental health workers as a group had a degree of disorder that fell in the middle degree of disorder range for posttraumatic stress disorder. The group mean FRI–A score was 17.85, which fell in the 12 to 24 range for mild degree of severity for stress disorder. The proportion of disaster mental health workers with some degree of severity for stress disorder was 64.7% ($n = 22$). Of the respondents, 35.3% ($n = 12$) fell in the doubtful degree of disorder range (less than 12), 44.1% ($n = 15$) fell in the mild degree of severity for stress disorder (12–24), 11.8% ($n = 4$) fell in the moderate degree of severity for stress disorder (25–39), and 8.8% ($n = 3$) fell in the severe degree severity for stress disorder (40–59). No respondents scored in the very severe degree of severity for stress disorder range (greater than 60).

Overall reported stress since the bombing was elevated. Of the respondents who answered the items, 55.9% ($n = 19$) reported stress-related problems since the bombing, 93.9% ($n = 31$) reported some degree of overall stress

TABLE 3.2
Disaster Mental Health Workers' Reaction to Bombing

Disaster Exposure		
Experienced disaster	35.3%	12
Injury to self	0	0
Injury to family member	2.9%	1
Death to family member	2.9%	1
Experienced loss or damage to property	2.9%	1
Estimated dollar amount of damage	0	0
Feared I would die	2.9%	1
Fearful someone I knew might die	61.8%	21
Stress Response		
Stress related problems since disaster	55.9%	19
Overall stress since disaster (> low)	93.9%	31
Level of stress related problems now	87.9%	29
Experienced delayed stress problems	48.5%	16

since the bombing, 87.9% (n = 29) reported some level of stress problems currently, and 48.5% (n = 16) experienced delayed stress problems (see Table 3.2).

Disaster Mental Health Work

The psychological impact of providing disaster mental health services was examined using CFS and BOS and by asking respondents several questions about the stressfulness of their disaster mental health work. The risk of compassion fatigue and risk for burnout for the disaster mental health workers as reflected in the mean scores for this sample suggest high risk of both compassion fatigue and burnout. The group mean compassion fatigue score was 36.82, which is in the high risk for compassion fatigue group that ranges from 36 to 40. The crisis counselors were distributed into the following risk groups based on their CFS scores: 11.8% (n = 4) were in the extremely low-risk group (26 or

TABLE 3.3
Degree of Severity of Disaster Worker Stress Response

Severity of Stress Response		
Mild to severe PTSD	64.7%	22
Frederick Reaction Index	mean 17.85	range 0–54
doubtful	35.3%	12
mild	44.1%	15
moderate	11.8%	4
severe	8.8%	3
very severe	0	

less), 14.7% (*n* = 5) were in the low-risk group (27–30), 23.5% (*n* = 8) were in the moderate-risk group (31–35), 29.4% (*n* = 10) were in the high-risk group (36–40), and 20.6% (*n* = 7) were in the extremely high-risk group (43 or more) for compassion fatigue. The risk of burnout mean score was 30.794, which is in the high risk for burnout grouping that ranges from 30 to 42. The crisis counselor BOS scores were distributed into the following risk groups: 23.5% (*n* = 8) are at extremely low risk (19 or less), 35.3% (*n* = 12) are in the moderate-risk group (25–29), 26.5% (*n* = 9) are in the high-risk group (30–42), and 14.7% (*n* = 5) are in the extremely high-risk group (43 or more) for burnout.

Disaster mental health work was evaluated as more stressful than other jobs by slightly more than half of the disaster mental health workers, or 52.9% (*n* = 18) of the respondents. Respondents evaluated disaster work as much less stressful than previous jobs, 2.9% (*n* = 1); less stressful, 8.8% (*n* = 3); about the same, 14.7% (*n* = 5); more stressful, 44.1% (*n* =15); much more stressful, 8.8% (*n* = 3); and 2.9% (*n* = 1) were missing data (see Table 3.4).

Practicing personal stress management activities was reported by 82.3% (*n* = 28) of respondents. Frequency of personal stress management activities was reported by 14.7% (*n* = 5) as none of the time; 2.9% (*n* = 1) as every other month; 5.9% (*n* = 2) as monthly; 44.1% (*n* = 15) as several times per week;

TABLE 3.4

Disaster Mental Health Workers' Crisis Counseling Experiences

Crisis counseling job more stress level compared to previous jobs		
Don't work in program	17.6%	6
Much less stressful	2.9%	1
Less stressful	8.8%	3
About the same stress	14.7%	5
More stressful	44.1%	15
Much more stressful	8.8%	3
Missing	2.9%	1
Personally practice stress management	82.3%	28
Participated in crisis counseling program stress	yes = 52.9%	27
management activities	no = 38.2%	13
	missing = 8.8%	3
Compassion fatigue (high risk)	mean = 36.82	
Extremely low risk	11.8%	4
Low risk	14.7%	5
Moderate risk	23.5%	8
High risk	29.4%	10
Extremely high risk	20.6%	7
Burnout (high risk)	mean = 30.79	
Low risk	23.5%	8
Moderate risk	35.3	12
High risk	26.5%	9
Extremely high risk	14.7	4

17.6% (n = 6) as daily; 11.8% (n = 4) as several times per day; one report was missing.

Counselors were asked to describe the types of personal activities they used to manage stress. The following practices were described:

> Friday night is my designated "destress" time. I spend it with a close friend. We have supper, then do crafts, watch TV or movies or talk. I also listen to relaxing music on my way to and from work.

> I went for a weekend in the woods twice, without a phone or other people. I did not have my home phone or my answering machine on for several months.

Other frequently listed personal stress-management activities included these:

Leisure and "diversion" activities: dinner; movies; social activities; reading; outdoor things such as walking or fishing; crocheting; making time for old hobbies

Family time: communication with my spouse regarding my feelings; time with family, especially children; games

Exercise: walking (most frequently mentioned), weightlifting, aerobic exercise and weight training, running, swimming, bicycling, dancing

Relaxation and meditation: Relaxation tapes, music, deep breathing, positive visualization, daydreaming, journaling, art/drawing, rest

Informal "group therapy" with coworkers: brainstorming, sharing information, consulting with other counselors

Personal counseling and personal session with my doctor

Prayer: church, spirituality growth groups, reading philosophy

Humor

Participation in stress-management training activities sponsored by the crisis counseling program was reported by 53% (n = 27). Not participating in the stress-management services was reported by 38.2% (n = 13) of respondents. The types of program-sponsored stress-management services staff reported using included these:

Debriefings with or without a facilitator: Some counselors went to one or two debriefings, others attended regularly, with a frequency of twice a week to once a month.

"Informal" debriefing and defusing among coworkers.

Training (frequently mentioned, with a wide variety of topics listed as being helpful and supportive).

Consultation and professional support.

Staff meetings.

The respondents were divided into two job classification groups based on the job title they reported in the survey: administration ($n = 4$) and direct services ($n = 28$). The job class of administrator scored significantly higher than direct service workers on compassion fatigue (CFS), burnout (BOS), Global Severity Index (GSI), and Positive Symptom Total Index (PSTI) on the Symptom Checklist 90–R.

Respondents who had worked longer with bombing survivors had higher mean distress scores than respondents working fewer months. The number of months working with bombing survivors was significantly correlated to compassion fatigue ($p = 0.001$) and burnout ($p = 0.008$), and approached significance with the FRI–A ($p = 0.07 > 0.05$).

Psychological Symptoms and Distress

The disaster mental health workers as a group would not be considered in the clinical range as measured with the SCL–90–R using nonpatient norms. A *portion* of the sample have scores that place them within the clinical range. The SCL–90–R GSI scores are well below the cut-off T score of 63, which establishes clinical caseness. The operational definition of caseness is individuals considered a case or positive risk based on the individual scoring at or above the 90th percentile for nonpatient norms. The GSI T score mean was 54.667. The mean Positive Symptom Total (PST) score was 55.39. The mean Positive Symptom Distress Index (PSDI) was 48.79. Fifteen workers (44.1%; $n = 15$) had caseness based on a GSI score or two-dimensional T scores greater than or equal to a T score of 63 (see Table 3.5).

The relationship between demographic variables of sex, age, ethnicity, and education with stress response to the bombing (FRI–A), stress response to working with survivors of the bombing (Compassion Fatigue Self-Test for Helpers), and general signs and symptoms of distress SCL–90–R were examined. Significant relationships between sex and general signs and symptoms of distress were found. The mean GSI, mean PST, and mean PSTI were greater

TABLE 3.5
Psychological Symptoms and Distress Level of Disaster
Mental Health Workers

Symptom and Distress Level SCL–90–R	mean	
Caseness (individuals considered a case or positive risk based on individuals scoring at or above the 90th percentile for nonpatient norms)	44.1	15
Global Severity Index T score	54.667	
Positive Symptom Total T score	55.39	
Positive Symptom Distress Index T score	48.79	

for male (n = 6) than for female respondents. Males had a significantly higher mean GSI score of 66.5, compared to females, who had a mean GSI of 52.03 (p = 0.009). Males had a higher mean PST score (64.3) than did females (mean PST of 53.4; p = .003), and a higher mean PSTI score (59) than females' mean PSTI score (46.51; p = 0.017).

Males also scored slightly higher on the FRI–A and lower on the CFS and BOS, although the differences were not significant. The mean FRI–A score for males was 24.33, and the FRI female mean score was 16.5. The mean CFS score for males was 34.5, for females it was 37.07. The mean BOS scores for males was 29.8, and for females, it was 31.0.

Differences between caucasian (n = 25) and other ethnic groups (n = 7) (Latino, African American, Native American, and other) on the GSI were found to be present. The mean GSI score for caucasian was 52.25, and for other ethnic groups it was 62.43. The difference in mean GSI score between other ethnic groups and caucasians approached significance (p = 0.065 > 0.05).

Social Support

The exchange of social support was measured in terms of respondents' perceptions that other people understood their experiences. This was assessed by asking whether respondents felt understood by people *not* involved in the bombing disaster; whether respondents felt understood by people who were involved in the bombing disaster; and whether respondents felt that people rejected their experience, feelings, or thoughts about the bombing. These three items were combined in an Empathy Index Score (Jenkins, 1996). Empathy scores ranged from 1 (not at all) to 4 (quite). In response to the question, "How well do people who were *not* involved in the bombing understand what you have experienced?" 20.6% (n = 7) responded not at all; 32.4% (n = 11), a little; 26.5% (n = 9), moderately; 2.9% (n = 1), quite well; and 17.6% (n = 6) were missing. The mean empathy value from others not involved was 2.14, with 71.8% (21) having experienced some degree of empathy from noninvolved others. In response to the question, "How well do people who *were also involved* in the bombing understand what you have experienced?" 5.9% (n = 2) responded a little; 17.5% (n = 6) moderately; 50% (n = 17) quite well; and 26.5% were missing. The mean empathy from involved others value was 3.6, with 73.5% (25) having experienced some degree of empathy from involved others. In response the question, "How frequently *have other people rejected* your experience, feelings, or thoughts about the bombing?" 52. 9% (n = 18) responded not at all; 20.6% (n = 7) answered a little of the time; 8.8% (n = 3), moderately frequently; 8.8% (n = 3), quite frequently; and 8.8% (n = 3) were missing. The mean empathy rejected value was 3.26, with 52.9% (18) experiencing no rejection of their experience, thoughts, or feelings. The mean Empathy Index Score for the sample was 3.061, which is in the moderate level of empathy range.

Respondents who believed that someone they knew might die as a result of the bombing experienced significantly greater levels of empathy from people involved in the bombing experience. When the sex of the respondents was considered in relationship to empathy experienced, males experienced higher levels of empathy from people not involved and lower levels of empathy from people involved than their female counterparts experienced. Males also experienced more rejection of their experience, feelings, or thoughts about the bombing than was experienced by females. These lower levels of empathy were not statistically significant but represent an interesting trend, especially when considering that males had more signs and symptoms of distress than females on all measurement scales except compassion fatigue and burnout.

Instruments

The instruments used to measure stress response to the bombing (FRI–A), stress response to working with survivors of the bombing (Compassion Fatigue Self-Test for Helpers), and general signs and symptoms of distress (SCL–90–R) are correlated at a statistically significantly level ($p \leq 0.05$; see Table 3.5). Different clusters of variables were significantly associated with the different measures. Significant differences between males and females were found on the SCL–90–R, as well as significant differences among job classifications. Significant differences in postbombing stress response between administrators and direct services workers were found on CFS and BOS and approached significance on the FRI–A. Exposure to disaster mental health work, measured in months working with victims affected by the bombing, was significantly associated with compassion fatigue and burnout and approached significance with the FRI–A. Each of the different instruments appears to measure a different domain of the respondent reaction to the disaster, disaster mental health work, and generalized psychological distress.

DISCUSSION

This study examined the effects of disaster crisis counseling work on mental health workers. The primary focus was the disaster experience, postdisaster stress response, interpersonal effects, and reactions of mental health workers providing crisis counseling services to victims of the Oklahoma City bombing. A secondary focus was to identify variables that may be associated with vulnerability to development of postdisaster stress response in workers involved in long-term mental health recovery activities. The result of such assessment can help mental health workers providing disaster crisis counseling services in identifying their vulnerabilities, stress responses, and effective interventions to mitigate stress responses during long-term disaster mental health recovery activities.

The Alfred P. Murrah Federal Building bombing resulted in many respondents experiencing fear that someone they knew might die as a result of the blast. The belief that someone they knew might die may be the most significant psychological feature of this bombing disaster. Many more respondents were fearful that others might die than were fearful for their own safety. This disaster affected the disaster mental health workers and appears not to have affected any subgroups of these workers significantly more than others. Of particular interest is that the postdisaster stress responses of the disaster mental health workers who personally experienced the bombing of the Alfred P. Murrah Federal Building were slightly but not significantly higher than those of the group of disaster mental health workers who did not experience the bomb blast. Certainly this last group experienced the bombing through media coverage and the profound impact the disaster had on the entire community.

Two factors were significantly associated with increased degree of severity of stress disorder: the job classification of administrator and the number of months providing disaster mental health services to bombing survivors. The administrators of the program may have had an increased degree of stress due to their role of providing administrative and clinical support to direct service workers seeking assistance with difficult cases and decisions. Thus, their stress may be related not to the number of actual cases with which they were working clinically but to the intensity or "trauma titer" of the cases brought to them for help. One might also consider the complexity, difficulty, and intensity of the cases brought to administrators for consultation. In such cases where victims were experiencing intense suffering and neither the clinician nor the supervisor could "fix" the situation, it is reasonable to assume that supervisors, as the supposed "experts," felt an intense sense of helplessness, one of the key criteria for the development of posttraumatic stress disorder.

Risk of compassion fatigue and burnout mean scores for the sample suggest high risk for both compassion fatigue or burnout. Increased number of months working with bombing survivors is significantly associated with higher risk for compassion fatigue and burnout. This suggests there may be a dose relationship between disaster mental health work and compassion fatigue and burnout. Increased duration of time providing crisis counseling and educational services to victims of the Alfred P. Murrah Federal Building bombing appears related to increased compassion fatigue. In their study of medical, mental health, and public safety personnel following a school shooting, Sloan, Razensky, Kaplan, and Saunders (1994) found that job stress dimensions described by Hartsough and Myers (1985) were significant predictors of traumatic stress response six months after the incident. Time pressure was most predictive, followed by quantitative work load, then qualitative work load—

corroborating the findings of this study related to quantity or "dose" of work contributing to risk of compassion fatigue and burnout.

A higher level of generalized distress for other ethnic groups (Latino, African American, Native American, and other) than Caucasians as measured by the GSI on the SCL–90–R approached significance. The higher generalized distress for other ethnic groups is not found in response to the disaster or disaster mental health work. This elevated general level of distress may have been present prior to the bombing. The predisaster generalized level of distress may be associated with experiences and conditions experienced by other ethnic groups and not experienced by the Caucasians. This predisaster generalized level of distress may be associated with the use of "forbearance" by other ethnic groups to cope with racism, sexism, and community violence (Snowdon, 1997).

The findings in this study are quite important in comparison to other studies of disaster mental health workers. This study found the highest proportion of disaster mental health workers with some degree of severity for stress disorder compared to disaster mental health workers in other studies reported in the literature. Lindstrom and Lundin (1982) found that 4 out of 13 (31%) people who provided rescue and health care assistance following a fire had General Health Questionnaire scores suggesting psychological disturbance. Hodgkinson and Shepherd (1994) found that 60% of social workers experienced significant levels of symptoms during their first year of disaster social work. A study of disaster social workers providing counseling to individuals and families following the Piper Alpha North Sea oil production and platform explosion and the Clapham Rail crash found higher mean and subscale Hopkins Symptom Checklist scores for the disaster social workers than for the general population. The differences found were small but highly significant. Nine months following the Northridge earthquake, disaster mental health workers were surveyed about their reactions to the earthquake and to providing disaster mental health services during a FEMA crisis counseling program. The proportion of disaster mental health workers with some degree of severity for stress disorder was 60.5%. The proportion of mental health workers who did not do disaster mental health work but experienced the earthquake was 52% (Wee & Myers, 1997). The proportion of disaster mental health workers providing services following the Alfred P. Murrah Federal Building bombing with some degree of severity for stress disorder is 64.7% ($n = 22$). Fifteen (44.1%) disaster mental health workers have caseness

Perhaps the most significant finding of this study is the severity of distress among disaster mental health workers as compared to the distress reported among emergency service workers in other studies. Since 1983, with the publication of Mitchell's (1983) seminal work on stress management for emergency service workers, a multitude of research projects have studied the effects of disaster on the responders. For example, in a study of disaster workers following the Piper Alpha disaster, a comparison of police officer controls and mortuary worker groups showed no significant changes in individual officers (Alexander & Wells, 1991). In a study of distress and health among paramedics in the Killeen shooting incident by Jenkins and Sewell (1993), questionnaires were completed by 37 EMTs, paramedics, and firefighters one week postincident and at a one-month follow-up. Depression, anxiety, hostility, and GSI scales increased significantly during the 8 to 10 days after the event. The mean severity of reported health problems was significantly higher in the month after the event than in the month before. In a study of stress response of emergency personnel responding to the I-880 collapse, researchers found that 9% were above thresholds established for case identification and would be considered moderate to high distress responders averaging 1.5 years postevent (Marmar, Weiss, Metzler, Ronfeldt, & Foreman, 1996). A study of the psychological reactions of rescue workers following a tornado found that 17% would qualify for PTSD diagnosis (McCammon, Durham, Allison, & Williamson, 1986). Scott and Jordon (1993), in a study of Los Angeles County firefighters after the Los Angeles civil disturbances, found that 27% of the firefighters who responded reported continuing symptoms of distress six months after the incident. In a survey three months following the L.A. civil disturbances, Wee, Mills, and Koehler (1994) found that 42% of the EMTs surveyed had some degree of severity of stress response. In a study of British soldiers whose duties included handling and identification of bodies following the Gulf War, Deahl, Gillham, Thomas, Searle, and Srinivasan (1994) found that 50% had evidence of psychological disturbance suggestive of PTSD. A study six months following a massacre found that 50% of the officers present at the incident had some degree of mild to severe PTSD (Mantel, Dubner, & Lipson, 1985). One month after the Bradford fire disaster, a study of police officers found that 35% would have met four criteria, and 21% met three of four criteria for DSM–III diagnosis of PTSD (Duckworth, 1986). These findings suggest that 56% of the Bradford police officers had some level of stress response following this event. Rescue and disaster workers following a railroad accident showed 70% expressing evidence of some strain and 35% showing at least moderate strain intensity (Raphael et al., 1984). *Following bombing of the Alfred P. Murrah Federal Building, 64.7% of the disaster mental health workers providing services had some degree of severity for stress disorder.*

The findings of this study suggest that the nature of the Alfred P. Murrah Federal Building bombing as a terrorist act, exposure to the bomb blast and its aftermath, the length of time providing disaster mental health services, and job duties providing disaster mental health services during long-term disaster recovery appear to have a similar and even more intense severity of stress response as the shorter-term, high-intensity rescue, disaster, and emergency work done by emergency service workers. *This severity of stress among the disaster mental health workers is higher than the distress levels found in almost all other groups of emergency and rescue workers studied in the last 16 years.* These results strongly suggest the need for further research of the impact of disaster crisis counseling on the workers providing the counseling. In addition, serious attention needs to be paid to developing effective stress management and prevention programs for these at-risk workers.

The disaster mental health workers of the Alfred P. Murrah Federal Building bombing crisis counseling program faced enormous challenges in providing crisis counseling following what was then called the worst terrorist attack in United States history. The disaster mental health workers were pioneers in the effort to bring support, understanding, reassurance, encouragement, and crisis counseling to the people of Oklahoma City and beyond who were affected by this bombing. The crisis counseling program provided stress management services and resources to the counselors involved, without which the level of stress could have gone even higher. The presence, level of stress, and distress of the disaster mental health workers should in no way interpreted as judgment or criticism of their efforts to ease human suffering. Rather, the risk for compassion fatigue and burnout might be viewed as evidence of the extraordinary empathy, sympathy, understanding, and energy devoted to caring for the children, mothers, fathers, sisters, brothers, families, neighbors, emergency service workers, and fellow human beings struck by this catastrophic disaster.

IMPLICATIONS FOR FUTURE RESEARCH

This study was of an exploratory nature with a small sample size composed of disaster mental health workers working in long-term mental health recovery. The disaster studied was a human-caused event that prior to September 11, 2001, was referred to as the worst terrorist event up until that time in the history of the United States. The fact that this disaster was an intentional terrorist act may have added to the intensity of its impact on the victims as well as on the disaster mental health workers involved.

Further research on stress reactions of disaster mental health workers in various *types* of disasters would help to identify those types in which disaster mental health workers are most at risk for stress-related problems. Such knowledge could guide the development of stress management practices and programs appropriate to the type of disaster and the risk intensity the disaster mental health workers would likely be facing. Thus, the disaster mental health workers would likely be at risk for fewer and a lower intensity of stress-related problems.

Further study of the effects of gender, ethnicity, and job class as they are related to the reactions of the disaster mental health workers is warranted based on the results of this study. In addition, the relationship of prior disaster experiences, the phase of disaster in which intervention is occurring, and the length of time providing disaster mental health services (dose relationship) to mental health worker stress response needs further study. The study of disaster mental health workers under real-life field conditions poses many challenges. Predisaster mental health assessment of mental health workers with postdisaster measurement of changes in stress response over time in relation to comparison controls would be highly desirable. The identification, standardization, and evaluation of various stress management programs as well as social supports are needed to assist in protecting the health of disaster mental health workers who will provide disaster mental health services in the future.

IMPLICATIONS FOR FUTURE PRACTICE

Assistance is needed for mental health workers providing disaster crisis counseling services in identifying their vulnerabilities, stress responses, and effective interventions to mitigate stress responses during long-term disaster mental health recovery activities. The development of interventions and programs to safeguard mental and physical health of disaster mental health workers during long-term disaster mental health recovery is in a developmental phase. Until research demonstrates clearly which interventions and programs are effective in mitigating and treating secondary posttraumatic stress, compassion fatigue, and burnout, care must be exercised by disaster mental health service workers and managers. Consideration must be taken about the nature of the disaster and how it can affect disaster mental health workers. The issues of human-caused versus natural disasters, the nature of the original and ongoing threat, the presence or absence of warning, the extent of deaths and injuries, as well as the disruption to housing and the environment must be considered in relation to the stress of the disaster mental health workers. Stress management programs to mitigate the impact of compassion fatigue and burnout need to be comprehensive and address differences in gender, ethnicity and job duties that may be related to primary and secondary PTSD. Last, but very important, is the perceived social support or empathy disaster mental health workers receive not only in the disaster itself but in their professional roles following the disaster.

Followup of disaster mental health workers once the crisis counseling program ends also must be considered. Disaster mental health workers may have continuing stress responses and distress associated with their individual history as well as their disaster experiences, and may have no source of support once the program ends. Activities to provide support and intervention to disaster mental health workers at one, three, and six months after the crisis counseling program ends might be considered to assess what the "cost of caring" has been and to provide assistance to those in need.

REFERENCES

Alexander, D. A., & Wells, A. (1991). Reactions of police officers to body-handling after a major disaster: A before-and-after comparison. *British Journal of Psychiatry, 159*, 547–555.

American Psychiatric Association. (1994). *Diagnostic and statistical manual of mental disorders* (4th ed.). Washington, DC: Author.

Armstrong, K., O'Callahan, W., & Marmar, C. R. (1991). Debriefing Red Cross disaster personnel: The multiple stressor debriefing model. *Journal of Traumatic Stress, 4*, 581–593.

Bartone, P., Ursano, R., Wright, K., & Ingraham, L. (1989). Impact of a military air disaster. *Journal of Nervous and Mental Disease, 177*, 317–328.

Berah, E., Jones, H., & Valent, P. (1984). The experience of a mental health team involved in the early phase of a disaster. *Australia and New Zealand Journal of Psychiatry, 18*, 354–358.

Deahl, M. P., Gillham, A. B., Thomas, J., Searle, M. M., & Srinivasan, M. (1994). Psychological sequelae following the Gulf War: Factors associated with subsequent morbidity and the effectiveness of psychological debriefing. *British Journal of Psychiatry, 165*, 60–65.

Department of Health and Human Services. (1988a). *Prevention and control of stress among emergency workers: A pamphlet for team managers* (DHHS Publication No. ADM 88–1496). Washington, DC: U.S. Government Printing Office.

Department of Health and Human Services. (1988b). *Prevention and control of stress among emergency workers: A pamphlet for team managers* (DHHS Publication No. ADM 88–1497). Washington, DC: U.S. Government Printing Office.

Derogatis, L. (1993). *SCL–90–R bibliography of research reports.* Minneapolis, MN: National Computer Systems.

Derogatis, L. (1994). *SCL–90–R Symptom Checklist–90–R: Administration coding, and procedures manual.* Minneapolis, MN: National Computer Systems.

Duckworth, D. (1986). Psychological problems arising from disaster work. *Stress Medicine, 2*, 315–323.

Durham, T. W., McCammon, S. L., & Allison, E. J., Jr. (1985, July). The psychological impact of disaster on rescue personnel. *Annals of Emergency Medicine, 14*(7), 664–668.

Eby, D. C. (1984). A disaster worker's response. In *Role stressors and supports for emergency workers.* (DHHS Publication No. ADM 85–1408). Rockville, MD: National Institute of Mental Health.

Federal Emergency Management Agency. (1987a). *FEMA workers can be affected by disasters.* (Brochure L–156). Washington, DC: FEMA & National Institute of Mental Health.

Federal Emergency Management Agency. (1987b). *Returning home after the disaster: An information pamphlet for FEMA disaster workers.* (Brochure l–157). Washington, DC: FEMA & National Institute of Mental Health.

Federal Emergency Management Agency. (1995, May 1). *Building inspection area.* Oklahoma City, OK: FEMA-GIS.

Federal Emergency Management Agency & Center for Mental Health Services. (1992). *Crisis counseling programs for victims of presidential declared disasters.* Washington, DC: Author.

Figley, C. R. (1982). *Traumatization and comfort: Close relationships may be hazardous to your health.* Keynote presentation at the Families and Close Relationships: Individuals in Social Interaction Conference, Texas Tech University, Lubbock, TX.

Figley, C. R. (1989). *Helping traumatized families.* San Francisco: Jossey-Bass.

Figley, C. R. (1993, February). Compassion stress and the family therapist. *Family Therapy News,* 1–8.

Figley, C. R. (1995). Compassion fatigue as secondary traumatic stress disorder: An overview. In C. R. Figley (Ed.), *Compassion fatigue* (pp. 1–20). New York: Brunner/Mazel.

Forman, W. C. (1986). Police stress response to a civilian aircraft disaster. In J. T. Reese & H. A. Goldstein (Eds.), *Psychological services for law enforcement* (pp. 423–429). Washington, DC: U.S. Government Printing Office.

Forstenzer, A. (1980). Stress: The psychological scarring of air crash rescue personnel. *Firehouse, 7,* 50–62.

Frederick, C. J. (1977). Current thinking about crisis or psychological interventions in United States disasters. *Mass Emergencies, 2,* 43–49.

Frederick, C. J. (1985). Children traumatized by catastrophic situations. In S. Eth & R. S. Pynoos (Eds.), *Post-traumatic stress disorder in children* (pp. 71–100). Washington, DC: American Psychiatric Press.

Green, B. L., & Gleser, G. C. (1983). Stress and long standing psychopathology in survivors of the Buffalo Creek disaster. In D. Ricks & B. S. Dohrenwend (Eds.), *Origins of psychopathology: Problems in research and public policy* (pp. 73–90). Cambridge, MA: University Press.

Hartsough, D. M., & Myers, D. G. (1985). *Disaster work and mental health: Prevention and control of stress among workers* (DHHS Publication No. ADM 85-1422). Rockville, MD: National Institute of Mental Health.

Hodgkinson, P. E., & Shepherd, M. A. (1994). The impact of disaster support work. *Journal of Traumatic Stress, 7*(4), 587–600.

Horowitz, M. J., Stinson, C., & Field, N. (1981). Natural disasters and stress response syndromes. *Psychiatric Annals, 21*(9), 556–562.

Jenkins, S. R. (1996). Social support and debriefing efficacy among emergency medical workers after a mass shooting incident. *Journal of Social Behavior and Personality, 11*(3), 447–492.

Jenkins, S. R., & Sewell, K. W. (1993, March). *Distress and health among paramedics in the Killeen shooting incident.* Paper presented at the Annual Meeting of the Socity for Behavioral Medicine, San Francisco.

Jordon, F. B. (1997). The role of the medical examiner/coroner in mass fatality disaster management. *National Foundation for Mortuary Care Disaster Management News, 1,* 1–3.

Kenardy, J. A., Webster, R. A., Lewin, T. J., Carr, V. J., Hazell, P. L., & Carter, G. L. (1996). Stress debriefing and patterns of recovery following a natural disaster. *Journal of Traumatic Stress, 9*(1), 37–49.

Lanning, J. K. S., & Fannin, R. A. (1988, August/September). It's not over yet. *Chief Fire Executive, 40*–44, 58–62.

Lindemann, E. (1944). Symptomatology and management of acute grief. *American Journal of Psychiatry, 101,* 141–148.

Lindstrom, B., & Lundin, T. (1982). Stress reactions among rescue and health care personnel after a major hotel fire. *Nord. Psykiatr. Tidss, 36* (Supplement 6).

Lystad, M. (1988). Perspectives on human responses to mass emergencies. In M. Lystad (Ed.), Mental health response to mass emergencies: *Theory and practice* (pp. 22–51). New York: Brunner/Mazel.

Mantell, M. (1986). San Ysidro: When the badge turns blue. In J. Reese & H. Goldstein (Eds.), *Psychological services for law enforcement* (U.S. Govt. Printing Office Publication No. 027-000-012-66-3). Washington, DC: U.S. Department of Justice, Federal Bureau of Investigation.

Mantel, M. R., Dubner, J. S., & Lipson, G. S. (1985). *San Yesidro massacre: Impact on police officers.* San Diego, CA: San Diego Police Department.

Marmar, C. R., Weiss, D. S., Metzler, T. J., Ronfeldt, H. M., & Foreman, C. (1996). Stress responses of emergency services personnel to the Loma Prieta earthquake Interstate 880 freeway collapse and control traumatic incidents. *Journal of Traumatic Stress, 9*(1), 63–85.

McFarlane, A. C. (1988). The longitudinal course of post traumatic morbidity: The range of outcomes and their predictors. *Journal of Nervous and Mental Disease, 176*(1), 30–39.

Miles, M. S., Demi. A. S., & Mostyn-Aker, P. (1984). Rescue workers' reactions following the Hyatt Hotel Disaster. *Death Education, 8,* 315–331.

Mitchell, J. T. (1983). When disaster strikes . . . the critical incident stress debriefing process. *Journal of Emergency Medical Services, 8,* 36–39.

Mitchell, J. T. (1986, September/October). Critical incident stress management. *Response,* 24–25.

Mitchell, J., & Bray, G. (1990). *Emergency services stress: Guidelines for preserving the health and careers of emergency services personnel.* Englewood Cliffs, NJ: Prentice-Hall.

Mitchell, J., & Everly, G. S. (2001). *Critical incident stress debriefing: An operations manual for the prevention of traumatic stress among emergency services and disaster workers* (3rd ed.). Ellicott City, MD: Chevron Publishing Company.

Moran, C., & Britton, N. R. (1994). Emergency work experience and reactions to traumatic incidents. *Journal of Traumatic Stress, 7*(4).

Myers, D. (1985a). Helping the helpers: A training manual. In D. M. Hartsough & D. G. Myers, *Disaster work and mental health: prevention and control of stress among workers.* (DHMS Publication No. ADM 85-1422). Rockville, MD: National Institute of Mental Health.

Myers, D. (1992). *Hurricane Andrew disaster field office stress management program after action report.* Washington, DC: FEMA.

Myers, D. (1993). *After action report: 1993 California winter storms.* Washington, DC: FEMA.

Myers, D. (1994a). *A stress management program for FEMA disaster workers* (Contract No. 93MF06480701D). Washington, DC: FEMA.

Myers, D. (1994b). *Disaster response and recovery: A handbook for mental health professionals.* (DHHS Publication No. SMA 94-3010). Rockville, MD: Public Health Service, Substance Abuse and Mental Health Services Administration, Center for Mental Health Services.

Myers, D. (1995). Worker stress during longterm disaster recovery efforts. In G. S. Everly (Ed.), *Innovations in disaster and trauma psychology, volume 1: Applications in emergency services and disaster response.* Baltimore: Chevron Publishing Corp.

Myers, D., & Zunin, L. M. (1993a). *After action report: 1993 Florida winter storms disaster field office stress management program.* Washington, DC: FEMA.

Myers, D., & Zunin, L. M. (1993b). *After action report: 1993 midwest floods central processing unite stress management program.* Washington, DC: FEMA.

Myers, D., & Zunin, L. (1994a). *Cumulative stress reactions.* Unpublished training materials.

Myers, D., & Zunin, L. (1994b). *Stress management program after action report: 1994 Northridge earthquake.* Washington, DC: FEMA & California Governor's Office of Emergency Services.

Oklahoma City Public Works Department. (1995). *Building inspection area.* Oklahoma City, OK: Geographic Information Systems.

Raphael, B. (1986). *When disasters strike. How individuals and communities cope with catastrophe.* New York: Basic Books.

Raphael, B., Singh, B., Bradbury, B., & Lambert, F. (1984). Who helps the helpers? The effects of a disaster on the rescue workers. *Omega, 14,* 9–20.

Robinson, R. (1989). Critical incident stress and psychological debriefing in emergency services. *Social Biology Resources Center Review, 3*(3), 1–4.

Rosensweig, M. A., & Vaslow, P. K. (1992). *Recommendations for reduction of stress among FEMA disaster workers.* Washington, DC: National Institute of Mental Health.

Scott, R. T., & Jordan, M. J. (1993, April). *The Los Angeles riots April 1992: A CISD challenge.* Paper presented at the Second World Congress on Stress, Trauma, and Coping in the Emergency Services. A meeting of the International Critical Incident Stress Foundation, Baltimore, MD.

Smith, S. M. (1983). Family disruption in the wake of natural disaster. In C. R. Figley & H. A. Goldstein (Eds.), *Psychological services for law enforcement* (pp. 423–429). Washington, DC: U.S. Government Printing Office.

Sloan, I. H., Rozensky, R. H., Kaplan, L., & Saunders, S. M. (1994). A shooting incident in an elementary school: Effects of worker stress on public safety, mental health, and medical personnel. *Journal of Traumatic Stress, 1,* 565–574.

Statistical Package for the Social Sciences. (1993). *SPSS for Windows: Release 6.0.* Chicago: SPSS Inc.

Taylor, A. J. W., & Frazer, A. G. (1982). The stress of post-disaster body handling and victim identification work. *Journal of Human Stress, 8*(4), 4–12.

Wee, D. F. (1990). *Cypress structure collapse: A survey of emergency service workers.* Unpublished manuscript. Available from Berkeley Mental Health, 2640 Martin Luther King Jr. Way, Berkeley, CA 94704.

Wee, D. F. (1994). Disasters: Impact on the law enforcement family. In J. T. Reese & E. Scrivner (Eds.), *Law enforcement family: Issues and answers.* Washington, DC: U.S. Department of Justice, Federal Bureau of Investigation.

Wee, D. F., & Mills, D. (1993a). Stress response of emergency medical services personnel following the Los Angeles civil disturbances. In *Medical care for the injured: The emergency medical response to the April, 1992 Los Angeles civil disturbance* (EMSA #393–01). Sacramento, CA: California Emergence Medical Services Authority.

Wee, D. F., & Myers, D. (1997). Disaster mental health: Impact on the workers. In K. Johnson (Ed.), *Trauma in the lives of children* (pp. 257–263). Alameda. CA: Hunter House.

Wee, D. F., Mills, D. M., & Koehler, G. (1999). The effects of critical incident stress debriefing (CISD) on emergency medical services personnel following the Los Angeles civil disturbances. *International Journal of Emergency Mental Health,* pp. 33–37.

Winget, C. N., & Umbenhauer, S. L. (1982). Disaster planning: The mental health workers a "victim-by-proxy." *Journal of Health and Human Resources Administration, 4,* 363–373.

Wraith, R., & Gordon, R. (1988). *Workers' responses to disaster.* Melbourne, Australia: Melbourne Royal Children's Hospital.

Zunin, L. M., Myers, D., & Cook, C. (1995). *Stress management final report: Oklahoma City federal building bombing.* Washington, DC: FEMA.

4

Secondary Traumatic Stress in Case Managers Working in Community Mental Health Services

LENORE MELDRUM
ROBERT KING
DARREN SPOONER

A mental disorder is prevalent, extensive, affects all age, social and cultural groups, and may be associated with chronic disability, handicap and invalidity as a result of symptoms which disrupt the capacity for satisfying family and personal relationships and enjoyment of work and leisure. (Mental Health Consumer Outcomes Taskforce, 1991, p vii)

Approximately 25% to 30% of the population of Australia is expected to meet the diagnostic criteria for a mental disorder every year (Treatment Protocol Project, 1997). These 4 to 5 million people are potential clients of community mental health services. Of this population sector, two thirds will have mild or transient disorders, and an even smaller proportion (1 in 6) will seek help from medical services, most often from their general practitioners (Treatment Protocol Project, 1997).

Of the remaining group, approximately 3% (549,000) of the Australian population has been identified as suffering from a "serious mental disorder" (Australian Bureau of Statistics, 1998; Treatment Protocol Project, 1997), which has been defined as a disorder that results in *lifelong disabling conditions that impair personal and social functioning* (Draine, 1997, p. 32). The severity of serious and persistent mental disorders is generally determined by diagnosis, disability, and duration of the illness (Mercier, 1994). Serious mental illness may be conceptualized as being chronically traumatic because of the profound impact psychosis and major mood disorders have on personal identity and daily functioning. Furthermore, people who suffer from major mental illness have high risk of exposure to acute traumatic incidents such as suicide attempts (their own or those of friends), physical and/or sexual assault, sudden homelessness, or forced admission to hospital.

Care of people with serious mental disorders was essentially undertaken in tertiary hospitals or asylums during the 1950s. Since that time, there has been a move in Australia towards a more balanced system of hospital and community care. This policy change has meant that most people with mental disorders live and are cared for in the community (Australian Health Ministers, 1992).

Case managers provide the core services of Australia's community-based state mental health service. Their target clients are people with serious mental illness and complex service needs who require more coordinated services than those offered by a private psychiatrist, family physician, or private psychiatrist (National Health Strategy, 1993). Case managers are mental health professionals with core training in nursing, psychology, social work, occupational therapy, or medicine who typically work in multidisciplinary teams but whose work involves high levels of autonomy and responsibility. They provide a range of "generic" services and ensure access to specialist services when required.

Recent research conducted in Queensland determined that functions of case managers working in community services included these: (a) individual psychotherapy and/or counseling, (b) assessment, (c) psychoeducation, (d) crisis intervention, (e) monitoring daily living skills, (f) monitoring medication, (g) support, (h) activities of daily living, as well as, (i) liaison with other care agencies (Yellowlees, Howgego, Meldrum, & Dark, 1997). One of the earliest published articles that identified problems of those working in the helping professions was on the concept of burnout (Maslach, 1976).

BURNOUT

Burnout has been described by Maslach and Jackson (1986, p. 1) as "a syndrome of emotional exhaustion, depersonalization and reduced personal accomplishment that can occur among individuals who do *people work* of some kind." Symptoms—including feelings of emotional numbing, loss of ability to feel and "care" for the problems of those being helped, trouble sleeping and concentrating, and being jumpy and easily startled—have been attributed to burnout. Burnout has been related to amount and type of work done; the caseload of distressing cases, which may be too many in number; or working over too long a period (Raphael, Meldrum, & Donald, 1993).

AUSTRALIAN STUDIES OF SECONDARY STRESS AND PARALLEL PROCESS REACTIONS

Studies of mental health workers after disasters have shown reactions to the trauma of client experiences, as identified by these workers and in symptomatic patterns reported by them. Raphael, Singh, Bradbury, and Lambert (1983–1984) studied a number of groups of workers after a rail disaster and found that support workers were more likely to feel depressed by the burden of the suffering of others.

Berah, Jones, and Valent (1984) carried out an in-depth study of 19 mental health workers in the aftermath of a bushfire disaster. Two thirds of these workers reported experiencing shock, uncertainty, depression, sadness, and helplessness, plus feelings of dependency and a need for team support. Fatigue, physical illness, and changed lifestyle behaviors were also described. Although these reactions were prominent after their first encounter with the disaster victims and diminished after three to four visits, more than half still experienced significant posttrauma reactions and fatigue at that time. Most reported this work to be an emotionally valuable experience, but they also found it frustrating, stressful, and depressing. They reported themselves to be "shocked, saddened and very tired."

Mental health professionals providing debriefing for bank workers after armed hold-ups have described an experience of parallel process. These workers experienced a reflection of the trauma effects and working through processes of their clients. (Talbot, 1990; Talbot, Manton, & Dunn, 1992). A survey conducted of mental health workers ($n = 149$) revealed that work with trauma victims was perceived as very to extremely stressful in 21.7% of instances, and if those who perceived their work as quite stressful were included, more than half (54.8%) of respondents clearly identified their work as significant in this way. A total of 35.1% reported being quite, very, or extremely emotionally drained (Raphael et al., 1993).

INTERNATIONAL STUDIES

Therapists working with families also may be traumatized by events that affect them or their families directly or through contact with traumatized clients (Carbonell & Figley, 1996). Symptoms of secondary stress in therapists have been well-documented as including intrusive images, physiological arousal, functional impairment, and compulsive behaviors (Figley 1995; Herman, 1992; McCann & Pearlman, 1990).

A significant minority of community psychiatric nurses were found to have high levels of stress and burnout compared with their hospital counterparts (Fagin, Brown, Bartlett, Leary, & Carson, 1995). Research in discipline-specific areas has found that all of the mental health professions are affected (Fagin, 1996; Sweeney & Nicols, 1996;). McCann and Pearlman (1990) confirmed that the impact of working with clients affected all aspects of a therapist's life, were cumulative, and had the possibility of permanently altering the therapist's cognitive schemata of dependency and trust, safety, power, independence, esteem, and intimacy—affecting their feelings, lives, and relationships.

A small study reporting on reactions paralleling victim responses described the effects on five nurse researchers of reviewing the case records of 1,215 rape crisis center victims. The nurses' reactions included anger, dreams, fear of physical injury, and sleep disturbances, as are commonly reported by rape victims themselves (Alexander, de Chesnay, Marshall, & Campbell, 1989). Mental health workers were found to be exposed to additional stressors more than other health workers by the nature of their professional care, dealing with troubled people over lengthy periods of time (Moore & Cooper, 1996).

A study of workers in a community mental health service working with clients with severe mental illnesses reported emotional exhaustion, depersonalization, and General Health Questionnaire score levels above the norms for the general population (Oliver & Kuipers, 1996). It also found that stress in community care teams in Great Britain was associated with high levels of burnout, high staff turnover, absenteeism, and job dissatisfaction (Blankertz & Robinson, 1997; Parker & Kulik, 1995). These levels were found to be higher than those of their professional counterparts working within hospital systems (Prosser et al., 1996; Wykes, Stevens, & Everitt, 1997). Discipline was found to be a major source of variance in a study of burnout among 445 team members from 57 community mental health teams in the United Kingdom (Onyett, Pillinger, & Muijen, 1997). From this data set the major sources of stress were identified as lack of resources and work overload (Onyett, Pillinger, & Muijen, 1995).

The impact of secondary traumatic stress (STS) on professional capability has not been addressed in many workplaces. Decreased staff morale—both of those suffering secondary stress and the ripple effect on other staff—is one of the first factors to be detected by management. Reduced professional functioning is shown in the decrease in quality and quantity of output, low motivation, increasing errors, avoidance of allotted tasks, and obsession regarding details (Yassen, 1995).

STS provides a somewhat more developed theoretical framework for understanding work-related stress. It posits a causal process, a characteristic symptomatic response that is directly linked to the causal process, and a phenomenology of illness that enables linkage to the relatively well-developed posttraumatic stress disorder (PTSD). Linkages with PTSD also suggest possible lines of intervention by drawing on the extensive PTSD treatment literature.

QUEENSLAND MENTAL HEALTH CASE MANAGER–SECONDARY TRAUMATIC STRESS SURVEY

This study set out to determine whether STS could provide a useful framework for measurement and conceptualization of stress among mental health workers. Community-based case managers were chosen as a focus for the study because of a broader interest in investigating the experience and role functioning of this relatively new but functionally critical occupational group. Many questions remain unanswered or have been the subject of a range of competing and speculative answers. The following are of particular importance:

1. What is the source of stress and burnout among mental health workers?
2. What is the relative importance of worker vulnerability and stressful experience?
3. What kinds of interventions might reduce stress and burnout among mental health workers?

These are somewhat interrelated questions and they share a common theme. This is that there does not appear to be a well-developed explanatory model for burnout. Although one often hears descriptive components such as *emotional exhaustion, depersonalization,* and *lack of personal accomplishment,* there is a notable lack of consensus concerning explanatory models. Factors that have been considered include these:

- work load (Duquette, Kerouac, Sandhu, & Beaudet, 1994; McLeod, 1997),
- role uncertainty (Duquette et al., 1994),
- characteristics of the client population (Prosser et al., 1997),
- low pay and low work status (McLeod, 1997),
- conflicts between work and home demands (Nolan, Cushway, & Tyler, 1995),
- individual coping strategies (Thornton, 1992), and
- inadequate community resources (Carson, Leary, de Villiers, Fagin, & Radmall, 1995).

The current study had four aims:

1. To develop a reliable means of measuring STS among mental health case managers;
2. To determine the prevalence of STS among mental health case managers in Australia;
3. To determine the extent to which STS is associated with occupational impairment among mental health case managers in Australia; and
4. To identify factors associated with increased risk for STS symptoms.

The study took the form of a survey employing a measure of STS, two concurrent measures (of emotional well-being and of role functioning and role support), and questions relating to factual matters associated with work role. The conclusions are based on an analysis of relationships between the various data sets obtained from the survey. The uniformity of the state mental health system under the National Mental Health Strategy permitted us to administer the survey nationally, and the data presented here are based on 300 returns from major cities and regional areas throughout Australia. (Scale development data relate to a subset of these returns.) The characteristics of the sample are set out in Table 4.1.

TABLE 4.1
Subject Pool Characteristics

Descriptives	
Age	
Range	22 to 69 years
Mean	39.2
SD	9.3
Professions (*n*)	
Psychiatrists	15
Psychologists	53
Social workers	58
Occupational therapists	34
Psychiatric nurses	117
Clinical nurse consultants	18
Other (i.e., welfare workers)	5
Work mode (*n*)	
Full-time	251
Part-time	49
Seniority Levels (*n*)	
PO1 (entry level/in-training)	6
PO2 (graduate entry-level)	181
PO3 (senior graduate/team leader)	82
PO4 (senior professional/manager)	20
PO5 (director)	2
PO6 (regional director)	3
Years of training	
Range	0 to 13 years
Mean	4.7
SD	1.8
Years of job experience	
Range	6 months to 51 years
Mean	12.4
SD	9

Source: Meldrum, King, and Spooner (1999).

SCALE DEVELOPMENT

The Florida Secondary Traumatic Stress Scale (Florida Scale) developed by Figley and Bride (1996) was used as a template for this study. The selection of this scale was considered appropriate because it had already undergone considerable development and corresponded closely with *DSM–IV* diagnostic criteria for PTSD (American Psychiatric Association, 1994). The Florida Scale was developed specifically for people who, through their occupations, were indirectly exposed to traumatic events. These included health professionals charged with the care of traumatized persons. The scale was designed to determine whether the carer met the symptom criteria specified by the *DSM–IV* for PTSD, and each item is linked directly to corresponding symptoms from criteria groups B, C, and D. The scale therefore might be expected to have a high level of concurrent validity with clinical diagnoses according to the DSM–IV. The first draft of the Florida Scale was reviewed by experts in the field of traumatology, modified, and reviewed a second time by additional experts before a third modification.

The modifications made in the development of the Queensland Mental Health Case Manager–Secondary Traumatic Stress Survey (QMHCM–STSS) were designed to preserve the essential features of the Florida Scale, especially the clear cross-referencing to *DSM–IV* diagnostic criteria, with minor item content changes relevant to the experience of mental health case managers. A four-point Likert-type scale replaced the three-point yes/no/maybe of the Florida Scale. Additional items were included following consultation with a panel of experienced mental health workers.

Twenty-seven of the scale items related closely to *DSM–IV* criteria B, C, and D for PTSD and were concerned with symptomatology in four conceptual clusters. Category B questions (20–25) in the new scale were concerned with intrusive and distressing recollections of the traumatic event; Category B questions (29–36) were concerned with the psychosensory media in which the trauma is reexperienced (i.e., smells, images, sounds, thoughts, memories and encounters with the original trauma victim); Category C questions (38–45) were concerned with avoidance of stimuli associated with the traumatic event; and category D questions (46–50) measured symptoms of arousal associated with recollections of the traumatic event.

Appendix 1 provides a summary of the essential features of the scale and its points of departure from the Florida Scale

INVESTIGATION OF THE PSYCHOMETRIC PROPERTIES OF THE SCALE

Subjects

The subjects were 300 mental health professionals from 41 mental health facilities in states and territories around Australia. All participants were involved in case management with psychiatric inpatients or outpatients, and were from adult or child and adolescent mental health services. Of the 233 who stated their gender, 160 were female and 73 were male, and ages ranged from 22 to 69 years (mean = 39.2, *SD* = 9.3). The sample consisted of the following professional subgroups: medical personnel (*n* = 15), psychologists (*n* = 53), social workers (*n* = 58), occupational therapists (*n* = 34), psychiatric nurses (*n* = 117), clinical nurse consultants/charge nurses (*n* = 18), and other personnel (i.e., welfare workers; *n* = 5). There were 251 full-time case managers and 49 part-time, and appointment levels ranged from PO1/in training to PO5/director. Years of training ranged from 0 to 13 (mean = 4.6, *SD* = 1.6), and years of experience as a case manager ranged from 6 months to 51 years (mean = 12.1, *SD* = 9.1).

PROCEDURE

Databases were obtained from state and territory mental health authorities detailing all metropolitan and rural mental health services in Australia. Recruiting letters were then mailed to the director of each service outlining the purpose of the study and the inclusion criteria. Services that agreed to participate then provided the research team with a list of case managers. A brief outline of the study, questionnaire completion instructions, the questionnaire, and a postage-paid envelope were mailed to each participant. A three-week return-by date was requested of all participants. To assist with the determination of concurrent validity and criterion validity, the questionnaire included a short form of the General Health Questionnaire (GHQ) and questions concerning the frequency of sick days during the previous month and a global self-evaluation of current coping at work. The Case Manager Personal Efficacy Scale (CMPES) was included in the data-gathering package (King, LeBas, & Spooner, 1997).

Results

Reliability
Reliability analysis suggests that the 27 items which corresponded with category B, C, and D symptoms of PTSD in *DSM–IV* may be regarded as constituting a reliable unidimensional scale.

Factor Structure
A confirmatory factor analysis was performed to cross-validate scale structure with *DSM–IV* diagnostic structure for PTSD. The four factors that emerged accounted for 58.1% common variance. The pattern matrix reflected a close to perfect match with the four conceptual clusters in the QMHCM–STSS.

TABLE 4.2
QMHW–STSS Categories and Diagnostic Criteria to be Met for STS
and Subclinical STS

Category		STS	Subclinical STS
A.	Experiencing a traumatic event	Yes	Yes
B.	Reexperiencing the traumatic event	Yes	Yes
C.	Persistent avoidance of stimuli associated with the event (8 items)	3 or more	2
D.	Persistent symptoms of arousal (5 items)	2 or more	1
E.	Duration of symptoms more than 1 month	Yes	No

Criterion, Concurrent, and Discriminant Validity

Subjects were divided into three groups—clinical secondary traumatic stress, subclinical secondary traumatic stress, and asymptomatic—according to which they met the modified *DSM–IV* PTSD criteria (Criteria A, B, C, D, and E). The *DSM–IV* diagnostic criteria for PTSD provided the basis for classification. The criteria for distinguishing STS from subclinical STS are set out in Table 4.2. Comparison of these groups with respect to both self-evaluation of occupational coping and general emotional health showed that the STS group was experiencing significantly more distress and impairment than those without STS symptoms

In view of the high reliability of the 27 symptom items as a unidimensional scale, the linear relation between this scale and the concurrent (GHQ) and criterion (global coping and sick day) variables was examined using a Pearson correlation. It was of particular interest in this analysis to determine whether a single, unidimensional scale would have equivalent validity to the symptom category criteria model employed by the *DSM–IV* and used in our initial analysis (refer to Table 4.2). The results of this analysis are reported in Table 4.3.

Correlational analysis revealed a significant linear relationship between the STS symptom scale and both GHQ scores and the single measure of occupational coping. Conversely, there was a weak and nonsignificant relationship between STS symptoms and sick days.

TABLE 4.3
Correlation Between STS Symptom Scores, GHQ, Sick Days,
and Occupational Coping

	GHQ	Sick Days	Occupational Coping
STS symptoms	.467*	.087	.351*
GHQ		.079	.472*
Sick days			.099

*$p < .001$

DISCUSSION

The QMHCM–STSS has high internal consistency and might be described as a reliable unidimensional scale. Its underlying factor structure closely approximates the organization of symptoms for PTSD in the *DSM–IV*, and it is reasonable to conclude that it provides a measure of a clinical entity that has very similar phenomenology to PTSD. Although the scale is essentially unidimensional, there is evidence that the relationship between scale scores and at least one criterion variable (sick days) is not linear. The use of a form of the *DSM–IV* diagnostic formula to determine whether scores reach a clinically significant threshold may be of value in some applications. The scale can be used to identify a group that meets symptom criteria for *DSM–IV* PTSD, and there is evidence of significantly greater impairment for this group when compared with the subclinical and asymptomatic groups. The scale therefore appears to have concurrent, criterion, and discriminant validity. Given the close relationship between this scale and the Florida Scale from which it was derived, it is likely that the original scale will have equivalent psychometric properties.

The strong face validity of the scale, deriving from its close linkage with *DSM–IV* diagnostic criteria, raises concerns about dissimulation or "faking bad." The existence of self-report measures of PTSD with good psychometric properties and high concurrent validity in relation to clinical diagnosis (Blanchard, Jones, Buckley, & Forneris, 1996; Norris & Perilla, 1996; Solomon et al., 1993), suggests that self report may be no more susceptible to dissimulation than clinical interview. However, with a population such as mental health case managers, who might be expected to have familiarity with diagnostic criteria, there is the possibility of a higher risk than might be the case with more naive populations. There is no reason to suspect dissimulation in this study; simply note that it is a consideration with scales of this kind.

PREVALENCE

Prevalence rates were determined using the categories of clinical STS, subclinical STS, and asymptomatic described previously. Across the sample we found that 17.7% of all case managers met symptom criteria for STS; another 18% were experiencing significant but subclinical levels of symptomatology; and the remaining 64.3% were experiencing low levels of symptoms, or were asymptomatic.

Diagnosis was not influenced by age, gender, occupational category, type of client (adult, adolescent, or child), level of appointment, or experience. It was found, however, that case managers working away from capital city environments were at greater risk of meeting symptom criteria or subclinical symptom criteria than were case managers working in the various state capitals. The prevalence rates among rural mental health workers (STS = 24.1%; sub-

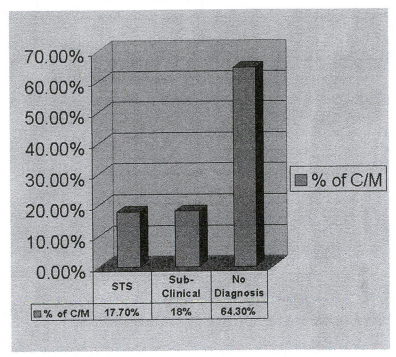

FIGURE 4.1. Diagnoses of mental health workers–STS survey.

clinical STS = 21.4%) were significantly higher ($c^2 = 7.55$, $p < .023$) than those for metropolitan workers (STS = 15.35%; subclinical STS = 15.81%). This comparison is presented in Figure 4.2.

Unfortunately, there is little normative data to assist in comparing the prevalence rates found in this sample with either population prevalence or prevalence among other high-risk groups. The closest equivalent data come from a study of trauma counselors in which it was reported that 14% experienced traumatic stress levels similar to PTSD (Arvay & Uhlemann, 1996). However comparison with PTSD point prevalence data is probably valid, especially when the comparison data were obtained through similar *DSM–IV* indexed self-report procedures. Comparative prevalence rates for PTSD are 29% for former POWs of World War II and the Korean War (Engdahl, Dikel, Eberly, & Blank, 1997), 10% for motor accident victims (Mayou, Tyndel, & Bryant, 1997), and 1.7% for women after childbirth (Wijma, Soderquist, & Wijma, 1997).

These comparisons suggest that the prevalence rate among mental health case managers is at least as high as that of trauma counselors, a recognized high-risk group. It is also well within the range that might be expected among people who have suffered direct exposure to significant trauma. In other words, it is sufficiently high to be a matter for serious concern.

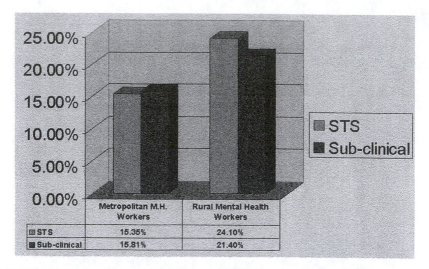

FIGURE 4.2. Metropolitan M.H. workers compared with rural M.H. worker–rates of STS.

OCCUPATIONAL IMPAIRMENT

The CMPES was used (King et al., 1997) as a measure of self-rated role performance and role support. This is a 17-item unidimensional scale (alpha = .78) that asks case managers to rate their current capacity to fulfill a number of basic work roles and to access professional role supports. Case managers also were requested to report on the number of days they had been absent from work as a result of illness during the past month and to provide a global rating of current work functioning.

One-way ANOVAs were calculated to determine if the STS group, the sub-clinical STS group, and the asymptomatic group, differed in their occupational impairment as indicated by their overall sense of occupational coping, time off from work sick, and their general psychological health (GHQ–12). Results of these comparisons are summarized in Table 4.4. Clinically significant distress or social/occupational impairment forms one of the formal *DSM–IV* criteria for PTSD, but might be conceptualized in terms of criterion validity in that people experiencing high levels of symptoms should experience distress or impairment, or both.

Responding on a 10-point Likert-type scale (1 = *coping just fine*, 10 = *dreadful*), the STS group had a lower sense of being able to cope at work than the asymptomatic group ($F_{2,243}$ = 15.33, $p < .001$). Second, the number of sick days during the month prior to completing the questionnaire differed significantly across the STS, subclinical STS and asymptomatic groups ($F_{2,242}$ = 4.53, $p < .01$). Post hoc Bonferroni *t*-tests showed that the STS group had more sick days than both the asymptomatic group and the subclinical group. Third, the

TABLE 4.4

Comparisons of Group Means for CMPES, Sick Days, and GHQ-12

	Asymptomatic	Subclinical STS	STS
CMPES	65.18	63.65	61.63 (a)
Sick days	.58	.37	1.1 (b)
GHQ	1.62	3.62(c)	5.37 (d)

[a]STS significantly poorer case manager self efficacy than asymptomatic $p < .037$
[b]STS significantly more sick days than asymptomatic $p < .008$ and subclinical STS $p < .01$
[c]Subclinical STS significantly more distressed than asymptomatic $p < .001$
[d]STS significantly more distressed than subclinical STS $p < .02$ and asymptomatic $p < .001$

three groups differed significantly in their general psychological health as measured by the GHQ ($F_{2,241} = 21.33$, $p < .001$). Again, post hoc Bonferroni *t*-tests revealed that the STS group was less psychologically healthy than both the subclinical STS group and the asymptomatic group, and the subclinical group was less healthy than the asymptomatic group ($p < .01$).

An item analysis from the CMPES revealed further factors that were related to STS. Subjects in the STS group were more likely to believe they had too many roles to be effective as a case manager ($F_{2,293} = 3.67$, $p < .027$) and to not know who to turn to for help or support if they were worried about a client ($F_{2,295} = 3.40$, $p < .035$). However, items such as the amount of supervision received, the amount of interdisciplinary liaison involved, role ambiguity, and time management were not related to the experience of traumatic stress. It was reported, however, by 22% of the respondents that they rarely or never "received sufficient regular supervision," with an additional 18% indicating they only sometimes were supported by regular supervision. The relationship between these findings and the levels of secondary traumatic stress was not shown to be statistically significant.

RISK FACTORS

As indicated, mental health workers in regional or rural areas were more likely to report clinically significant levels of STS than were workers in capital cities. This suggests that working in a regional setting should be considered a risk factor, at least in the Australian context.

Item analysis of the CMPES provided additional data relevant to interpretation of this risk factor. Regional workers were significantly more likely to state that support services were not available for clients in crisis than were their capital city counterparts ($t_{296} = 2.13$, $p < .034$). This finding suggests that these workers were more likely to bear the brunt of the burden of care for clients in crisis, and as such either were more frequently exposed to traumatic events or were relatively alone in dealing with traumatic events.

Mental health workers in regional Australia tend to work in small teams and often cover large geographical areas on their own. Whereas the major cities can draw on the support of crisis teams and acute beds, crisis teams frequently are unavailable in rural areas, and acute beds may be hundreds of kilometers from the location of the crisis.

The only other risk factor able to be identified from the variables included in this study was the quality of the trauma to which the case manager had been vicariously exposed. Respondents were invited to identify one or more of nine categories of secondary trauma to which they had been exposed:

- actual death (including suicide)
- the threat of death (including suicide ideation)
- serious injury
- the threat of serious injury (including self-harm)
- threat to their physical well-being
- threat to the physical well-being of a loved one
- threat of major mental breakdown
- horrific mental/physical/sexual abuse
- highly disturbing/bizarre/horrific thoughts.

Although all nine were commonly experienced, only two were associated with STS.

One-way ANOVAs revealed that threats of death (including suicidal ideation; $F_{2,296} = 3.30$, $p < .04$) and threats to physical well-being ($F_{2,293} = 3.18$, $p < .05$) were significantly related to the prevalence of STS. In contrast, there were no between-group differences found for the other traumatic events. It is not clear why threats to life and physical well-being were more likely to be associated with STS than other disturbing events. It is possible that case managers have developed effective coping mechanisms for dealing with disturbed thought processes and with accounts of past abuse, but are less able to deal with reports of current or recent trauma. However, whatever the reasons, it is important for supervisors and case managers themselves to be aware of the possible impact of secondary exposure to threats to life and physical well-being.

CONCLUSION

In view of the sample size and questionnaire return rate, the researchers are reasonably confident that this data set provides a broadly representative sample of mental health case managers in Australia. However, as with any study of this kind, the possibility of systematic sample bias as a result of relevant differences between responders and nonresponders cannot be excluded.

It is likely that the measure of STS used has broadly equivalent diagnostic fidelity to that which might be achieved by clinical interview. This is based on evidence of validation of self-report measures of PTSD constructed along similar lines in close correspondence with *DSM–IV* criteria. The QMHCM–STS scale is believed to be reliable, and it appears to have good concurrent validity

We believe that the results reported provide a scientifically acceptable estimate of the prevalence of STS among mental health case managers in Australia. The results indicate that approximately 18% of mental health case managers are experiencing symptoms which in quantity, quality, and intensity are equivalent to those experienced by people who meet criteria for a diagnosis of PTSD.

This finding provides a quantitative basis for assertions that stress is an occupational factor in mental health case management and suggests the need for further attention to means of minimizing risk. PTSD often is debilitating, with an uncertain prognosis and variable treatment response. Clearly, there is both a public interest and a public duty involved in protecting of the emotional well-being of those people who undertake work providing care to the mentally ill.

We believe this study provides support for the more general proposition that secondary traumatic stress provides a valid conceptual framework for the evaluation of workplace stress with this population. The symptom criteria used in secondary stress appear to be sensitive to workplace stress, and there is evidence of linkage between the symptoms and secondary exposure to traumatic events. It must be noted, however, that the link is relatively modest, and it is clear that secondary exposure alone is but one of a number of relevant variables.

Notwithstanding the value of the data reported in this study, a number of important questions remain which require investigation before STS can be evaluated in relation to mental health case managers.

1. There is a lack of normative data; therefore, comparison of the rates of STS we have recorded with those from other occupational groups is not possible. The only real comparison point is with population prevalence rates for PTSD, and even here the data are quite variable.
2. It remains unclear as to the extent to which STS is best understood as a specific stress reaction and the extent to which it is better understood as a generalized stress condition. The evidence in this study suggests that secondary stressors are significant, but they account for quite a small amount of the variance of the data. This survey gathered little information of other factors that contribute to the symptom clusters or the relevance of predisposing factors. This is a key issue in determining the role of workplace factors and the degree and type of occupational health and safety intervention that is most appropriate.
3. Finally, this study has investigated STS in a cross-sectional manner. We were unable to determine the duration or course of symptoms. Informa-

tion of this type is essential to any serious planning in relation to intervention for prevention or amelioration of symptoms.

The QMHCM–STSS has a number of potential applications. These may be summarized as follow:

1. *Research applications*: To date, little is known about the prevalence of STS. The availability of a scale with good psychometric properties enables studies to be undertaken which might identify environments or population subgroups in which risk is high. Although this scale was developed for a specific application, its psychometric properties are unlikely to be adversely affected by the minor modifications required for application in other settings. The scale also has potential as a means of measuring the impact of workplace changes on the well-being of staff exposed to STS and of determining which kinds of work stress are most likely to lead to significant ongoing consequences for emotional health and well-being. It also may be of value in relation to research investigating the efficacy of interventions designed to prevent or ameliorate STS.
2. *Local personnel management and occupational health and safety processes*: The instrument has the potential to enable workplace managers to determine the emotional well-being of specific staff members or groups of staff members and to initiate and monitor changes designed to enhance well–being.
3. *National and state health policy*: The instrument has the potential to provide government and policymakers with epidemiological information relevant to implementation and evaluation of policies regarding workplace risk exposure and risk minimization.

RECOMMENDATIONS FOR MINIMIZING LEVELS OF SECONDARY TRAUMATIC STRESS IN COMMUNITY MENTAL HEALTH CASE MANAGERS

Although much work remains to be done, this study suggests a few possible directions for those who want to develop means of minimizing risk:

1. Some forms of secondary exposure have a stronger association with major symptoms than others. This aspect may vary from site to site, and local levels of traumatic events should be clearly identified.
2. Exposure to clients who have been in life-threatening situations or have experienced threats to their physical well-being were the only two conditions significantly associated with STS symptoms. Regular reporting procedures of such events should become standard practice in all community mental health services. Case managers who report such events

should be supported, and the impact of the exposure should be monitored through the professional supervision process.

3. Supervisors must be alert to such exposures and be prepared to offer effective support or access to appropriate counseling when such exposures occur. Supervisors may require specialist training in assessment of and response to posttrauma reactions and PTSD among professional staff

4. There is evidence that STS is not simply a function of secondary exposure to trauma but also is linked to access or otherwise to resources that might assist in a crisis situation. Provision of resources that guarantee appropriate support for case managers whose clients are in crisis should be a priority for all mental health services.

5. The evidence that regional workers are more at risk than workers in major cities is probably linked with this issue. It is probable that case managers who feel they are able to do something effective following exposure are less at risk of STS than case managers who feel helpless. This has implications for organization and deployment of resources, especially in rural areas. The utilization of technology such as video conferencing to enable rural case managers to discuss stress-related issues with other professionals could be expected to reduce such isolation.

6. There is some evidence that STS may be associated with organizational climate. Case managers with a clinical level of STS report greater difficulty with complex and competing role demands than do those less affected by STS symptoms. Caution must be exercised with respect to relating causal inference to this variable, as it is possible that the general decline in emotional functioning associated with STS results in lowered ability to manage complex roles. However, in the light of previous reports that role complexity and role ambiguity are significant work stressors, attention to this issue is warranted as a possible means of minimizing STS. Professional development and staff supervision should aim to ensure that roles and role responses are clear. Service management should aim to ensure clear and open lines of communication and accountability.

7. The grouping of a range of disciplines into generic teams may add to the levels of stress experienced because of the loss of professional identification and loss of traditional reporting and supervision practices. It is recommended that community mental health services give greater priority to the manner in which teams are composed, trained, and managed. Included in the management process must be a level of psychological support. Appropriate training must be provided for team leaders in team leadership and the management of multidisciplinary professional staff. If the discipline senior or team leader cannot provide effective professional and psychological support, there should be a procedure by which the process may be outsourced to a private agency.

APPENDIX 4.1
Item Comparison Between Queensland Mental Health Case Manager -Secondary Traumatic Stress Scale and Florida Secondary Traumatic Stress Scale

Part A. Have you had contact with someone who has experienced, witnessed, or been confronted with an event or events that involved the following? *(three additional items and three modifications)*

1	2	3	4
Never	Once or twice	Several times	Many times
Actual death *(including suicide)*			
The threat of death *(including suicide ideation)*			
Serious injury			
The threat of serious injury *(including self harm)*			
Threat to their physical well-being			
Threat to the physical well-being of a loved one.			
Threat of major mental breakdown			
Horrific mental/physical/sexual abuse			
Highly disturbing/bizarre/horrific thoughts			

Based on that contact, did the traumatized person's response involve the following? *(5 additional items)*

1	2	3	4
No	A little	Quite a lot	Very much so
A feeling of intense fear.			
A feeling of helplessness.			
A feeling of horror.			
14. *Feelings of anger*			
15. *Feelings of guilt*			
16. *A mental breakdown*			
17. *Intense depression*			
18. *Denial of event or events*			

Part B. Have you persistently experienced any of the following as a result of contact with the traumatized person? (*1 additional item*)

Distress due to repeated and unwanted images associated with the person.
Distress due to repeated and unwanted thoughts associated with the person.
Distress due to repeated and unwanted sensations associated with the person.
Distress due to repeated dreams associated with the person.
Have you acted or felt as if the contact with the traumatized person and what she or he experienced were happening in your mind (e.g., feelings of reliving the experience, flashbacks, or images of all or part of the experiences)?
24. *Have you ever experienced any significant lowering or instability of mood associated with thoughts or images of the person?*

Have you experienced intense psychological distress when exposed to reminders of the contact with the traumatized person and what the traumatized person experienced? (*2 additional items*)

A memory.
An image.
A thought.
A picture.
A sound.
A smell.
35.   *Repeated encounters with the person*
36.   *Encounters with similar people or situations*

Part C. Have you experienced any of the following since the contact? *(1 additional item)*

Efforts to avoid thoughts, feelings, or conversations associated with contact with the traumatized person and what he/she experienced.
Efforts to avoid activities, places, or people that remind you of contact with the traumatized person and what the he/she experienced.
An inability to recall an important aspect of contact with the traumatized person and what she/he experienced.
A noticeable reduction in interest or participation in activities you once enjoyed.
A feeling of separation or withdrawal from others.
A restricted range of emotions.
A sense of mortality (could die at any time).
45.   *A sense of relief at cancelled or missed appointments by the traumatized person or by other persons who may serve as reminders*

Note: Parts D and E have remained unchanged.

REFERENCES

Alexander, J. G., de Chesnay, M., Marshall, E., & Campbell, A. R. (1989). Parallel reactions in rape victims and rape researchers. *Violence and Victims, 4*(1), 57–62.

American Psychiatric Association. (1994). *Diagnostic and statistical manual of mental disorders* (4th ed.). Washington DC: Author.

Arvay, M. J., & Uhlemann, M. R., (1996). Counsellor stress in the field of trauma: A preliminary study. *Canadian Journal of Counselling, 30*(3), 193–210.

Australian Bureau of Statistics. (1998). *ABS statsite: Australia in brief.* Canberra, Australia: Commonwealth of Australia.

Australian Health Ministers. (1992). *National mental health policy.* Canberra, Australia: Australian Government Publishing Service.

Berah, E., Jones, H. J., & Valent, P. (1984). The experience of a mental health team involved in the early phase of a disaster. *Australian and New Zealand Journal of Psychiatry, 18,* 354–358.

Blanchard, E. B., Jones, A. J., Buckley, T. C., & Forneris, C. A. (1996). Psychometric properties of the PTSD Checklist (PCL). *Behavior Research and Therapy, 34*(8), 669–673.

Blankertz, L. E., & Robinson, S. E. (1997). Turnover intentions of community mental health workers in psychosocial rehabilitation services. *Community Mental Health Journal, 33*(6), 517–529.

Carbonell, J. L., & Figley, C. R. (1996). When trauma hits home: Personal trauma and the family therapist. *Journal of Marital and Family Therapy, 22*(1), 53–58.

Carson, J., Leary, J., de Villiers, N., Fagin, L., & Radmall, J. (1995). Stress in mental health nurses: Comparison of ward and community staff. *British Journal of Nursing, 4*(10), 579–582.

Draine, J. (1997). A critical review of randomized field trials of case management for individuals with serious and persistent mental illness. *Research on Social Work Practice, 7*(1), 32–52.

Duquette, A., Kerouac, S., Sandhu, B. K., & Beaudet, L. (1994). Factors related to nursing burnout: A review of empirical knowledge. *Issues in Mental Health Nursing, 15*(4), 337–358

Engdahl, B., Dikel, T. N., Eberly, R., & Blank, A., Jr. (1997). Posttraumatic stress disorder in a community group of former prisoners of war: A normative response to severe trauma. *American Journal of Psychiatry, 154*(11), 1576–1581

Fagin, L., Brown, D., Bartlett, H., Leary, J., & Carson, J. (1995). The Claybury Community Psychiatric Nurse Stress Study: Is it more stressful to work in hospital or the community? *Journal of Advanced Nursing, 22*(2), 347–358.

Fagin, L., Carson, J., Leary, J., De-Villiers, N., Bartlett, H., O'Malley, P., West, M., McElfatrick, S., & Brown, D. (1996). Stress, coping and burnout in mental health nurses: Findings from three research studies. *International Journal of Social Psychiatry, 42*(2), 102–111.

Figley, C. R. (1995). Compassion fatigue: Toward a new understanding of the costs of caring. In B. H. Stamm (Ed.), *Secondary traumatic stress: Self-care issues for clinicians, researchers and educators* (pp. 3–28). Lutherville, MD: The Sidran Press.

Figley, C. R., & Bride, B. (1996). *Development of the Secondary Traumatic Stress Disorder Scale*. Psychosocial Stress Research Program, Florida State University.

Herman, J. L. (1992). *Trauma and recovery*. New York: Basic Books.

King, R., Le Bas, J., & Spooner, D. (1997, August). Mental Health Case Manager Personal Efficacy Scale. Paper presented at the Mental Health Services Conference, Sydney, Australia.

Maslach, C. (1976). Burned-out. *Human Behaviour, 5,* 16–22.

Maslach, C., & Jackson, S. E. (1986). *The Maslach Burnout Inventory: Manual* (2nd ed.). Palo Alto, CA: Consulting Psychologists Press.

Mayou, R., Tyndel, S., & Bryant, B. (1997). Long term outcome of motor vehicle accident injury. *Psychosomatic Medicine, 59*(6), 578–584.

McCann, I. I., & Pearlman, L. A. (1990). Vicarious traumatisation: A framework for understanding the psychological effects of working with victims. *Journal of Traumatic Stress, 3,* 131–149.

McLeod, T. (1997). Work stress among community psychiatric nurses. *British Journal of Nursing, 6*(10), 569–574

Meldrum, L., King, R., & Spooner, D. (1999, March). *Secondary stress in Australian mental health workers*. Paper presented at the American Psychological Association/National Institute of Occupational Safety and Health–Work Stress and Health '99 Conference, Baltimore, MD.

Mental Health Consumer Outcomes Task Force. (1991). *Mental health statement of rights and responsibilities*. Canberra, Australia: Australian Government Printing Service.

Mercier, C. (1994). Improving the quality of life of people with severe mental disorders. *Social Indicators Research, 33,* 165–192.

Moore, K. A., & Cooper, C. L. (1996). Stress in mental health professionals: A theoretical overview. *International Journal of Social Psychiatry, 42*(2), 82–89.

National Health Strategy. (1993). Help where help is needed: Continuity of care for people with chronic mental illness. In *National health strategy issues paper No 5*. Canberra, Australia: Treble Press.

Nolan, P., Cushway, D., & Tyler, P. (1995). A measurement tool for assessing stress among mental health nurses. *Nursing Standard, 9*(46), 36–39.

Norris, F. H., & Perilla, J. L. (1996). The revised Civilian Mississippi Scale for PTSD: Reliability, validity, and cross-language stability. *Journal of Traumatic Stress, 9*(2), 285–298

Oliver, N., & Kuipers, E. (1996). Stress and its relationship to expressed emotion in community mental health workers. *International Journal of Social Psychiatry, 42*(2), 150–159.

Onyett, S., Pillinger, T., & Muijen, M. (1995). *Making community mental health teams work*. London: Sainsbury Centre for Mental Health.

Onyett, S., Pillinger, T., & Muijen, M. (1997). Job satisfaction and burnout among members of community mental health teams. *Journal of Mental Health, 6*(1), 55–66.

Parker, P. A., & Kulik, A. (1995). Burnout, self and supervisor-rated job performance, and absenteeism among nurses. *Journal of Behavioral Medicine, 18*(6), 581–599.

Prosser, D., Johnson, S., Kuipers, E., Szmukler, G., Bebbington, P., & Thornicroft, G. (1997). Perceived sources of work stress and satisfaction among hospital and community mental health staff, and their relation to mental health, burnout and job satisfaction. *Journal of Psychosomatic Research, 43*(1), 51–59.

Prosser, D., Johnson, S., Kuipers, E., Szmukler, G., Bebbington, P., & Thornicroft, G. (1996). Mental health, "burnout' and job satisfaction among hospital and community-based mental health staff. *British Journal of Psychiatry, 169*(3), 334–337.

Raphael, B., Meldrum, L., & Donald, M. (1993, April). *Mental health professionals and traumatic stress*. Paper presented at the Stress and Trauma in the Workplace Conference, Adelaide, Australia.

Raphael, B., Singh, B., Bradbury, L., & Lambert, F. (1983–1984). Who helps the helpers? The effects of a disaster on the rescue workers. *Omega, 14*(1), 9–20.

Solomon, Z., Benbenishty, R., Neria, Y., Abramowitz, M., Ginzburg, K., & Ohry, A. (1993). Assessment of PTSD: Validation of the revised PTSD Inventory. *Israeli Journal of Psychiatry and Related Science, 30*(2), 110–115

Sweeney, G., & Nichols, K. (1996). Stress experiences of occupational therapists in mental health practice arenas: A review of the literature. *International Journal of Social Psychiatry, 42*(2), 132–140.

Talbot, A. (1990). The importance of parallel process in debriefing crisis counsellors. *Journal of Traumatic Stress, 3*, 265–278.

Talbot, A., Manton, M., & Dunn, P. J. (1992). Debriefing the debriefers: An intervention strategy to assist psychologists after a crisis. *Journal of Traumatic Stress, 5*(1), 45–62.

Thornton, P. I. (1992). The relation of coping, appraisal, and burnout in mental health workers. *Journal of Psychology, 126*(3), 261–271.

Treatment Protocol Project. (1997). *Management of mental disorders*. Paper presented at the World Health Organisation Collaborating Centre for Mental Health and Substance Abuse, Darlinghurst, Australia.

Wijma, K., Soderquist, J., & Wijma, B. (1997). Posttraumatic stress disorder after childbirth: A cross sectional study. *Journal of Anxiety Disorders, 11*(6), 587–597.

Wykes, T., Stevens, W., & Everitt, B. (1997). Stress in community care teams: Will it affect the sustainability of community care? *Social Psychiatry and Psychiatric Epidemiology, 32*(7), 398–407.

Yassen, J. (1995). Preventing secondary traumatic stress disorder. In C. R. Figley (Ed.), *Compassion fatigue: Coping with secondary traumatic stress disorder in those who treat the traumatized* (pp. 178–208). New York: Brunner/Mazel.

Yellowlees, P., Howgego, I., Meldrum, L., & Dark, F. (1997, August). *Case manager functions in community mental health services*. Paper presented at the Mental Health Services Conference, Sydney, Australia.

5

Measuring Compassion Satisfaction as Well as Fatigue: Developmental History of the Compassion Satisfaction and Fatigue Test*

B. HUDNALL STAMM

Compassion is feeling and acting with deep empathy and sorrow for those who suffer. It is a necessary although not sufficient ingredient of helping. This book is about helping those who themselves suffer in their effort to help others. Yet, the helper's motivation to help is shaped, in part, by the satisfaction derived from the work of helping others. The satisfaction, labeled here as compassion satisfaction, plays a vital role in the equation of human services. This chapter chronicles the theoretical thinking that led to the expansion of the Compassion Fatigue Self Test (Figley, 1995a, 1995b; Figley & Stamm, 1996) to the Compassion Satisfaction and Fatigue Test (Stamm & Figley, 1996). In many ways, it is a philosophical story with a quantitative editor. The theory of secondary or vicarious traumatization records the deleterious effects of being in harm's way as an act of compassion. We have come to know that this saga can be heroic, tragic, or even dangerous (Brady, Guy, Poelstra, & Brokaw, 1999;

---

*The opinions or assertions contained herein are the private ones of the author, and are not to be considered as official or reflecting the views of the Institute of Rural Health Studies or Idaho State University.

Figley, 1995a, 1995b; Follette, Polusny, & Milbeck, 1994; Ghahramanlou & Brodbeck, 2000; McCann & Pearlman, 1990; Pearlman & Saakvitne, 1995; Schauben, & Frazier, 1995; Stamm, 1995, 1997, 1999). Yet, people continue to do the work set before them, and to do it well. What sustains a person to continue in the face of potential distress? Most people are glad they could help. Clearly, there is an aspect of *compassion satisfaction* that is compelling.

LIFE IS DIFFICULT

Certainly, those of us who work with or around trauma—whether as caregivers, teachers, clergy, public safety, or reporters, or in other roles—can affirm the difficulty inherent in being human. There is a clear awareness of the pain documented by the research. In a random sample of American adults, 60.7% of men and 51.2% of women reported experiencing at least one event that would meet the A1 criterion of the diagnosis for posttraumatic stress disorder (PTSD; Kessler, Sonnega, Bromet, Hughes, & Nelson, 1995). Overall, the estimated lifetime prevalence of PTSD among American adults is 7.8%. Most of those who have PTSD—88% of the women and 79% of the men—also have at least one comorbid disorder, usually another anxiety disorder, depression, or substance abuse. The rates of exposure can be unfathomable for those who live in extreme situations, such as those brought about by severe poverty, famine, captivity, or war. Beyond the obvious psychological consequences of traumatic exposure, trauma is powerfully related to physical health problems (Friedman, & Schnurr, 1995; Lessman, Li, Hu, & Drossman, 1998; Schnurr, Friedman, Sengupta, Jankowski, & Holmes, 2000; Schnurr & Jankowski, 1999). There is also an elevated risk of suicide among those with a trauma history (Davidson, Hughes, Blazer, & George, 1991; Ferrada-Noli, Asberg, Ormstad, Lundin, & Sundbom, 1998; Flannery, Singer, & Wester, 2001; Kotler, Iancu, Efroni, & Amir, 2001; Krug et al., 1998; Lambert & Fowler, 1997).

If life is so difficult, why are most people all right? Why is everyone not a patient? Everyone is at risk, but the risks are compounded for those who work around trauma; there is the risk for direct personal exposure and then there is the risk of work-related secondary exposure. In the face of this compound risk, how do people stay sufficiently healthy to do their work? It would seem that the human spirit, although clearly breakable, is remarkably resilient. According to Kessler, Sonnega, Bromet, Hughes, and Nelson (1995), being exposed to a traumatic stressor is not a guarantee that one will develop a diagnosable pathology. As previously noted, the exposure rates are 50% to 60%, but the rate of qualifying for PTSD at least sometime during one's life is only 7.8%. What in the path between the event and PTSD protects us? According to King, King, Fairbank, Keane, and Adams (1998), it is hardiness and social support. The path between hardiness, good social support (functional and structural), and PTSD is characterized by an inverse relationship: Good hardiness and social support are associated with less PTSD.

THE ROLE OF HARDINESS

What does all of this mean for the person who works around trauma? Likely it means much the same as it does for the traumatized person: Terrible things can happen to us in the course of our personal lives and in our work. In work, as in our personal lives, we are potentially better off when hardiness and a good social support network sustain us.

King and colleagues (1998) defined hardiness as being characterized by (a) control, (b) commitment, and (c) change as challenge. In a previous article (Stamm & Pearce, 1995) and its revision (Stamm, 1999a), I proposed that caregivers were at risk for developing negative reactions to their patients' difficult material when their competency and control were at risk. I suggested that questions of competency, at least in part, arise from the professional's feelings of lack of control of traumatic material. Further, I proposed that these factors could be enhanced and sustained by positive collegial support, which are important elements of structural and functional social support. In a later paper (Rudolph, Stamm, & Stamm, 1997), my colleagues and I examined functional and structural social support and issues of living, such as amount of time spent working, sleeping, visiting with family and friends, doing paperwork, continuing education, availability of shopping, libraries, food, and even accessing the Internet. Those who had more time to sustain relationships and do basic self-care tasks seemed to be less at risk for the negative effects of caregiving. In Rudolph and Stamm (1999), we proposed that corporate and institutional accommodations that enhance control can protect workers.

CAN THE CURRENCY FLOW BOTH WAYS?

If trauma challenges control and lack of control causes psychological distress, it begs the question of why so many people who work around trauma are doing well. Is it the sustaining positive resources? Slowly, it became clear that, to understand the negative "costs of caring," it is necessary to understand the credits or positive "payments" that come from caring. This concept was sharpened during my work as a consultant with the South African KwaZulu-Natal Programme for Survivors of Violence. Its founder, Craig Higson-Smith, and colleagues provide a variety of psychosocial services, ranging from youth clinics to classes for mothers, psychotherapy referrals, self-sufficiency through gardening, and helping people prepare to testify before the South African Truth and Reconciliation Commission (Burnette, 1997; Stamm, Higson-Smith, Stamm, & Terry, 1996).

Around the globe, in warfare and low-level warfare periodic eruptions of extreme violence lead to temporary mass migrations of people. For people working in these types of settings, helping is an exercise in discerning how to shore up the psyche while understanding when psychotherapy is a moot point in the face of sheer survival. In these conditions, exposure to PTSD Criterion A1 (American Psychiatric Association, 2000) events is guaranteed. Frustration is guaranteed when warfare coexists with the activities of peacemaking and humanitarian aid. Yet, most of the people who work in these conditions press on, often with joy. What I observed in South Africa, as well as in other settings, was not a negation of the struggle, but a celebration of hope. I had to wonder, were we asking only half of the question?

We knew to ask, "I feel estranged from others," but did we know to ask, " I feel connected to others"? Given the scale (see Compassion Fatigue Self Test; Figley, 1995a, pp. 13–14), a "no" answer was possible, but it was uninterpretable. Did "No, I do not feel estranged from others" mean the same thing as "I feel connected to others," or did it reflect some anhedonia that prevented a person from knowing what he or she felt at all? Or, did it reflect a burnout state, in which the respondent simply did not care? The dilemma presented by interpreting this negation is a classic problem of Boolean logic. If cows are black and this cow is a not-black cow, is the cow white? The answer is that the cow could be white, or that white is a fallacious assumption based on insufficient data—for example, the cow could be black with white spots. Clearly, the way we asked the questions showed we had no idea about what was happening to providers on the positive side of their work. And, if there was a protective aspect of being satisfied with doing the work of caring, it would be impossible to understand the negative aspects of caring without knowing about the positive.

Moreover, psychometric problems occurred by asking only negative questions. The negative, symptom-focused format could create a response bias producing a response set that artificially inflated or deflated negative reporting. Finally, there was additional evidence that including positive questions was warranted, because some providers who were doing well were put off by the negative questions' implication that there had to be something wrong.

Originally, we countered this concern by using other measures that included positive items (Rudolph, Stamm, & Stamm, 1995). Yet, this proved unsatisfying because it was difficult to match concepts across the measures. We still had no idea whether the not-black cows were white. At the same time, we were considering this dilemma: I was asked to develop a program evaluation to address whether the installation of a telehealth program could reduce caregiver stress (see Forkner, Reardon, & Carson, 1997, for a description of the program). We spent a great deal of time designing the assessments in order to protect the caregivers. We suspected that some people in the rural area we were assessing were struggling with extreme isolation brought about by cuts in health care funding. Yet, if we did identify compassion fatigue in the course of the program evaluation, it could potentially endanger the caregiver's good status with his or her employer. Thus, to protect the workers, it was necessary to address both the positive and negative aspects of caregiving.

With Dr. Figley's encouragement, I developed a series of positive questions parallel to the negative aspects of caregiving. At his suggestion, I named the new subscale *Compassion Satisfaction*. The initial pilot testing was done with a focus group of graduate psychology and social work students. After making adjustments, the measure was used with a variety of health care providers in a small study.

ESTABLISHING THE MEASURE

The results of the early study were encouraging, yet the sample size was far too small to judge the quality of the measure. The basic psychometric properties of the original two subscales (compassion fatigue and burnout) were published (Figley, 1995a; Stamm & Figley, 1996). Thus, the task was to confirm the psychometric properties of the two original scales and test the new Compassion Satisfaction subscale. We started with two samples: the health care providers in the original study and data from a study of caregivers and caregivers in training ($n = 210$; $n = 160$) in the United States and 50 professionals with unknown country of origin who submitted their tests through the Internet (Rudolph, Stamm, & Stamm, 1997).

Three colleagues offered to share their raw data for psychometric purposes. Data were collected in South Africa among bank workers trained as debriefers for bank robberies (Ortlepp, 1998), caregivers from various mental health agencies in South Africa ($n = 20$; Higson-Smith, 1997), and rape crisis workers in Canada ($n = 30$; identity protected). All of the data were pooled, except for those from the caregivers in South Africa. The South African caregiver sample was handled separately because these professionals worked in low-level warfare circumstances. Although these groups differed based on country of origin, all were fluent English speakers; they did not differ on a number of demographic characteristics, including age and sex; and all worked in positions of similar status within their respective countries. Multivariate analysis of variance did not provide evidence of differences based on country of origin, type of work, or sex when age was used as a control variable.

The combined sample was 374. The average age was 35.4 years (SD = 12.16), with a median age of 36. There were 121 (33%) males, 207 (56%) females, and 46 (11%) did not identify sex. Caregivers in training accounted for 102 (27%) of the sample; 30 (8%) were Red Cross or similar crisis workers, 130 (35%) were business people who volunteered as debriefers, and 62 (16%) were working trauma professionals (see Table 5.1).

Table 5.1
Demographics of combined sample

Age	Sex	Type of Work	Country of Origin
Mean 35.4	Males *n* = 121 (33%)	Trauma Professional *n* = 62 (16%)	USA Rural–Urban Mix *n* = 160 (43%)
Median 36	Females *n* = 207 (56%)	Business volunteer *n* = 130 (35%)	Canada–Urban *n* = 30 (8%)
SD 12.16	Unknown *n* = 46 (11%)	Red Cross or similar volunteer *n* = 30 (8%)	South Africa–Urban *n* = 130 (35%)
		Caregivers in training *n* = 102 (27%)	Internet (unknown origin) *n* = 50 (13%)

As previously noted, the lay mental health caregivers in rural Africa (*n* = 20) were not compiled with the other data because their work environment included low-level warfare. Two scales (Compassion Fatigue [CF] and Burnout [BO]) were given to these workers, who had completed a minimum of three months on the job. A second testing was given three months later. The mean scores on CF and BO did not vary across time (CF$_1$ mean = 45 [*SD* 14.4]; CF$_2$ = 44 [*SD* 13.6]; BO$_1$ mean = 32 [SD 11.3]; BO$_2$ mean = 28.86 [*SD* 9.6]). The overall alphas for the scales ranged from .87 to .90 (see Table 5.2). These results are preliminary, but they are consistent with the findings of Figley and Stamm (1996), who reported reliabilities of .85 to .94 on a sample of 142 psychotherapy practitioners.

Table 5.2
Alpha reliabilities, mean scores, standard deviations, and scale interpretation

Scale	Alpha	Mean	Standard Deviation	Interpretation
Compassion satisfaction	.87	92.10	16.04	Higher score is better satisfaction with ability to caregiver (e.g., derives pleasure from helping, likes colleagues, feels good about ability to help, makes contribution).
Burnout	.90	24.18	10.78	Higher score is higher risk for burnout (e.g., feels hopeless and unwilling to deal with work, onset gradual as a result of feeling one's efforts make no difference or very high workload).
Compassion fatigue	87	28.78	13.15	Higher score is higher risk for compassion fatigue (e.g., symptoms of work-related PTSD, onset rapid as a result of exposure to highly stressful caregiving).

CONCEPTUAL RELATIONSHIP BETWEEN COMPASSION FATIGUE AND COMPASSION SATISFACTION

One of the most intriguing questions raised by this line of inquiry is whether a person could be at high risk for experiencing compassion fatigue and, at the same time, still experience high compassion satisfaction. At this point, the hypothesis is that there is a balance between the two. For example, from discussions with caregivers in various humanitarian settings, we came to understand that they believe they have CF, but many of them like their work because they feel positive benefits from it. They believe what they are doing is helping a group of people and, in some ways, that it is even redemptive. Certainly, they believe it is the right thing to do. In situations like these, in which the belief system is being well maintained with positive material, perhaps a person's resiliency is enhanced (Pearlman & Sackvitne, 1990). However, if CF and BO are combined, there may be no energy available to sustain the vision of a better world in which one could find satisfaction.

Burnout, characterized by exhaustion, seems to make it impossible to envision a world in which one is not overwhelmed by an inability to be efficacious (Demerouti, Bakker, Nachreiner, & Schaufeli, 2001; Lee & Ashforth, 1990). This lack of efficacy (individual or corporate) likely colors negatively a person's view of his or her current fit with a personal belief system. Compassion satisfaction (CS) may be the portrayal of efficacy: Indeed, CS may be happiness with what one can do to make the world in which one lives a reflection of what one thinks it should be.

FUTURE DIRECTIONS

The Compassion Satisfaction and Fatigue Test (CSF Test) is being used in a number of research studies around the world and in a variety of fields. The question remains open as to whether it is a good measure of the constructs it seeks to test. There is no extant measure against which to gauge the CSF Test. The body of research that is beginning to emerge will not only add to our understanding of the statistical adequacy of the measure, it will add to our understanding of professional quality of life, and the constructs of compassion fatigue, compassion satisfaction, and burnout.

However, a number of questions are in immediate need of addressing before confidence can be placed in the CSF Test as a measure of reality. These questions are varied and include those listed here:

1. How does this measure of CF compare with other measures of traumatic stress?
2. Does the underlying factor structure support the subscales?

3. Is the measure sensitive to change across time?
4. How do the constructs of CF, CS, and burnout relate to one another?
5. Do the theoretical constructs make sense across differences in age, race, gender, and culture?
6. Are there differences between people based on age, race, gender, or culture?
7. Do CF, CS, and BO constructs that apply to people with a Western, individualist orientation apply to those with a collectivist, group orientation?
8. Do the constructs measured by the test apply equally to those with an external orientation (extraverted) as to those with an interior orientation (introversion)?
9. Do the constructs apply equally well across a variety of different professions, such as caregivers, teachers, public safety workers, news reporters, clergy, and volunteers?
10. Is there a quantifiable relationship between CF, CS, and BO that could predict potential risks and protective factors concurrently?

If these quantitative and construct validity questions can be addressed, the options for research across the spectrum of traumatic stress-related work are broad. In the meantime, the measure may be helpful to those who draw upon their compassion to help those who are suffering as a way to evaluate their own risk of burnout or compassion fatigue. In addition and probably of equal importance, these workers can consider their potential for deriving satisfaction from their work.

Thus, there are two uses for the CSF Test: for research to assist in establishing the constructs of secondary exposure to trauma (e.g., compassion fatigue or vicarious traumatization) and as a personal exploration of one's risk for the positive and negative aspects of helping. To facilitate these activities, the test is reprinted here as Appendix 5A, with a permission to reprint on the test itself.[1] Knowing how working with trauma affects us should help individuals, as well as employers, identify and put into place practices and policies that enhance the probability of satisfaction and reduce the risk of burnout and compassion fatigue. That will be very satisfying, indeed.

---

1. Updates and additional information about the test are available at http://www.isu.edu/~bhstamm/ts.htm

COMPASSION SATISFACTION AND FATIGUE (CSF) TEST

Helping others puts you in direct contact with other people's lives. As you probably have experienced, your compassion for those you help has both positive and negative aspects. This self-test helps you estimate your compassion status: How much at risk you are of burnout and compassion fatigue and also the degree of satisfaction with your helping others. Consider each of the following characteristics about you and your **current** situation. Write in the number that honestly reflects how frequently you experienced these characteristics in the last week. Then follow the scoring directions at the end of the self-test.

0 = Never	1 = Rarely	2 = A few times
3 = Somewhat often	4 = Often	5 = Very often

Items About You

1. I am happy.
2. I find my life satisfying.
3. I have beliefs that sustain me.
4. I feel estranged from others.
5. I find that I learn new things from those I care for.
6. I force myself to avoid certain thoughts or feelings that remind me of a frightening experience.
7. I find myself avoiding certain activities or situations because they remind me of a frightening experience.
8. I have gaps in my memory about frightening events.
9. I feel connected to others.
10. I feel calm.
11. I believe I have a good balance between my work and my free time.
12. I have difficulty falling or staying asleep.
13. I have outbursts of anger or irritability with little provocation.
14. I am the person I always wanted to be.
15. I startle easily.
16. While working with a victim, I thought about violence against the perpetrator.
17. I am a sensitive person.
18. I have flashbacks connected to those I help.
19. I have good peer support when I need to work through a highly stressful experience.
20. I have had first-hand experience with traumatic events in my adult life.
21. I have had first-hand experience with traumatic events in my childhood.
22. I think I need to "work through" a traumatic experience in my life.
23. I think I need more close friends.
24. I think there is no one to talk with about highly stressful experiences.
25. I have concluded that I work too hard for my own good.
26. Working with those I help brings me a great deal of satisfaction.
27. I feel invigorated after working with those I help.
28. I am frightened of things a person I helped has said or done to me.
29. I experience troubling dreams similar to those I help.
30. I have happy thoughts about those I help and how I could help them.

10 = 0

86 – X

20 = ✓

_0_ 31. I have experienced intrusive thoughts of times with especially difficult people I have helped.

_0_ 32. I have suddenly and involuntarily recalled a frightening experience while working with a person I helped.

_1_ 33. I am preoccupied with more than one person I help.

_0_ 34. I am losing sleep over a person I help's traumatic experiences.

x _3_ 35. I have joyful feelings about how I can help the victims with whom I work.

_0_ 36. I think I might have been "infected" by the traumatic stress of those I help.

x _1_ 37. I think I might be positively "inoculated" by the traumatic stress of those I help.

_1_ 38. I remind myself to be less concerned about the well-being of those I help.

_1_ 39. I have felt trapped by my work as a helper.

_0_ 40. I have a sense of hopelessness associated with working with those I help.

✓_1_ 41. I have felt "on edge" about various things, and I attribute this to working with certain people I help.

✓_2_ 42. I wish I could avoid working with some people I help.

x _2_ 43. Some people I help are particularly enjoyable to work with.

_2_ 44. I have been in danger working with people I help.

✓_0_ 45. I feel that some people I help dislike me personally.

Items About Being a Helper and Your Helping Environment

x _5_ 46. I like my work as a helper.

x _4_ 47. I feel I have the tools and resources I need to do my work as a helper.

✓_2_ 48. I have felt weak, tired, and run down as a result of my work as helper.

✓_0_ 49. I have felt depressed as a result of my work as a helper.

x _4_ 50. I have thoughts that I am a "success" as a helper.

✓_0_ 51. I am unsuccessful at separating helping from my personal life.

x _2_ 52. I enjoy my coworkers.

x _2_ 53. I depend on my coworkers to help me when I need it.

x _5_ 54. My coworkers can depend on me for help when they need it.

x _3_ 55. I trust my coworkers.

✓_2_ 56. I feel little compassion toward most of my coworkers

x _5_ 57. I am pleased with how I am able to keep up with helping technology.

✓_1_ 58. I feel I am working more for the money or prestige than for personal fulfillment.

x _4_ 59. Although I have to do paperwork that I don't like, I still have time to work with those I help.

✓_1_ 60. I find it difficult separating my personal life from my helper life.

x _5_ 61. I am pleased with how I am able to keep up with helping techniques and protocols.

✓_0_ 62. I have a sense of worthlessness/disillusionment/resentment associated with my role as a helper.

✓_0_ 63. I have thoughts that I am a "failure" as a helper.

✓_0_ 64. I have thoughts that I am not succeeding at achieving my life goals.

✓_4_ 65. I have to deal with bureaucratic, unimportant tasks in my work as a helper.

✓_5_ 66. I plan to be a helper for a long time.

Scoring Instructions

Please note that research is ongoing on this scale, and the following scores are theoretically derived and should be used only as a guide, not as confirmatory information.

1. Be certain you respond to all items.
2. Mark the items for scoring:
   a. Put an x by the following 26 items: 1–3, 5, 9–11, 14, 19, 26–27, 30, 35, 37, 43, 46–47, 50, 52–55, 57, 59, 61, and 66.
   b. Put a check by the following 16 items: 17, 23–25, 41, 42, 45, 48, 49, 51, 56, 58, 60, and 62–65.
   c. Circle the following 23 items: 4, 6–8, 12, 13, 15, 16, 18, 20–22, 28, 29, 31–34, 36, 38–40, and 44.
3. Add the numbers you wrote next to the items for each set of items and note:
   a. *Your potential for compassion satisfaction (x)*: 118 and above = extremely high potential; 100–117 = high potential; 82–99 = good potential; 64-81 = modest potential; below 63 = low potential.
   b. *Your risk for burnout (check)*: 36 or less = extremely low risk; 37–50 = moderate risk; 51–75 = high risk; 76–85 = extremely high risk.
   c. *Your risk for compassion fatigue (circle)*: 26 or less = extremely low risk, 27–30 = low risk; 31–35 = moderate risk; 36–40 = high risk; 41 or more = extremely high risk.

X = High Potential (compassion)
✓ = Extreme low risk (Burnout)
O = Extreme low risk (Compassion Fatigue)

REFERENCES

American Psychiatric Association. (2000). *Diagnostic and Statistical Manual of Mental Disorders (text revision)* (4th ed.). Washington, DC: Author.

Brady, J. L., Guy, J. D., Poelstra, P. L., & Brokaw, B. F. (1999). Vicarious traumatization, spirituality, and the treatment of sexual abuse survivors: A national survey of women psychotherapists. *Professional Psychology: Research and Practice, 30,* 386–393.

Burnette, E. (1997, September). Community psychologists help South Africans mend. *The American Psychological Association Monitor.*

Davidson, J. R. T., Hughes, D., Blazer, D. G., & George, L. K. (1991). Post-traumatic stress disorder in the community: An epidemiological study. *Psychological Medicine, 21*(3), 713–721.

Demerouti, E., Bakker, A. B., Nachreiner, F., & Schaufeli, W. B. (2001). The job demands-resources model of burnout. *Journal of Applied Psychology, 86,* 499–512.

Ferrada-Noli, M., Asberg, M., Ormstad, K., Lundin, T., & Sundbom, E. (1998). Suicidal behavior after severe trauma, Part 1: PTSD diagnoses, psychiatric comorbidity, and assessments of suicidal behavior. *Journal of Traumatic Stress, 11*(1) 103–112.

Figley, C. R. (1995a). *Compassion fatigue: Coping with secondary traumatic stress disorder in those who treat the traumatized.* New York: Brunner/Mazel.

Figley, C. R. (1995b). Compassion Fatigue. In B. H. Stamm (Ed.), *Secondary traumatic stress: Self-care issues for clinicians, researchers, and educators* (pp. 3–28). Lutherville, MD: Sidran Press.

Figley, C. R., & Stamm, B. H. (1996). Psychometric review of the Compassion Fatigue Self Test. In B. H. Stamm (Ed.), *Measurement of stress, trauma & adaptation.* Lutherville, MD: Sidran Press.

Flannery, D. J., Singer, M. I., & Wester K. (2001). Violence exposure, psychological trauma, and suicide risk in a community sample of dangerously violent adolescents. *Journal of the American Academy of Child and Adolescent Psychiatry, 40,* 435–442.

Follette, V. M., Polusny, M. M., & Milbeck, K. (1994). Mental health and law enforcement professionals: Trauma history, psychological symptoms, and the impact of providing services to child sexual abuse survivors. *Professional Psychology, 25,* 275–282.

Forkner, M. E., Reardon, T. & Carson, G. D. (1997). Experimenting with feasibility of telemedicine in Alaska: Successes and lessons learned. *Telemedicine Journal, 2, 233–240.*

Friedman, M. J., & Schnurr, P. P. (1995). The relationship between trauma, post-traumatic stress disorder and physical health. In M. J. Friedman, D. S. Charney & A. Y. Deutch (Eds.), *Neurobiological and clinical consequences of stress: From normal adjustment to PTSD.* Philadelphia: Lippincott-Raven.

Ghahramanlou, M., & Brodbeck, C. (2000). Predictors of secondary trauma in sexual assault trauma counselors. *International Journal of Emergency Mental Health, 2,* 229–240.

Higson-Smith, C. (1997). *Monitoring of the psychosocial health of trauma workers in KwaZulu-Natal.* Unpublished manuscript.

Kessler, R. C., Sonnega, A., Bromet, E., Hughes, M., & Nelson, C. (1995). Post-traumatic Stress Disorder in the National Comorbidity Survey. *Archives of General Psychiatry, 52,* 1048–1059.

King, L., King, D., Fairbank, J., Keane, T., & Adams, G. (1998). Resilience-recovery factors in post-traumatic stress disorder among female and male veterans: Hardiness, post war social support and additional stressful life events. *Journal of Personality and Social Psychology, 74*(2), 420–434.

Kotler, M., Iancu, I., Efroni, R., & Amir, M. (2001). Anger, impulsivity, social support, and suicide risk in patients with posttraumatic stress disorder. *Journal of Nervous and Mental Disorders, 189,* 162–167.

Krug, E., Kresnow, M., Peddicord, J. P, Dahlberg, L. L., Powell, K. E., Crosby, A. E., & Annest, J. L. (1998). Suicide after natural disasters. *New England Journal of Medicine, 338*(6), 373–378.

Lambert, M. T., & Fowler D. R. (1997). Suicide risk factors among veterans: Risk management in the changing culture of the Department of Veterans Affairs. *Journal of Mental Health Administration, 24,* 350–358.

Lee, R. T., & Ashforth, B. E. (1990). On the meaning of Maslach's three dimensions of burnout. *Journal of Applied Psychology, 75,* 743–747.

Lessman, J., Li, Z., Shiming, J. B., & Drossman, D. A. (1998). How multiple types of stressors impact on health. *Psychosomatic Medicine 60,* 175–181.

McCann, I. L., & Pearlman, L. A. (1990). Vicarious traumatization: A framework for understanding the psychological effects of working with victims. *Journal of Traumatic Stress, 3,* 131–149.

Ortlepp, K. (1998). Non-professional trauma debriefers in the workplace: *Individual and organisational antecedents and consequences of their experiences.* Unpublished doctoral dissertation, University of the Witwatersrand, Johannesburg, South Africa.

Pearlman, L., & Saakvitne, K. (1995). *Trauma and the therapist: Countertransference and vicarious traumatization in psychotherapy with incest survivors.* New York: Norton.

Rudolph, J. M., & Stamm, B. H. (1999). Maximizing human capital: Moderating secondary traumatic stress through administrative & policy action. In B. H. Stamm. (Ed.), *Secondary traumatic stress: Self-care issues for clinicians, researchers and educators* (2nd ed.). Lutherville, MD: Sidran Press.

Rudolph, J. M., Stamm, B. H., & Stamm, H. E. (1997, November). *Compassion fatigue: A concern for mental health policy, providers and administration.* Poster presented at the 13th Annual Conference of the International Society for Traumatic Stress Studies, Montreal, Ontario, Canada.

Schauben, L. J., & Frazier, P. A. (1995). Vicarious trauma: The effects on female counselors of working with sexual violence survivors. *Psychology of Women Quarterly, 19*(1), 49–64.

Schnurr, P. P., Friedman, M. J., Sengupta, A., Jankowski, M. K., & Holmes, T. (2000). PTSD and utilization of medical treatment services among male Vietnam veterans. *Journal of Nervous and Mental Disorders, 8,* 496–504.

Schnurr, P. P, & Jankowski, M. K. (1999). Physical health and post-traumatic stress disorder: review and synthesis. *Seminar in Clinical Neuropsychiatry, 4,* 295–304.

Stamm, B. H. (Ed.). (1995). *Secondary traumatic stress: Self-care issues for clinicians, researchers and educators.* Lutherville, MD: Sidran Press.

Stamm, B. H. (1997, Spring). Work-related secondary traumatic stress. *PTSD Research Quarterly, 8,* 2. Retrieved September 23, 2001, from http://www.ncptsd.org/research/rq/rqpdf/V8N2.PDF

Stamm, B. H. (1998, August). Improving care with technology: Reducing military caregiver stress. In R. Ax (Chair), *Federal telehealth—Issues and initiatives.* Paper presented at the 106th Annual Convention of the American Psychological Association, San Francisco.

Stamm, B. H. (1999). Creating virtual community: Telehealth and self care updated. In B. H. Stamm. (Ed.), *Secondary traumatic stress: Self-care issues for clinicians, researchers and educators* (2nd ed.; pp. 179–207). Lutherville, MD: Sidran Press.

Stamm, B. H. (Ed.). (1999). *Secondary traumatic stress: Self-care issues for clinicians, and educators* (2nd ed.). Towson, MD: Sidran Press.

Stamm, B. H., & Figley, C. R. (1996). *Compassion satisfaction and fatigue test.* Retrieved September 23, 2001, from http://www.isu.edu/~bhstamm/tests.htm

Stamm, B. H., Higson-Smith, C., Terry, M. J., & Stamm, H. E. (1996, November). *Politically correct or critically correct? Community and culture as context.* Symposium at the 12th Annual Conference of the International Society for Traumatic Stress Studies, San Francisco.

Stamm, B. H., & Pearce, F. W. (1995). Creating virtual community: Telemedicine applications for self-care. In B. H. Stamm. (Ed.), *Secondary traumatic stress: Self-care issues for clinicians, researchers and educators.* Lutherville, MD: Sidran Press.

Part II

TREATMENT AND PREVENTION INNOVATIONS

Introduction to Part II: Treatment and Prevention Innovations

The next five chapters apply contemporary knowledge, theory, and assessment to preventing and treating compassion fatigue and related problems. The first chapter is a good example of this integration. Three traumatologists came together from three different countries (the United States, Canada, and Australia) to devise a comprehensive program of treatment for professional caregivers. The next two chapters focus on humor and silence as indicators of compassion fatigue. The two final chapters, although focusing on preparing for two separate and very different traumatic events (war versus disasters), harmonize advice on self-monitoring and self-care. Together, these five chapters serve as an important handbook for practitioners who work with the suffering on a regular basis. The goal, of course, is to keep them on the job and thriving.

6

ARP: The Accelerated Recovery Program (ARP) for Compassion Fatigue*

J. ERIC GENTRY
ANNA B. BARANOWSKY
KATHLEEN DUNNING

"The professional work centered on the relief of the emotional suffering of clients automatically includes absorbing information that is about suffering. Often it includes absorbing that suffering as well." (Figley, 1995, p. 2)

"The only resource we had to help us cope with this emotional, physical and spiritual distress was ourselves." (Bloom, 1997, p. 112)

In his pivotal book *Compassion Fatigue* (1995), Figley conceptualized an issue that has plagued many clinicians, emergency response workers, and other care-providers who work with traumatized populations. This work provided the language for the feelings of these challenged service providers. It then became exceedingly clear that the next step was developing strategies for addressing and resolving the distress resulting from exposure to trauma experienced directly by another.

Exposure to trauma can result in the symptoms now synonymous with Post-Traumatic Stress Disorder (Janoff-Bullman, 1992; Rando, 1996). When indi-

---

* Based on a symposium presented at the International Society for Traumatic Stress Studies, Montreal, Quebec, November 1997.

viduals bring their traumatic stories to a caregiver a "radiating distress" can pass over onto another human being and may impact upon them through a process of secondary traumatization. When this occurs the caregiver is no longer able to function effectively due to the overwhelming nature of com- passion fatigue. Compassion fatigue is a combination of secondary traumati- zation and burnout precipitated by services that bring professionals in direct contact with traumatized persons (Beavan & Stephans, 1999). When the pro- fessionals themselves are overwhelmed by their work who is left to care for them?

The primary focus of the ARP program is facilitation of a recovery process of the compassion fatigued service provider. Essentially, this implores profes- sionals to learn to attend to each other, recognizing and accepting individual vulnerabilities while entrusting trained clinicians in a process of recovery. The treatment program presented is directed at professionals who up to the present day have had little recourse for the alleviation of symptoms that arise as a direct result of their essential work.

COMPASSION FATIGUE: WHAT IS IT?

Compassion fatigue (CF) (Figley, 1995) is the convergence of primary of traumatic stress, secondary traumatic stress (Landry, 1999; Stamm, 1995) and cumulative stress/burnout (Maslach, 1982) in the lives of helping profession- als and other care providers. Secondary Trauma occurs when one is exposed to extreme events directly experienced by another. Burnout is a state of physi- cal, emotional, and mental exhaustion caused by a depletion of ability to cope with one's everyday environment (Figley & Kleber, 1995; Friedman, 2000). When helping others precipitates a compromise in our own well-being we are suffering from CF. "By understanding . . . Compassion Fatigue, [as] the natu- ral, predictable, treatable, and preventable consequences of [caregiving] we can keep these caring professionals at work and satisfied with it" (Figley, 1995).

The symptoms of CF can mimic, to a lesser degree, those of the trauma- tized people we are working with. Vicarious traumatization (Clemens, 1999; McCann & Pearlman, 1990) is a related term that also depicts this phenomena of the transmission of traumatic stress by observation and/or "bearing wit- ness" to the stories of traumatic events. Secondary traumatic stress occurs when one is exposed to extreme events directly experienced by another and is overwhelmed by this secondary exposure to trauma (Figley & Kleber, 1995). Several theories have been offered but none have been able to conclusively demonstrate the mechanism which accounts for the transmission of traumatic stress from one individual to another. Figley (1995) hypothesizes that the caregiver's empathy level with the traumatized individual plays a significant role in this transmission. The Baranowsky and Gentry model, includes the conceptualization of primary traumatic stress as a latent vulnerability to CF or Secondary Traumatic Stress (STS) (Baranowsky & Gentry, 1999a, 1999b; Gentry & Baranowsky, 1999; Rosenheck & Nathan, 1985; Solomon, 1990; Solomon, Kotler, & Mikulincer, 1988)

Burnout, or cumulative stress, is the state of physical, emotional, and mental exhaustion caused by a depletion of ability to cope with one's environment resulting from our responses to the on-going demand characteristics (stress) of our daily lives (Maslach, 1982). High levels of cumulative stress in the lives of caregivers negatively affects their resiliency therefore making them more susceptible to CF. The silencing response (Baranowsky, this volume; Danieli, 1984, 1996) is an inability to attend to the stories or experiences of others and instead to redirect to material that is less distressing for the professional. This occurs when another's experiences and stories are overwhelming, beyond our scope of comprehension and desire to know, or simply spiraling past our sense of competency. The point at which we may notice our ability to listen becoming compromised is the point at which the silencing response has weakened our efficacy.

Secondary traumatization and burnout, the two components of CF, affect most every caregiver at some point in his or her professional cycle leaving them challenged to reach out for help—a difficult position for many care providers to be in. Fear of judgment, reprisal, or ridicule; fear of exposing oneself; illusions of omnipotence and difficulty trusting other professionals seem to contribute to the silencing response and often prevent us from reaching out for the help we need.

Figley (1996) defines CF as "a state of tension and preoccupation with the individual or cumulative trauma of clients as manifested in one or more ways:

- Re-experiencing the traumatic events,
- Avoidance/numbing of reminders of the traumatic event,
- Persistent arousal
- Combined with the added effects of cumulative stress (burnout)." (p. 11)

These symptoms reflect the PTSD triad of symptoms: intrusion, avoidance and hypervigilance. CF also includes burnout symptoms. In addition, there are elements unique to CF which require additional consideration and sensitivity. The primary categories are described as: 1) intrusive thoughts, images and sensations; 2) avoidance of people, places, things and experiences which elicit memories of the traumatic experience, and 3) negative arousal in the forms hypervigilance, sleep disturbances, irritability and anxiety. These symptoms combine to form a state of physical, emotional, cognitive and spiritual volatility in traumatized individuals, families and groups (Janet, 1889; van der Kolk, 1996) and are hypothesized to encompass the primary CF symptomology. Persons who work closely with traumatized groups and individuals are vulnerable to the contagion of this volatility. Some caregivers appear to be more resilient than others to the transmission of traumatic stress, however, any caregiver who continually works with traumatized individuals is vulnerable to feeling overwhelmed at some point in his or her professional life.

Compassion Fatigue is a relatively recent construct although it is likely that the problem has been in existence as long as humans have cared for one another. The research in this area and the results suggests that CF is a very real concern and one that may result in diminished capacity to function at work, home, and within personal relationships. CF has many symptoms that can parallel PTSD (American Psychiatric Association, 1994) symptoms of the traumatized people with whom caregivers are working. While CF has been most often written about in the rubric of psychotherapy as emotional contagion passed from client to clinician, there is growing evidence to support the transgenerational and societal transmission of this condition (Baranowsky, this volume; Baranowsky et al., 1998; Bloom, 1997; Danieli, 1985, 1996). Professionals other than therapists, psychologists, and psychiatrists who may be vulnerable to the effects of CF include physicians, nurses, other physical healthcare professionals, police, legal council, clergy, emergency service responders, CISD members, journalists, trauma researchers and other individuals whose work brings them in direct contact with highly distressed individuals or materials related to extremely disturbing events.

Other target symptoms of CF include:

- Increased negative arousal
- Intrusive thoughts/images of another's critical experiences (or caregiver's own historical traumas)
- Difficulty separating work from personal life
- Lowered frustration tolerance. Increased outbursts of anger or rage
- Dread of working with certain individuals
- Marked or increasing transference/countertransference issues with certain individuals
- Depression
- Perceptive/"assumptive world" disturbances (i.e., seeing the world in terms of victims and perpetrators coupled with a decrease in subjective sense of safety)
- Ineffective and/or self-destructive self-soothing behaviors
- Hypervigilance
- Decreased feelings of work competence
- Diminished sense of purpose/enjoyment with career
- Reduced ego-functioning (time, identity, volition)
- Lowered functioning in nonprofessional situations
- Loss of hope

These symptoms constitute an interconnecting weave of responses or be- haviors that warn us of CF. They may appear singly or in combination with other symptoms. Any of these symptoms could signal the presence of CF. Utilizing the Compassion Fatigue Scale–Revised (see Appendix 6.1) facilitates the means of identifying the existence and degree of CF in the professional caregiver. The following self-test was designed to assist caregivers in their ability to identify the symptoms of CF in themselves. This test is a modified version of the original found in Figley (1995).

WHO IT AFFECTS?

Empathy is the tool that many service providers use to establish a relation- ship. Over time, working in continuously emotionally charged situations, this empathy can become overtaxed and exhausted even when the professional is diligently maintaining self-care skills.

There are two main groups of people that are typically impacted by CF: 1) those who aid in a professional capacity; and 2) family and friends of those in need. CF may occur in a wide range of persons involved in providing aid to others (Jay, 1991). We have found that it is most prevalent among profession- als and personal family members, friends, and associates of trauma survivors (Beaton & Murphy, 1995; Baranowsky & Gentry, 1999a, 1999b; Gentry & Baranowsky, 1999). Therapists, psychologists, social workers, disaster relief workers, 911 operators, journalists/reporters, lawyers, nurses, doctors, emer- gency care professionals, police, help-line attendants, crisis shelter workers, among others, are all susceptible to CF (Friedman, 2000).

First-hand exposure to trauma in the caregiver's life further heightens vul- nerability to CF (Solomon, Kotler, & Mikulincer, 1988; Solomon, 1990; Rosenheck & Nathan, 1985). Yet, in the emerging field of traumatology many care providers have such experience. It is not uncommon to find ex-substance abusers counseling those currently trying to break away from using. Like- wise, it is not uncommon to find those who are personally knowledgeable about trauma trying to aid others who have faced terrible events (Pearlman & MacIan, 1995).

THE ROAD BACK HOME

We have used the metaphor of "The Road Back Home" to describe our program because CF seems to rob the professional of their sense of well-be- ing, comfort, purpose, identity and empowerment; all the qualities that one associates with being "at home." The experience of being "at home" in our bodies, our work, our thoughts and our spirit seem to diminish as the symptoms of CF increase. The program we have created is designed with the hope of assisting helping professionals, to move rapidly toward comfort and empowerment in their professional and personal lives. Our program will challenge and assist the helping professional in finding their own personal "road back home."

THE ACCELERATED RECOVERY PROGRAM (ARP) MODEL

Gentry, Baranowsky and Dunning (1997) developed the Accelerated Program for Compassion Fatigue (ARP) while visiting Florida State University (FSU) on a Green Cross Scholar's Project under the direction of Dr. Charles Figley. The ARP is a five (5)-session model for the treatment of the deleterious effects of CF in the lives of professionals who encounter trauma secondarily through their work (Baranowsky & Gentry, 1999a, 1999b; Gentry & Baranowsky, 1999). Since its inception in 1997, hundreds of caregivers have successfully resolved their symptoms of CF and have re-created their professional and personal lives to remain resilient to these effects. We are excited to be able to offer information about this program and its development in the hope that you will receive the same gifts.

Early 1997, the development team began preliminary trials with the ARP. During this time, it became apparent that CF was responsive to intervention and may even be the incentive that leads to the enhancement of professional skills and personal life enrichment in the same way that a crisis may precipitate change and growth in a patient or client's lives. Although the ARP was first developed as a standardized individual treatment model the program ideas were furthered through a "train the trainer" model as well as small and large workshop models. By the spring of 1999, the authors were contacted by caregivers in Oklahoma City requesting that we create both a one-day and a three-day group model of the ARP. We were, at first, skeptical that we could condense this rich material into a group model. After continued support from the professionals in Oklahoma City and after providing a training for Certified Compassion Fatigue Specialists during which the group model was workshopped, we have been able to condense the techniques and concepts into the one-day "group model" and a three-day "Retreat/Workshop."

All ARP models were designed to address prevention and treatment of CF for a broad range of professionals of all types. The ARP was designed to be powerfully introspective and interactive. Its purpose was to provide participants with the raw materials to begin to develop resiliency and prevention skills from CF. In addition, the program offers an opportunity to review personal and work history to the present and assist in the process of movement toward a more intentional and less reactive professional and personal life.

The ARP is designed to assist those working in high-stress/high-demand careers. It is not a panacea or a "cure-all." There will be many who, once introduced to the ARP concepts find that they will need and want to pursue further training and treatment to resolve symptoms of compassion fatigue and other complexities in order to gain the skills necessary to retain resiliency.

PRIMARY ARP PROGRAM ELEMENTS

The ARP was originally developed as a brief (five session) treatment program designed to assist professionals in reducing the intensity, frequency and duration of symptoms associated with CF. Whether the program is presented to individuals, trainers, or in small to large group workshop formats all elements are covered. Treatment sessions are standardized and directed toward the completion of all major objectives.

Program goals include:

- ✓ Symptom identification
- ✓ Recognize compassion fatigue triggers
- ✓ Identify and utilize resources
- ✓ Review personal and professional history to the present day
- ✓ Master arousal reduction methods
- ✓ Learn grounding and containment skills
- ✓ Contract for life enhancement
- ✓ Resolve impediments to efficacy
- ✓ Initiate conflict resolution
- ✓ Implement supportive aftercare plan—utilizing the PATHWAYS self-care program

ARP COMPONENTS

The ARP follows a standardized component treatment model that covers the following elements:

1. *Therapeutic Alliance*—This is especially important in a model that offers care for professionals who generally view themselves as care providers and hence are resistant to seek help for themselves. The developers asked themselves, what does it mean for a care provider to leave his or her identification of caregiver to seek out care? It became a central tenet of the program that each individual who completed the ARP would be treated with great respect and an understanding of the unique challenge of a professional asking for help.

2. *Assessment - Quantitative*—The ARP utilizes a CF assessment profile, a

carefully constructed assessment package that allows us to consider many of the aspects of CF, silencing, primary trauma exposure, emotional disturbance, and stressors that may be impacting on the professional's life functioning. Some of these are in the experimental stages (i.e., TRS, SRS, GCS) and are used to determine change over time as opposed to diagnosis (Baranowsky & Gentry, 1999a, 1999b; Gentry & Baranowsky, 1999).

   Assessment - Qualitative—The Qualitative Assessment portion of the work consists of a participant interview recognizing the importance of depathologized, collaborative, strength-based approaches with participants.

3. *Anxiety Management*—Each ARP participant is exposed to a variety of anxiety reduction tools to assist with the management of stress and lowering of negative arousal. Many cutting edge approaches commonly utilized in the field of traumatic stress have been incorporated into this component of the training.

4. *Narrative*—The power of story and the restorative quality of personal self-awareness clearly aids in rebuilding professional and personal life quality. As with trauma survivors, so with those with CF or secondarily wounded, the story becomes a component of the journey back to wellness (Herman, 1992; Dietrich et al., 2000).

5. *Exposure/Resolution of Secondary Traumatic Stress (STS)*—Using "exposure" methods in the treatment of anxiety disorders and PTSD in particular is common (Rothschild, 2000; Rosenbloom & Williams, 1999). Hence, it was believed that exposure methods could also be the hallmark of efficacious treatment for CF. Although there are many new techniques in which we achieve exposure/resolution (Dietrich et al., 2000) most are based on the early work of Wolpe (1969), *The Practice of Behavior Therapy*.

6. *Cognitive Restructuring (Self-care and Integration)*—What we say to ourselves creates an internal environment in which we may flourish or flounder. If we have been through a difficult experience we may believe from that moment on that "we live in a dangerous world." This belief may persist even when we are with people we love in a safe physical environment. In this case we feel we are NOT SAFE even when we are. What we say to ourselves may make all the difference in breaking down negative beliefs. Getting a reality check helps but, *even better,* challenging the internal dialogue may help to shift our automatic thoughts and beliefs to one of a more honest and harmonious inner world. We use "letter from the 'Great Supervisor'" and Video-Dialogue with "critical self" to accomplish this in our program.

7. *PATHWAYS - Self-directed Resiliency and Aftercare Plan*—The PATHWAYS is an integral component of the ARP and constitutes an aftercare element that reinfuses the individual's life with a sense of personal com-

mitment to wellness and responsibility for making this happen through-out the program and into the future.

PATHWAYS - AFTERCARE RESILIENCY MODEL

The ARP attempts to further address CF in professional caregivers by en-couraging mastery of the PATHWAYS which represents the self-care, after-care prevention portion of this program. There are five identified pathways which enhance skills development and act as a buffer, preventative medicine and means of distress resolution. Below are listed five (5) areas which we have found and which research supports to be instrumental in the development of healthy lifestyles with minimal distress and optimal satisfaction (Herman, 1992; Kabat-Zinn, 1990; Rosenbloom & Williams, 1999; Rothschild, 2000; Williams & Sommer, 1994):

1. Resiliency Skills
2. Self-management and Self-care
3. Connection with Others
4. Skills Acquisition
5. Conflict Resolution

The professional will be challenged to address five primary pathways as they relate to his or her wellness in both professional and personal lives:

1. *Resiliency Skills - Non-anxious Presence and Self-validated Caregiving*: The ARP developers believe that professionals who are able to develop and maintain the essential skills of "non-anxious presence" and "self-vali-dated caregiving" will enjoy an increased sense of resiliency to CF. The ARP is designed to challenge the caregiver to integrate these concepts into their lives thereby moving from reactivity towards intentionality.
2. *Self-management and Self-care:* We challenge ARP participants to ask them-selves what leads them to feel overextended in their work or personal lives? What boundaries need to be implemented or reinforced? What self-care or self-soothing skills need to be developed, implemented, re-instated, or reorganized?
3. *Connection with Others:* Reaching out to others is extremely important for the professional who is attempting to recover from CF. Developing a personal "therapeutic community" is also mandatory in the prevention of CF. Breaking isolation and constriction can often provide immediate lessening of the problems associated with CF. The professional will be challenged to identify and develop underutilized resources for support, nurturance, and enrichment.

4. *Skills Acquisition:* Becoming well-skilled in our field of choice acts as a buffer to CF. When we do not receive adequate training or supervision we become vulnerable to feelings of inadequacy and low self-esteem. We encourage professionals to gain mastery in helping endeavors and to ask themselves what steps need to be taken to get this training?

5. *Conflict Resolution:*

   i. *Internal:* Many professionals know exactly what they need to do for themselves but they find themselves, during the whirlwind of the day, unable to implement these strategies. Internal conflicts result in an energy drain of valuable resources away from current-day issues to past, unresolved personal issues. What symptoms do you recognize when you are caught in internal conflicts?

   ii. *External - Resolution of Primary Traumatic Stress:* A noteworthy number of caregivers have had personal experience with trauma. When this is the case, the primary trauma may become re-triggered through professional work. In order for us to be most effective and least reactive in our work it becomes important to resolve our own past traumas.

DISCUSSION AND TREATMENT RESPONSIVENESS

The good news is that in preliminary testing, compassion fatigue appeared to be very responsive to ARP treatment. When helping professionals make the crucial first step of reaching out to ask for help, they are already well on their way to recovery. Many helping professionals who have successfully resolved their symptoms of CF credit this reaching out as one of the most important personal and professional moves of their career. Not only do these professionals report a marked reduction in CF symptoms, they also state that they feel more empowered, more energetic, and enlivened with a strong sense of self-worth.

This program addresses the symptoms of CF and identifies primary trauma where relevant. All participants are informed that primary trauma may need to be addressed first before commencing with the ARP protocol (Gallo, 1997). The program attempts to deal holistically with CF and underlying unresolved trauma using the essential elements of this program.

The ARP program has now been offered successfully to individuals, groups and communities in Canada, Tasmania and the United States. A "train the trainer," model is being offered for clinicians wishing to aid Compassion Fatigued Professionals through the Traumatology Institute's "Certified Compassion Fatigue Specialist" (CCFS) program. Individuals requiring such services can acquire names of CCFSs in their vicinity. Workshops are being offered in private and public facilities for both overview (1-day ARP) and more intensive (3-day ARP) models. Group models are most suitable for larger organizations, such as hospitals, police departments, social work agencies and other related services where caregivers have become compassion fatigued through their work. For example, training clinicians through employee assistance programs to aid hospital staff is an excellent means to maintain high functioning and reduce employee turnover. Training materials for clinicians interested in treating CF in themselves and others are also available (Baranowsky & Gentry, 1999a,1999b; Gentry & Baranowsky, 1999).

CONCLUSIONS

The ARP combines several brief trauma protocols, a comprehensive assessment package, and a self-administered self-care plan (PATHWAYS). This constellation of treatment/training strategies, distilled into program components and goals seems to have combined to provide an effective means for resolution of CF symptoms.

At this time, there is little empirical data on the efficacy, utility, and/or safety of this approach, however the protocol elements utilized in this program have shown promise in each of these areas (Dietrich, 2000; Figley & Carbonell, 1995; Friedman, 2000; Ochberg, 1993). Therefore, the authors of this program offer this protocol to compassion fatigued professionals as an approach to alleviate symptoms and reinforce resiliency. From the time of this publication, the ARP is the first comprehensive treatment program of its kind. We hope that clinicians will join us in beginning to utilize this protocol to assist compassion fatigued professionals on "the road back home."

APPENDIX 6.1

Compassion Fatigue Scale–Revised
Compassion Fatigue Scale–R is based on an earlier Compassion Fatigue Scale (Figley, 1995).

Compassion Fatigue Self Test–Revised for Care Providers (CF–R)
Self Test
The following self test was designed to assist caregivers identify the symptoms of Compassion Fatigue in themselves. This test is a modified version of the original found in *Compassion Fatigue* (Figley, 1995).

Consider each of the following items about you and your work/life situation. Write in the number that best reflects your experience using the following rating system, where 1 signifies rarely or never and 10 means very often.

Answer all items, even if they do not seem applicable. Then read the instructions to get your score.

1 = Rarely/Never (N/A) —2—3—4—5—6—7—8—9— 10 = Very Often
                                    Sometimes

_____ 1. I force myself to avoid certain thoughts or feelings that remind me of a frightening experience.

_____ 2. I find myself avoiding certain activities or situations because they remind me of a frightening experience.

_____ 3. I have gaps in my memory about frightening events.

_____ 4. I feel isolated from others.

_____ 5. I have difficulty falling or staying asleep.

_____ 6. I have outbursts of anger or irritability with little provocation.

_____ 7. I startle easily.

_____ 8. While caring for a victim I thought about violence against the perpetrator.

_____ 9. I have had flashbacks connected to my clients.

_____10. I have had first-hand experience with traumatic events in my adulthood.

_____11. I have had first-hand experience with traumatic events in my childhood.

_____12. I have thought that I need to "work through" a traumatic experience in my life.

_____13. I am frightened of things a client has said or done to me.

_____14. I experience troubling dreams similar to those of a client of mine.

_____15. I have experienced intrusive thoughts after working with especially difficult clients/patients.

_____16. I have suddenly and involuntarily recalled a frightening experience while working with a client/patient.

_____17. I am losing sleep over a client's traumatic experiences.

_____18. I have thought that I might have been "infected" by the traumatic stress of my clients/patients.

_____19. I remind myself to be less concerned about the well-being of my clients/patients.

_____20. I have felt trapped by my work.

_____21. I have felt a sense of hopelessness associated with working with clients/patients.

_____22. I have been in danger working with clients/patients.

_____23. I have thought that there is no one to talk with about highly stressful work experiences.

_____24. I have felt "on edge" about various things and I attribute this to working with certain clients/patients.

_____25. I have frequently felt weak, tired, or rundown as a result of my work as a caregiver.

_____26. I have felt depressed as a result of my work.

_____27. I feel I am unsuccessful at separating work from personal life.

_____28. I have a sense of worthlessness/disillusionment/resentment associated with my work.

_____29. I feel that I am a "failure" in my work.

_____30. I have thoughts that I am not succeeding at achieving my life goals.

Scoring Instructions:

(i) Be certain you responded to all items. (ii) Add the numbers you wrote next to the items. (iii) Note your risk of *Compassion Fatigue:* 94 or less = Low risk; 95 to 128 = Some risk; 129 to 172 = Moderate risk; 173 or more = High risk.

*Note. Items 1 through 22 are reflective of post-traumatic and/or secondary traumatic stress. Items 23 to 30 reflect the issue of burnout. The complete scale represents Compassion Fatigue.

REFERENCES

American Psychiatric Association. (1994). *Diagnostic and statistical manual of mental disorders* (4th ed.) (pp. 424–429). Washington, DC: Author.

Baranowsky, A. B. (This Edition). The silencing response in clinical practice: On the road to dialogue. In C. R. Figley (Ed.), *Treating compassion fatigue*. New York: Brunner-Routledge.

Baranowsky, A. B., & Gentry, J. E. (1999a). *Compassion satisfaction manual*. Toronto, Ontario, Canada: Psych Ink Resources.

Baranowsky, A. B., & Gentry, J. E. (1999b). *Workbook/journal for a compassion fatigue specialist*. Toronto, Ontario, Canada: Psych Ink Resources.

Baranowsky, A. B., Young, M., Johnson-Douglas, S., Williams-Keeler, L., & McCarrey, M. (1998). PTSD transmission: A review of secondary traumatization in Holocaust survivor families. *Canadian Psychology, 39,* 247–256.

Beaton, R. D., & Murphy, S. A. (1995). Working with people in crisis: Research implication. In C. F. Figley (Ed.), *Compassion fatigue: Coping with secondary traumatic stress disorder in those who treat the traumatized*. New York: Brunner/Mazel.

Beavan, V., & Stephens, C. (1999). The characteristics of traumatic events experienced by nurses on the accident and emergency ward. *Nursing Praxis in New Zealand, 14,* 12–21.

Bloom, S. (1997). *Creating sanctuary: Toward an evolution of sane societies*. New York & London: Routledge.

Callahan, R. J. (1994, September). *The five-minute phobia cure: A reproducible revolutionary experiment in psychology based upon the language of negative emotions*. Paper presented at the International Association for New Science, Fort Collins, CO.

Clemens, L. A. (1999). Secondary traumatic stress in rape crisis counselors: A descriptive study. California State University. Master's Thesis. Available UMI order No. AAD13-96034.

Danieli, Y. (1984). Psychotherapists' participation in the conspiracy of silence about the Holocaust. *Psychoanalytic Psychology, 1,* 23–42.

Danieli, Y. (1985). The treatment and prevention of long-term effects and intergenerational transmission of victimization: A lesson from Holocaust survivors and their children. In C. R. Figley (Ed.), *Trauma and its wake: The study and treatment of post-traumatic stress disorder* (pp. 295–313). New York: Brunner/Mazel.

Danieli, Y. (1996). Who takes care of the caretakers?: The emotional consequences of working with children traumatized by war and communal violence. In R. J. Apfel & B. Simon (Ed.), *Minefields in their hearts: The mental health of children in war and communal violence* (pp. 189–205). New Haven, CT: Yale University Press.

Dietrich, A. M., Baranowsky, A. B., Devich-Navarro, M., Gentry, E., Harris, C. J., & Figley, C. R. (2000). A review of alternative approaches to the treatment of post traumatic sequelae. *Traumatology, 6,* 251–271.

Figley, C. R. (1995). Compassion fatigue as secondary traumatic stress disorder: An overview. In C. R. Figley (Ed.), *Compassion fatigue: Coping with secondary taumatic stress disorder in those who treat the traumatized* (pp. 1–20). New York: Brunner/Mazel.

Figley, C. R., Baranowsky, A. B., & Gentry, I. E. (in press). Compassion Fatigue Scale–Revised. In C. R. Figley (Ed.), *Compassion fatigue: Volume II.* New York: Brunner/Mazel.

Figley, C. R., & Kleber, R. J. (1995). Beyond the "victim": Secondary traumatic stress. In R. J. Kleber, C. R. Figley, & B. P. R. Gersons (Eds.), *Beyond trauma: Cultural and societal dynamics* (pp. 75–98). New York: Plenum.

Friedman, M. J. (2000). PTSD diagnosis and treatment for mental health clinicians. In M. Scott & J. Palmer (Ed.), *Trauma and post-traumatic stress disorder* (pp. 1–14). New York: Cassell.

Gallo, F. P. (1997, March). Reflections on active ingredients in efficient treatments of PTSD, Part I. *International Electronic Journal of Innovations in the Study of the Traumatization Process and Methods for Reducing or Eliminating Related Human Suffering.* [On-line serial] Available: Traumatology Forum - Green Cross Forum.

Gentry, J. E., & Baranowsky, A. B. (1999). *Treatment manual for accelerated recovery from compassion fatigue.* Toronto, Ontario, Canada: Psych Ink Resources.

Gentry, E., Baranowsky, A. B., & Dunning, T. (1997, November). *Compassion fatigue: Accelerated Recovery Program (ARP) for helping professionals.* Paper presented at the meeting of the International Society for Traumatic Stress Studies on Linking Trauma Studies to the Universe of Science and Practice, Montreal, Quebec, Canada.

Gentry, J. E., & Schmidt, I. M. (1996). *Safety reconnaissance for trauma survivors.* Paper presented at the Sixth Annual Conference for Treating Traumatic Stress and Dissociation, Morgantown, WV.

Herman, J. L. (1992). *Trauma and recovery.* New York: Basic Books.

Holmes, D. & Tinnin, L. (1995). *On hearing voices: Video-dialogue technique.* MDTV, West Virginia University closed-circuit telemedicine training.

Janet, P. (1889). *L'Automatisme psychologique.* Paris: Felix Alcan. Reprint: Societe Pierre Janet, Paris, 1973.

Janoff-Bullman, R. (1992). *Shattered assumptions: Towards a new psychology of trauma.* New York: Free Press.

Jay, J. (1991). Terrible knowledge. *Family Therapy Networker, 15,* 18–29.

Kabat-Zinn, J. (1990). *Full catastrophe living.* New York: Delta Books.

Landry, L. P. (1999). Secondary traumatic stress disorder in the therapists from the Oklahoma City bombing. University of North Texas. Doctoral Dissertation. Available UMI order No. AAT99-81105.

Maslach, C. (1982). *Burnout—The cost of caring.* Englewood Cliffs, NJ: Spectrum.

McCann, I. L., & Pearlman, L. A. (1990). Vicarious traumatization: A framework for understanding the psychological effects of working with victims. *Journal of Traumatic Stress, 3,* 131–149.

Ochberg, F. M. (1993). Gift from within. Posttraumatic therapy. In J. P. Wilson & B. Raphael (Eds.), *International handbook of traumatic stress syndromes* (pp. 773–783). New York: Plenum.

Pearlman, L. A., & MacIan, P. S. (1995). Vicarious traumatization: An empirical study of effects of trauma work on trauma therapists. *Professional Psychology: Research and Practice, 26,* 558–565.

Rando, T. A. (1996). On treating those bereaved by sudden, unanticipated death. *In Session: Psychotherapy in Practice, 2,* 59–71.

Rosenbloom D., & Williams M. G. (1999). *Life after trauma: A workbook for healing.* New York: Guilford.

Rosenheck, R., & Nathan. P. (1985). Secondary traumatization in children of Vietnam veterans. *Hospital and Community Psychiatry, 5,* 538–539.

Rothschild, B. (2000). *The body remembers: The psychophysiology of trauma and trauma treatment.* New York: Norton.

Shapiro, F. (1995). *Eye movement desensitization and reprocessing: Basic principles, protocols, and procedures.* New York: Guilford.

Solomon, Z. (1990). Does the war end when the shooting stops? The psychological toll of war. *Journal of Applied Social Psychology, 20,* 1733–1745

Solomon, Z., Kotler, M., & Mikulincer, M. (1988). Combat-related posttraumatic stress disorder among second-generation Holocaust survivors: Preliminary findings. *American Journal of Psychiatry, 7,* 865–868.

Stamm, B. H. (Ed.). (1995). *Secondary traumatic stress: Self-care issues for clinicians, researchers, and educators.* Lutherville, MD: Sidran Press.

Tinnin, L. (1994). *Time-limited trauma therapy for dissociative disorders.* Bruceton Mills, WV: Gargoyle Press.

van der Kolk, B. (1996). *Traumatic stress: The effects of overwhelming experience on mind, body and society.* New York: Guildford.

Williams, M. B., & Sommer, J. F. (1994). *Handbook of post-traumatic therapy.* Westport, CT: Greenwood Press.

7

Humor as a Moderator of Compassion Fatigue

CARMEN C. MORAN

This chapter looks at the role of humor in extreme environments, particularly those involving emergency rescue workers and people in related helping professions. The term *emergency worker* is used to refer to the variety of professionals who are called upon to respond to emergency incidents such as major accidents, melees, and conflicts, as well as those who deal with the physical and psychological aftermath of these incidents. Humor is often regarded as one of the highest forms of coping with life stress (Andrews, Pollack, & Stewart, 1989; Freud, 1905; Martin, 1996; Vaillant, 1977). In extreme environments, especially those involving traumatic stressors, the role of humor can be covertly acknowledged while being overtly ignored. For emergency workers and helping professionals exposed to others' trauma, there is a dual expectation about the role of humor. First, there is a general expectation that gallows humor is to be found in most emergency environments, an expectation reinforced by novels, television programs, and movies. Second, there is an expectation that workers in these environments will be sensitive to the suffering of others, hence laughter in the face of tragedy is viewed with suspicion.

DEFINING HUMOR

Humor cannot be defined easily and the phenomenon is so complex that no single definition would suffice. There are various aspects to humor, and at times writers may be talking about sense of humor, appreciation of humor, or generation of humor (Bizi, Keinan, & Beit-Hallahmi, 1988; Cherkas et al., 2000; Martin & Lefcourt, 1983; Yates, 2001). Sense of humor can be seen as a personality predisposition, which might be measured as a propensity to laugh at certain things, including oneself (e.g., Martin & Lefcourt, 1984; Ruch, 1998). Appreciation of humor refers to the ability to see humor in the environment (Moran & Massam, 1999), and generation of humor refers to the tendency to make humorous comments or behave in a humorous manner (e.g., Thorson & Powell, 1993, 1996). In recent years, there have been many claims for the positive effects of humor on health and well-being, but these claims frequently have gone beyond the research evidence or do not distinguish between aspects of humor. When considering humor in emergency work, it seems reasonable to assume that different aspects of humor will serve different functions, some of which will be more beneficial than others.

COPING IN THE EMERGENCY CONTEXT

The stereotype of the hardy emergency worker who is oblivious to stress has been rejected over recent years, but there is a risk of it being replaced with another stereotype of the vulnerable worker-victim (Moran, 1998a). To assume everyone feels the same way after traumatic incidents is to minimize the extreme suffering of some individuals.

Over the last two decades, a growing body of research has regularly documented the occurrence of posttraumatic symptoms as a result of emergency work incidents (e.g., see Paton & Violanti, 1996). Traumatic stress reactions may arise as a result of direct threat to emergency workers' well-being—for example, when a firefighter is trapped by fire or a welfare worker is physically threatened. In other cases, traumatic reactions can result because emergency workers are constant witnesses to others' trauma. This latter type of traumatic stress reaction has been identified by different terms, including *compassion fatigue, secondary traumatic stress* (Figley, 1995), and *vicarious traumatization* (McCann & Pearlman, 1990). Taylor has used the term *tertiary victim* to refer to emergency personnel who develop stress symptoms as a result of working with disaster victims and their relatives (Taylor, 1996). Although terms vary and emphasize features of special relevance for certain professions, they reflect the common awareness that exposure to others' trauma can lead to a set of symptoms similar to those of posttraumatic stress disorder (PTSD). In the context of emergency and rescue work, this may also be called *critical incident stress* (Mitchell, 1988). Despite the increased recognition of risk, there is still debate over how to predict those most at risk (Moran & Shakespeare-Finch, in press). The nature of emergency work is such that studies of vulnerability and coping cannot adopt controlled conditions in the same way other studies of stress and coping can.

People's coping preferences do not necessarily predict which coping strategies will be used in specific situations (Carver, Scheier, & Weintraub, 1989). Coping style is not a good predictor of posttrauma symptoms (Shalev, 1996), and current tools for assessing coping are limited (de Ridder, 1997). Emergency workers are not necessarily a homogenous group (Paton & Smith, 1996), and individual differences will contribute to reactions to incidents and effectiveness of organizational interventions (Moran, 1998a). Despite these limitations in our knowledge of coping, there is a widespread belief, albeit informal, that "a sense of humor" helps.

Discussing personal coping strategies in emergency environments requires some caution, and this is particularly necessary when discussing the use of humor. Placing emphasis on individual coping may be seen by employees as giving employers an opportunity to blame the victim. In the particular case of humor, there is an additional risk of appearing to trivialize the issue. In the popular media, there has been a burgeoning view that humor can help almost unreservedly. At the same time, studies of humor are seldom found in most academic stress journals or monographs, especially those that deal with traumatic stress. This chapter thus proceeds with two cautions. First, understanding the role of humor in extreme environments will not be sufficient to understand the complex relationship between trauma, coping, and traumatic reactions. Second, humor is itself a complex phenomenon and cannot be reduced to a simple notion such as "sense of humor" or ability to "see the funny side of things." It is a pervasive component of human functioning that warrants further study to help us understand how and when humor helps us cope with the extreme demands and challenges of life.

THEORIES OF HUMOR

There are many theories of humor, not all of which are immediately relevant to the emergency context. Over a decade ago, Haig (1988) recognized over 100 theories of humor involving a diversity of perspectives, such as linguistic, sociological, psychological, anthropological, and theatrical. The focus has been narrowed here to the relationship of humor to stress and coping, and the relevance of humor in the emergency environment. Many theories of humor propose that humor provides some form of tension release and allows a reinterpretation of a given situation or event (Koestler, 1964; Martin & Lefcourt, 1983; Moran, 1998b). Tension release occurs as a rebound reaction to an initial increase in arousal that accompanies much humor—for example, during the build up of a joke and during vigorous laughter. Reinterpretation occurs as a result of humor providing a link between two normally unassociated items or contexts. That is, humor permits things to be seen in a new light because it allows the unexpected association of two normally unrelated or even conflicting scenarios. This unexpected association is commonly referred to as *incongruity*. Koestler (1964) referred to this as a "bisociation of ideas" and regarded it as a fundamental characteristic of humor. In certain circumstances, incongruity might be expected to increase distress, but in a humorous framework it adds to the pleasure (Nerhardt, 1970). Latta (1999) more recently reinterpreted this incongruity as a cognitive shift that happens to be pleasurable in the humor context. Although the fundamental role of incongruity in humor is still being debated today, incongruity seems to characterize much humor that is relevant to stress research.

Another important component of humor is aggression. Koestler believed aggression was also fundamental to humor. Aggression in humor may be pleasurable for its own sake, as it allows us to express feelings that we might not deal with otherwise. This expression of aggression may also lead to tension reduction, which is the real source of pleasure (Burger, 1993). Deckers and Carr (1986) noted when subjects were asked to rate cartoons, they rated those with characters experiencing pain as funnier than those with characters not experiencing pain. However, the present author found that when subjects were asked to identify with the characters in cartoons, cartoons with obvious victims and aggressors were rated as less funny (Moran, 1996). Thus, in some contexts aggressive humor is not funny. Aggressive humor can be healthy or harmful, liberating or offensive.

Mikes (1971) observed the most aggressive jokes are better than the least aggressive wars. While accepting this view, it is also fair to argue that in emergency and helping environments the value of aggressive humor can be constrained by many factors. Aggression may be a reaction to dealing with the harm done to others. For example, counselors dealing with victims of child abuse may experience aggressive feelings toward perpetrators. The value of using humor to cope with this type of aggression has not been established, and any potential therapeutic effect may become compromised by feelings of guilt and concerns over the spread of humor to include the victim. Aggressive humor in the emergency environment may be more likely to be directed at an organization rather than an emergency situation. Indeed, humor in organizational contexts frequently reflects an aggressive component. Humor may provide a way of challenging official guidelines without attacking the organization (Mulkay, 1988). A study of staff in a psychiatric hospital found humor was used by those in subordinate positions to cope with feelings of aggression that could not be expressed openly (Coser, 1960). Masten (cited in Martin, 1989) found that children from high-stress families who scored high on humor use were more competent than their low-humor siblings or counterparts. A similar effect might occur within organizations. That is, if an organization is stressed, humor may help individuals function more competently within that organization.

HUMOR AND PHYSICAL WELL-BEING

Many claims have been made for the health-enhancing effects of humor, especially laughter. These claims have sometimes exceeded our knowledge of the changes brought about by laughter, but research is increasingly indicating that humor is health-enhancing. The study of humor and its relationship to health is not new, but many authors take as their starting point the writings of Norman Cousins (1979), in which he documented the way humorous films and belly laughter contributed to his recovery from ankylosing spondylitis, a condition causing considerable pain and debility.

The physical effects of laughter appear to be similar to those of exercise, including increased muscle tension, heart rate, and respiration rate, all of which demonstrate a rebound reduction similar to a relaxation effect (Fry, 1994). The beneficial effects of humor extend to the immune system. Laughter has been shown to be accompanied by changes to salivary IgA, an immune enhancer related to the respiratory system. Humor also leads to changes in catecholamines, and it is speculated that this means release of endorphins. Whether these changes have longer term consequences has not been established (Lefcourt, Davidson, & Keuneman, 1990). In the emergency context, therefore, humor may help reduce physical symptoms of stress in the short term as well as contribute to longer term health by supporting immune function. Given the relationship between stress and illness, any factors that help maintain health are to be encouraged in occupations known to be stressful. In addition, the putative role of humor in contributing to health supports the contention that humor is a nontrivial component of human functioning and warrants organizational support.

HUMOR AND COGNITIVE REFRAMING

Cognitive reframing is one of the most popular components of current psychological treatments of emotional and stress-related disorders. Because humor can result in a reduction of tension and a reinterpretation of events, it can be neatly accommodated into many stress management or therapy programs with these objectives. In a nontherapy context, dispositional sense of humor has been shown to mitigate the effects of stress (Lefcourt et al., 1990; Martin & Dobbin, 1988). People with a high sense of humor do not experience fewer stressors; rather they show less disturbance as a result of them (Martin & Lefcourt, 1983; Nevo, Keinan, & Teshimovsky-Arditi, 1993; Nezu, Nezu, & Blissett, 1988).

The therapeutic value of humor is often evaluated in terms of how it helps people process negative information. However, dispositional humor characteristics interact with the way both negative and positive information is processed (Moran & Massam, 1999). The difference lies in the type of humor being measured. Coping humor, which reflects attempts to see the funny side of things, appears to filter out negative information. In contrast, humor bias, which reflects a tendency to pay attention to humor in the environment, appears to filter in positive information. The first finding (coping humor filters out negative information) matches the common view that coping humor helps people diffuse emotions in stressful situations or helps them remain in difficult situations (Dixon, 1980; Lefcourt, Davidson, & Shepherd, 1995; Moreall, 1987). Lefcourt and colleagues believed humor could act as a form of emotion-focused coping that allows people to process information about catastrophic events but not to the extent they become overwrought. Coping humor can also protect people from the full impact of personal criticism (Dews, Kaplan, & Winner, 1995). Jablonksi and Zillman were concerned this moderating aspect of coping humor might be so effective that it negates valuable negative reactions to circumstances. They found violent films were rated less stressful when viewed with a humor component, potentially trivializing the violence (Jablonksi & Zillman, 1995). In cases where it would seem useful to confront the unpleasant aspects of an event, using humor to escape from unpleasantness may be inappropriate.

Moran (1990) has noted how emergency workers often use the phrase "things can't be that bad if I can still laugh," which could be seen as a positive reframing of unpleasant and potentially traumatic events. In the emergency context, humor may also serve more specific functions, such as challenging self-defeating thoughts relating to the current scenario. For example, in a large-scale disaster, the humorous statement "well, I picked a great shift to be on today" could indirectly challenge the self-defeating statement "I'll never be able to help everyone." Both statements acknowledge the extent of suffering and the difficulty of the helping task, but the amusing irony of the former helps prevent the worker feeling a failure even before starting the helping task. The impossibility of helping everyone is reframed into the more humorous/ironic statement, which implies the more positive one: "I'm going to be working extremely hard helping people today."

In some extreme circumstances humor may be used to provide distance from, rather than reframing of, events. Lewis (1997) has discussed the impact of an extreme version of gallows humor, the killing joke exemplified in Freddy Kreuger's humor in the *Nightmare on Elm Street* movies. Lewis argued that laughing at the killing joke allows the audience to suspend sympathy for victims by identifying temporarily with something that is beyond human. That is, Lewis believed this "sadistic" humor gives participants a temporary experience of disaffiliation from the human race, which is perceived as pleasurable. The less sadistic but nevertheless sick humor found in emergency contexts may also serve a similar function of providing distance from horrific circumstances without the nihilism implied in killing jokes. In my own work, I have consistently noted that those using humor are often highly sensitive to their surroundings, can switch from humor to sorrow very quickly, and sometimes they cannot laugh—for example, with certain incidents involving children or large-scale disasters. The research literature that will emerge from the New York World Trade Center disaster will probably indicate an initial absence of laughter in those working at the scene, even those normally known to joke at the macabre.

Humor is not the only reframing technique with the potential to be insensitive. Taylor and Frazer (1982) discussed the way workers handling bodily remains after a major accident focused away from the fact that they were human parts, and those who were able to do this successfully also showed less distress. In both humorous and nonhumorous reframing, individuals may appear insensitive to outsiders, but workers within the field will frequently recognize the function such reframing serves. This recognition may be less likely if other workers have little grassroots experience of the types of traumatic events faced and the need for occasional escape. A difficulty can arise, of course, if workers are unable to acknowledge the circumstances of their work and continually escape through humor. For some, humor may be too effective in blocking out unpleasant stimuli and emotional reactions to them.

HUMOR AND COMMUNICATION

Communication is an important part of emergency work, both at the time of an incident and in the aftermath. In some cases humor may create a sense of belonging, a unique identity, and a private means of communication. Humor within organizations may help individuals engage in otherwise stressful collaborative activities (Mulkay, 1988). Palmer (1983) documented how paramedics use terms such as *crispy critter* for a fatal burn victim and *greenie* for a body that has started to decompose prior to discovery. These terms have an obvious humorous component, going beyond a private language. This humor acknowledges the horrific state of human remains while signaling that the worker is not focusing on that horror any further for the present time.

The reciprocal understanding of how colleagues are using humor can contribute to emotional bonding. Kuhlman (1988) described humor among staff in a maximum security forensic unit as an emotional language. Thus, humor may help to deal with emotions at an individual level as well as contribute to a social understanding at a broader level. Furthermore, the social benefits of humor may contribute positive features to the work environment. As Kuhlman noted, certain work environments provide little or no sense of accomplishment for staff and consequently staff rely on each other for this. In emergency work, certain traumatic incidents can be very public, and the media may present a graphic picture of devastation that takes away any sense of achievement from those who have put in effort to control or mitigate the effects of the incident. Private humor among emergency workers may help diffuse feelings of failure and restore a sense of positive experience in emergency work.

Humor may also enhance performance of certain tasks—for example, those requiring creativity, problem solving, and memory skills. Johnson (1990) proposed that humor in educational settings can increase comprehension, enhance memory retention, and improve faculty ratings. Peer ratings of humor have been shown to correlate with ratings of performance under the stressful conditions of combat training, but both humor and performance ratings may reflect a global positive view of peers (Bizi et al., 1988). There is no direct evident yet that humor has a performance-enhancing effect in emergency work, but there is a frequently quoted view that humor helps the emergency worker focus on the task at hand rather than on his or her emotions or the awful nature of the task (Moran, 1990). As one worker noted of emergency work, "crying does not seem to help us do it better whereas laughing does" (Steele, 1989, p. 488).

HUMOR AND EMERGENCY EXPERIENCE

Researching humor in emergency contexts and distinguishing between types of humor use can be difficult because of the often ephemeral nature of such humor. It can be difficult to know what questions to ask about humor. Moran (1990) asked permanent volunteer emergency workers with a mean length of 13 years of experience for examples of humor in a rescue context. Fifteen subjects completed the item, but only five gave any detailed descriptions. In most cases the scenarios described something funny occurring rather than humor being deliberately evoked. This was not just a function of being asked to write about humor, because the same pattern was noted in interviews. Nevertheless, participants generally acknowledged that humor was being used to cope with situations. Humor probably arises spontaneously during the emergency incident, in contrast to more deliberate humor that may be used back at the depot or office. In the field, humor may appear to be a reaction to a simple stimulus—for example, the dishevelled appearance of a colleague at the end of a rescue operation—but factors contributing to the laughter may be more complex. The knowledge that a colleague is safe or a dispute settled can contribute to laughter and accompanying tension relief. Others at the scene may come up with witty comments that add to the humor and also serve as a sign that it is permissible to laugh (Moran & Massam, 1997).

The emergency scene can be charged with tension, having features of the unexpected, the exaggerated, and the extreme. The circumstances may be such that humor is inappropriate, or that there is simply nothing to evoke humor in the circumstances. Humor should not be regarded as a constant part of the emergency environment. Emergency work, even in busy organizations, does not place consistent demands on its workers. In each emergency organization particular characteristics of that organization will contribute to when and what type of humor is used. It is doubtful whether organizations have a formal attitude to the appropriateness of humor (as they may have for other coping strategies). Acceptance of humor is probably passed on during training and group activities. Rosenberg (1991) described how trainee paramedics informally learn how and when to use humor from their more experienced colleagues. Colleagues act as models for the humor, and over time it becomes easier for trainees to make jokes themselves.

The importance of role models and permission to laugh may be especially important with more traumatic or horrific incidents. During CNN coverage of the New York World Trade Center disaster in September 2001, there was little or no humor, even mild, visible, or audible for the first four days of television coverage. The first notable reference to humor was the mention of the priest's eulogy at the funeral of Reverend Mychal Judge, New York Fire Department chaplain. The priest humorously recalled how the chaplain used to place his hands on people to bless them "even when they didn't want to be blessed" (CNN, 2001a).

Pogrebin and Poole (1988) listed four types of humor in police work: jocular aggression, audience degradation, diffusion of danger or tragedy, and normative neutralization. Group norms will have a strong influence on the acceptance of humor, and the type of humor used may involve implicit rules, which will vary across contexts and possibly across professions and organizations.

Emergency workers frequently mention how they restrict their humor to situations out of the range of public hearing (McCarroll, Ursano, Wright, & Fullerton, 1993). In some cases this is because the public may not recognize the need for humor to relieve tension or that the content of the humor may appear tasteless. "Outsiders" may emphasize the need for good taste, as a CNN reporter did when commenting on the body retrieval process at the World Trade Center: "I can assure you the body parts are being treated with the greatest respect" (CNN, 2001b). Alexander and Wells (1991) studied police officers working on the Piper Alpha disaster (a 1988 oil rig explosion in the North Sea that left 165 dead) and noted, although they used humor to cope with handling body parts, they were aware that such humor would be seen as tasteless or offensive by outsiders. Similarly, paramedics considered humor should be restricted to the emergency environment particularly because "other people would not appreciate it or get the point, they would think you were sick" (Rosenberg, 1991, p. 199). The increased ability of the media to participate in and broadcast disaster recovery activity, albeit at a distance via sensitive equipment, will probably have a constraining effect on the behavior of emergency workers and the coping strategies they are prepared to reveal.

Removing humor from the emergency environment may reduce the social bonding that can occur with shared humor. Thompson and Solomon (1991) observed that police volunteers were an extroverted, well-knit team with many jokes and friendly banter. The friendly environment may then make it easier to ask for and give support. Humor can be both a means and a consequence of socialization in the emergency context.

GALLOWS HUMOR

The type of humor used in emergency environments is frequently referred to as gallows humor. Gallows humor takes its name from jokes about the condemned man on the gallows (Freud, 1905). Often it is the condemned man who is generating the joke—for example, by asking the hangman if the scaffold is safe. The term has been more widely used to refer to situations of a hopeless victim, extending into chronic situations and harsh settings, including emergency work environments. It is found in situations where people have to persist in working even though the nature of the work is incongruous. As Kuhlman (1988, p. 1085) noted, "it . . . offers a way of being sane in insane places." Such humor is seen to reflect a sensitive awareness of the nature of circumstances while at the same time providing a healthy confrontation with them. Janoff (1974) argued that those who use gallows humor have a darker vision than most and their humor indicates a "terrible candour concerning the most extreme situations" (p. 303). Those who use humor in emergency work may be signaling to others just how much they recognize the horrors of their tasks. However, we should be cautious in assuming this is always the function of humor in such circumstances.

HUMOR AS A SIGN OF DISTRESS

In highly charged and stressful situations, excessive humor can be a sign of distress. The question arises as to what "excessive" means. In some cases, such as within psychotherapy, any humor might be regarded suspiciously in the belief it stops a person acknowledging anxiety (Kubie, 1971). In such cases, therapists may see their role as helping patients face their anxiety rather than suppress it with humor. Even in studies that have shown humor reduces distress, there are concerns that the nature of change may be limited to certain measures. For example, physiological indices of stress have been reduced, while psychological ones remained unchanged (White & Camarna, 1989). Humor may also block more general communication within a therapeutic relationship (Thomson, 1990). Haig (1988) saw overuse of humor as a form of denial that helps the person avoid dealing with problems. Mulkay (1988) argued that humor can be a form of inaction and withdrawal. Humor may also be used in a deliberate effort to appear normal (Skevington & White, 1998). Given these possibilities, a therapist would need to evaluate humor with respect to both the circumstances of the person using humor and the other coping functions it may be replacing.

In emergency work, humor may be used as an avoidance technique. There are other reasons to be cautious about humor in the emergency environment. As Robinson (1991) argued, humor may be used to curry favor with other workers. She argued it can be particularly inappropriate when used without regard to the situation, timing or individuals present; when it becomes annoying and tiresome; when it interferes with job performance; and when there is an overreliance on humor for stress relief to the exclusion of other strategies. Overholser (1992) also questioned the value of humor when it is overused, referring to this as the "Uncle Joe Syndrome," which causes a person to lose social attractiveness.

McCarroll and colleagues (1993) noted that some people are frightened by their own humor, thinking they have gone too far over the edge. On the other side, Robinson (1991) argued that those lacking in humor should not be seen as abnormal. From a clinical perspective, lack of humor is less frequently cited as a cause for concern within a therapeutic encounter than is excessive humor. In contrast to a lack of humor, loss of humor usually is a sign of serious distress.

HUMOR, THERAPY, AND COMPASSION FATIGUE

The use of humor in general therapy is not new (e.g., the Provocative Therapy of Farrelly & Brandsma, 1974). The role of humor in treating symptoms of trauma, primary or secondary, is less established. In part this may be because it can seem insensitive to mention humor in the same setting as trauma, so author-therapists do not draw attention to this aspect of their work. At an informal level, it is widely acknowledged that humor occurs during debriefing sessions after traumatic incidents and contributes to the sessions' effectiveness. In the literature on traumatic stress, loss of humor may be listed as part of the symptomatology. Loss of humor may be part of a general reduction in emotionality that occurs with these syndromes, as well as be exacerbated by specific symptoms of major depression.

Some researchers have explored whether humor has a differential effect on anxiety and depression, but this has not been consistently delineated. Nezu and associates (1988) argued that such a differentiation is likely, and using humor in the wrong instances could be harmful. Specifically, they considered humor might have an adverse effect on people already high in anxiety, because of their heightened arousal. Recall, humor has been found to cause an initial increase in arousal, followed by a rebound relaxation effect. The initial effect of humor, therefore, may serve to heighten arousal further in already highly aroused individuals, with detrimental consequences. In contrast to anxiety, Nezu argued, depression is characterized by low arousal, and thus people with depression may benefit more from the increase in arousal accompanying humor. Unfortunately, this argument cannot be sustained, as clinical workers will have already anticipated, because people may be both anxious and depressed at the same time (as the new "mixed anxiety depressive disorder" proposed in the *DSM–IV* acknowledges). Nevertheless, the arguments by Nezu and colleagues highlight the need to consider specific symptom patterns and their relationship to humor responses, rather than assume a global effectiveness of humor. In particular, we need to be extremely cautious about using humor where severe depression is present. Anhedonia, a loss of pleasure in things that once gave pleasure, may occur in people suffering trauma-related symptoms and severe depression. To present humorous material to these people who are no longer able to laugh and who recognize this loss may exacerbate their pain. Although other writers have argued that humor serves the therapeutic role of jostling people out of their depression (e.g., Farrelly & Brandsmar, 1974), a beneficial effect may be restricted to particular stages of depression or particular types.

There is always a concern that if anxiety is very high, humor may contribute to hysterical laughter. Nevertheless, it is my experience that laughter usually makes anxious people feel better. Techniques used in the treatment of anxiety have more than a passing similarity to some of the techniques of humor. For example, I have found the techniques of cognitive therapy to parallel those of humor: Selective abstraction, arbitrary inference, overgeneralization, polarization, exaggeration, and personalization can be used to highlight self-defeating thinking and also to help people laugh at their self-handicapping cognitive styles (Moran, 1998b). The value of humor in the treatment of anxiety disorders, however, is not sufficient to warrant its unqualified recommendation in cases of secondary traumatic stress.

Emergency workers and those in many related helping professions typically begin their careers with the expectation of coping. It is important to have their experiences of trauma validated. Depending on how humor is used, it may be seen to challenge the validity of these experiences. In such cases, humor would be better directed toward dealing with symptoms in the here-and-now, rather than be directed toward past experiences. Other intervention techniques might be more appropriate to help people find meaning in past trauma, and humor workers would need to be cognizant of these interventions and their goals.

Across a variety of severe conditions, the use of humor to enhance coping with current difficulties has been demonstrated—for example, with the gastric-intestinal disorders that can accompany AIDS (AIDS Newsletter, 1996), the disability of arthritis (Skevington & White, 1998), and the stereotype of victim in women with breast cancer (Ryan, 1997). This may be one of the strengths of humor; it helps us deal with circumstances that have consequences in the immediate sense. That is, humor may not be the tool to use for finding meaning in past circumstances, but it may be the tool to use to reframe the impact of day-to-day stressors, to reduce tension, and to enhance social support. That said, we must also recognize that humor has been used in the most dire ongoing circumstances that have threatened meaning, such as the Holocaust and Stalin's oppression of Jews in Soviet Russia. Such use of humor is indicated in books with the titles *The Jokes of Oppression* (Harris & Rabinovich, 1988) and *Laughter in Hell: The Use of Humor in the Holocaust* (Lipman, 1991). It is important to recognize the jokes in these books were generated by those being oppressed.

FINAL COMMENTS

There are many books, workshops, and organizations established to help people learn to appreciate and express humor. It is beyond the scope of this chapter to add to this information other than to encourage the extension of therapy and stress management techniques into the areas covered by humor. Using humor may require a context of permission, permission from oneself as well as from others. Permission will come as a result of recognizing the potential benefits of humor. Humor may encourage emotional expression, enhance social support, allow reframing of circumstances, facilitate communication, aid physiological functioning, and provide ways of dealing with difficult organizations.

It is important to reiterate that humor is a vast and complex phenomenon. We have not considered important factors such as gender differences, cultural attitudes to humor, or humor intended to hurt others. Even within "healthy humor," different aspects of humor do not necessarily have the same effects. Despite the growing body of research in this area, it is still unclear which aspects of humor are most beneficial to well-being. Laughter appears highly promising as a means of inducing beneficial physical change, but not all humor is accompanied by laughter and not all laughter reflects the perception of humor. Using humor to cope (by trying to see a funny side of things) may help filter out sad information, but forming a coherent narrative about traumatic events may require a person to focus on sadness. Negative emotions are not always bad.

Recent research suggests humor production—that is, generating humor in social contexts—may be the best humor-related predictor of psychological well-being (Moran & Massam, 1997; Overholser, 1992). It is possible that humor production is effective because it increases social attractiveness and therefore increases social support. If this is so, the beneficial effect of humor is indirect rather than direct. These concluding remarks are not intended to negate the earlier focus on direct benefits of humor. Rather, they are offered in acknowledgment of the complexity of the topics of humor, emergency work, and secondary traumatic stress. There is considerable scope for humor to help.

Although observing the amount of suffering about us may challenge our ability to cope at times, humor can help sustain us in our work. It may prevent us becoming secondary victims of trauma, as well as help us continue to work with those who are primary victims. It is important, therefore, that we maintain our humor without guilt. As Mahatma Gandhi said, "If I had no sense of humor, I would long ago have committed suicide."

REFERENCES

AIDS Newsletter. (1996). Sydney, Australia: AIDS Support Group.

Alexander, D. A., & Wells, W. (1991). Reactions of police officers to body-handling after a major disaster: A before and after comparison. *British Journal of Psychiatry, 159,* 547–555.

Andrews, G., Pollack, C., & Stewart, G. (1989). Determination of defensive style by questionnaire. *Archives of General Psychiatry, 46,* 455–460.

Bizi, S., Keinan, G., & Beit-Hallahmi, B. (1988). Humor and coping with stress: A test under real-life conditions. *Personality and Individual Differences, 9,* 951–956.

Burger, J. (1993). *Personality* (3rd ed.). Pacific Grove, CA: Brooks/Cole.

Carver, C., Scheier, M., & Weintraub, J. (1989). Assessing coping strategies: A theoretically based approach. *Journal of Personality and Social Psychology, 56,* 267–283.

Cherkas, L., Hochberg, F., MacGregor, A., Snieder, H., & Spector, T. (2000). Happy families: A twin study of humour. *Twin Research, 3,* 17–22.

CNN (2001a). *America under attack: The day after.* Broadcast Wednesday, September 12, 2001.

CNN (2001b). *America under attack: America's new war.* Broadcast Monday, September 17, 2001.

Coser, R. L. (1960). Laughter among colleagues: Staff of a mental hospital. *Psychiatry, 23,* 81–99.

Cousins, N. (1979). *The anatomy of an illness, as perceived by the patient.* New York: Norton.

de Ridder, D. (1997). What is wrong with coping assessment: A review of conceptual and methodological issues. *Psychology and Health, 12,* 405–415.

Deckers, L., & Carr, D. (1986). Cartoons varying in low level pain-ratings, not aggression rating, correlate positively with funniness ratings. *Motivation and Emotion, 10,* 207–216.

Dews, S., Kaplan, J., & Winner, E. (1995). Why not say it directly? The social functions of irony. *Discourse Processes, 19,* 347–367.

Dixon, N. F. (1980). Humour: A cognitive alternative to stress? In I. G. Sarason & C. D. Spielberger (Eds.), *Stress and Anxiety, 7* (pp. 281–289). Washington, DC: Hemisphere.

Farrelly, F., & Brandsma, J. (1974). *Provocative psychotherapy.* Millbrae, CA: Celestial Arts.

Figley, C. R. (1995). Compassion fatigue as secondary traumatic stress disorder: An overview. In C. R. Figley (Ed.), *Compassion fatigue: Coping with secondary traumatic stress disorder in those who treat the traumatized* (pp. 1–20). New York: Bruner/Mazel.

Freud, S. (1905/1976). *Jokes and their relation to the unconscious.* (P. Strachey, Trans.). London: Penguin.

Fry, W. (1994). The biology of humor. *Humor, 7,* 111–126.

Haig, R. A. (1988). *The anatomy of humor: Biopsychosocial and therapeutic perspectives.* Springfield, IL: Charles C. Thomas.

Harris, D. A., & Rabinovich, I. (1988). *The jokes of the oppression.* Northvale, NJ: Aronson.

Janoff, B. (1974). Black humor, existentialism and absurdity: A generic confusion. *Arizona Quarterly, 30,* 293–304.

Jablonksi, C., & Zillman, D. (1995). Humor's role in the trivialisation of violence. *Medienpsychologie-Zeitschrift-fur-Individual and Massen-kommunikation, 7,* 122–133.

Johnson, H. A. (1990). Humor as an innovative method for teaching sensitive topics. Special issue: Faculty and staff development in geriatric education. *Educational Gerontology, 16,* 547–559.

Koestler, A. (1964). *The act of creation.* London: Hutchinson.

Kubie, L. (1971). The destructive potential of humor in psychotherapy. *American Journal of Psychotherapy, 172*, 861–866.

Kuhlman, T. L. (1988). Gallows humor for a scaffold setting: Managing aggressive patients on a maximum-security forensic unit. *Hospital & Community Psychiatry, 39*, 1085–1090.

Latta, R. L. (1999). *The basic humor process: A cognitive shift theory and the case against incongruity.* Berlin, Germany: Mouton de Gruyter.

Lefcourt, H. M., Davidson, K., & Kueneman, K. (1990). Humor and immune system functioning. *Humor 3*, 305–321.

Lefcourt, H. M., Davidson, K., & Shepherd, R. (1995). Perspective-taking humor: Accounting for stress moderation. *Journal of Social and Clinical Psychology, 14*, 373–391.

Lewis, P. (1997). The killing jokes of the American Eighties. *Humor, 10*, 251–283.

Lipman, S. (1991). *Laughter in Hell: The use of humor in the holocaust.* Northvale, NJ: Aronson.

Martin, R. A. (1989). Humor and the mastery of living: Using humor to cope with the daily stresses of growing up. In P. E. McGhee (Ed.), *Humor and children's development: A guide to practical applications* (pp. 35–154). New York: Haworth.

Martin, R. A. (1996). The Situational Humor Response Questionnaire (SHRQ) and Coping Humor Scale (CHS): A decade of research findings. *Humor, 9*, 251–272.

Martin, R. A., & Dobbin, J. P. (1988). Sense of humor, hassles and immunoglobulin A: Evidence for a stress-moderating effect of humor. *International Journal of Psychiatry in Medicine, 18*, 93–105.

Martin, R. A., & Lefcourt, H. M. (1983). Sense of humor as a moderator of the relation between stressors and moods. *Journal of Personality and Social Psychology, 45*, 1313–1324.

Martin, R. A., & Lefcourt, H. M. (1984). Situational Humor Response Questionnaire: Quantitative measure of sense of humor. *Journal of Personality and Social Psychology, 47*, 145–155.

McCann, I. L., & Pearlman, L. A. (1990). Vicarious traumatization: A framework for understanding the psychological effects of working with victims. *Journal of Traumatic Stress, 3*, 131–149.

McCarroll, J. E., Ursano, R. J., Wright, K. M., & Fullerton, C. S. (1993). Handling bodies after violent death: Strategies for coping. *American Journal of Orthopsychiatry, 63*, 209–214.

Mikes, K. (1971). *Laughing matter: Towards a personal philosophy of wit and humor.* New York: Library Press.

Mitchell, J. T. (1988, December). Development and functions of a critical incident stress debriefing team. *Journal of Emergency Medical Services*, 43–46.

Moran, C. C. (1990). Does the use of humour as a coping strategy affect stresses associated with emergency work? *International Journal of Mass Emergencies and Disasters, 8*, 361–377.

Moran, C. C. (1996). Short term mood change, perceived funniness and the effect of humour stimuli. *Behavioral Medicine, 22*, 32–38.

Moran, C. C. (1998a). Stress and emergency work experience: A non-linear relationship. *Disaster Prevention and Management, 7*, 38–46.

Moran, C. C. (1998b). Cognitive behaviour therapy for emotional disorders: The role of humour. *Australian Journal of Comedy, 4*, 89–102.

Moran, C. C., & Massam, M. (1997). An evaluation of humour in emergency work. *The Australasian Journal of Disaster and Trauma Studies, 3*. http://massey.ac.nz/`trauma/

Moran, C. C., & Massam, M. (1999). Differential influences of coping humor and humor bias on mood. *Behavioral Medicine, 25*, 36–42.

Moran, C. C., & Shakespeare-Finch, J. (in press). A trait approach to post-trauma vulnerability and growth. In D. Paton, J. M. Violanti, & L. M. Smith (Eds.), *Promoting capabilities to manage stress perspectives on resilience.* Springfield IL: Charles C. Thomas.

Moreall, J. (1987). *The philosophy of humor and laughter.* Albany, NY: State University of New York Press.

Mulkay, M. (1988). *On humour, its nature and its place in modern society.* Cambridge, U.K.: Polity Press.

Nerhardt, G. (1970). Humor and the inclination to laugh: Emotional reactions to stimuli of different divergence from a range of expectancy. *Scandinavian Journal of Psychiatry, 2,* 185–195.

Nevo, O., Keinan, G., & Teshimovsky-Arditi, M. (1993). Humor and pain tolerance. *Humor, 6,* 71–88.

Nezu, A. M., Nezu, C. M., & Blissett, S. E. (1988). Sense of humor as a moderator of the relation between stressful events and psychological distress: a prospective analysis. *Journal of Personality and Social Psychology, 54,* 520–525.

Overholser, J. C. (1992). Sense of humor when coping with life stress. *American Journal of Sociology, 47,* 799–804.

Palmer, C. E. (1983). A note about paramedics' strategies for dealing with death and dying. *Journal of Occupational Psychiatry, 56,* 83–86.

Paton, D., & Smith, L. (1996). Psychological trauma in critical occupations: Methodological and assessment strategies. In D. Paton & J. Violanti (Eds.), *Traumatic stress in critical occupations: Recognition consequences and treatment.* Springfield, IL: Charles C. Thomas.

Paton, D., & Violanti, J. (Eds.). (1996). *Traumatic stress in critical occupations: Recognition consequences and treatment.* Springfield, IL: Charles C. Thomas.

Pogrebin, P., & Poole, E. D. (1988). Humor in the briefing room. *Journal of Contemporary Ethnography, 17,* 189–194.

Robinson, V. M. (1991). *Humor and the health professions* (2nd ed.). Thorofare, NJ: Slack Inc.

Rosenberg, L. (1991). A qualitative investigation of the use of humor by emergency personnel as a strategy for coping with stress. *Journal of Emergency Nursing, 17,* 197–203.

Ruch, W. (Ed.). (1998). *The sense of humour: Explorations of a personality characteristic.* Berlin, Germany: Mouton de Gruyter.

Ryan, C. A. (1997). Reclaiming the body: The subversive possibilities of breast cancer humor. *Humor, 10,* 187–205.

Shalev, A. (1996). Stress versus traumatic stress: From acute homeostatic reactions to chronic psychopathology. In B. van der Kolk, A. McFarlane, & L. Weisaeth (Eds.), *Traumatic stress: The effects of overwhelming experience on mind, body and society.* New York: Guilford.

Skevington, S. M., & White, A. (1998). Is laughter the best medicine? *Psychology and Health, 13,* 157–169.

Steele, C. (1989, November). In defence of "black humour." *The Psychologist,* 488.

Taylor, A. J. W. (1996). Disaster and victim classification. In D. Paton & N. Long (Eds.), *Psychological aspects of disasters* (pp. 26–39). Palmerston North, New Zealand: Dunmore Press.

Taylor, A. J. W., & Frazer, A. G. (1982). The stress of post-disaster body handling and victim identification work. *Journal of Human Stress, 8,* 4–12.

Thompson, J., & Solomon, M. (1991). Body recovery teams at disasters: Trauma or challenge? *Anxiety Research,* 235–244.

Thomson, B. (1990). Appropriate and inappropriate uses of humor in psychotherapy as perceived by certified reality therapists: A delphi study. *Journal of Reality Therapy, 10,* 59–65.

Thorson, J., & Powell, F. (1993). Development and validation of a multidimensional sense of humor scale. *Journal of Clinical Psychology, 49,* 13–23.

Thorson, J., & Powell, F. (1996). Women, aging and sense of humor. *Humor, 9,* 169–186.

White, S., & Camarena, P. (1989). Laughter as a stress reducer in small groups. *Humor, 2,* 73–79.

Vaillant, G. (1977). *Adaptation to life.* Boston: Little Brown.

Yates, S. (2001). Finding your funny bone: Incorporating humour into medical practice. *Australian Family Physician, 30,* 22–24.

8

The Silencing Response
in Clinical Practice:
On the Road to Dialogue*

ANNA B. BARANOWSKY

Pat[1] listened, steeling herself to the story unfolding before her. She winced as she heard about the AIDS diagnosis, certain of the all-consuming illness and loss to follow. Her client's lover had the diagnosis confirmed. Her client, Jim, was probably HIV-positive as well, thought Pat. She cursed him in her mind for his carelessness, blaming him subconsciously for a disease he did not want, a disease he had taken precautions against. Outwardly, Pat went through consoling motions, saying it was tragic and sad. Then she quickly changed the session's focus by asking about their last session, trying to fault his depression and fatigue on poor vocational choices. Pat, a seasoned therapist, was unable to listen to the disturbing turn her client's life had taken and redirected the focus to reduce her own uneasiness.

The vignette above is a classic example of the silencing response and its ability to clip clinical potency and curtail therapeutic work.

*This article is dedicated to the caring professionals who willingly offered their services to victims and their loved ones, following the 2001 terrorist attack on the World Trade Center and the Pentagon. Special thanks to the Green Cross Director Dr. Charles Figley, Green Cross Scholar Kathy Dunning, and Associate Director of the Traumatology Insitute Eric Gentry for their comments in the development of this chapter and the Silencing Response Scale.
1. The people and places described in the vignettes are fictional and used for illustration purposes only. Any resemblance to persons living or deceased is purely coincidental.

Treating Post-Traumatic Stress Disorder (PTSD) often takes many hours of close attention to the stories, thoughts, and emotions that our clients bring to us. Yet it is not always possible to listen, fully honoring the courage and willingness of those who come to us trusting in our ability to help. Instead, there are times when the stories are overwhelming, beyond our scope of comprehension and desire to know, or simply spiraling past our sense of competency. That is the point at which we may notice our ability to listen becomes compromised. It is precisely at those times, when we feel overwhelmed and in need of skills, that we are left most vulnerable to the silencing response (SR).

This chapter is an exploration into compassion-fatigued caregivers who become vulnerable to utilizing the silencing response with their clients, as a means of ending their own discomfort and pain. The construct of compassion fatigue (Figley, 1995) informs us of the potential negative consequences of working with highly distressed or traumatized persons (Clemens, 1999). Compassion fatigue is a combination of secondary traumatic stress and burnout, both of which negatively impact on caregiving skills. The silencing response is a reaction based on a series of assumptions that guide the caregiver to redirect, shutdown, minimize, or neglect the traumatic material brought by another to the care provider.

I believe that all care providers are vulnerable to the silencing response, and do not at any point want to convey blame, guilt, or shame to those caregiver's who rely on this response. The primary purpose of this article is to identify, acknowledge, and address the impact of the SR on the caregiver's work, but never to fault. Recognizing "silencing" in one's own work is a practice in self-exploration. Dealing with silencing by addressing this tendency and negotiating a way back toward dialogue, honesty, and therapeutic efficacy demands the practice of courage. The secondary purpose of this article is to present the Silencing Response Scale, psychometric properties of the scale, and preliminary study findings.

DEVELOPMENT OF THE SILENCING RESPONSE AS A MANIFESTATION OF COMPASSION FATIGUE

Pat had been working effectively with Jim over several months prior to his troubling discovery. She had successfully assisted him with career decisions and helped alleviate motivational blocks. However, following the last session with Jim, Pat was unable to take her mind off of the encroaching disease. She felt plagued with thoughts of helplessness and images of decaying humanity and the pain of slow death. Her self-defense included unconscious attempts to minimize AIDS-related discussions. Despite her efforts, she became secondarily traumatized, or compassion fatigued, through her work with Jim.

Compassion fatigue (CF) is a construct introduced by Figley (1995) that rests on an earlier term, secondary traumatization, as a precursor and subcomponent of compassion fatigue. Figley (1996) defined compassion fatigue this way:

> A state of tension and preoccupation with the individual or cumulative trauma of clients as manifested in one or more ways: (1) reexperiencing the traumatic events, (2) avoidance/numbing of reminders of the traumatic event, and (3) persistent arousal. (p. 11)

Compassion fatigue occurs when an individual becomes secondarily traumatized during exposure to traumatic incidents directly experienced and relayed by another. The reverberation of another's trauma in a caregiver's life can take the form of PTSD-like symptomatology that mimics the other's disturbances. In fact, the wording in the *DSM–IV* Criterion A-1 of PTSD suggests that individuals may be traumatized by witnessing events that occur to another. PTSD symptoms may develop in response to "learning about unexpected or violent death, serious harm, or threat of death or injury experienced by a family member or other close associates" (American Psychiatric Association, 1994, p. 424). In addition, vulnerability to compassion fatigue becomes heightened when, caregivers are overwhelmed by unsupportive or emotionally toxic environments (Beavan & Stephens, 1999).

Another related term is *vicarious traumatization* (VT), used by McCann and Pearlman, (1990) which stands for the transformation that occurs when an individual begins to change in a manner that mimics a client's trauma-related symptoms. VT is a constructivist model in which the individual's inner experience and worldview are changed as a direct result of secondary exposure to trauma through his or her work. The individual begins to interpret and relate to the world in a new manner as the inner experience is altered by exposure to trauma work (Pearlman & McCann, 1995).

Figley (1995) noted that the number of persons seriously affected by traumatic events is greatly underestimated, largely due to the fact that "empathic induction of . . . [another's] experiences results in considerable emotional upset" (p. 4). It is precisely this human characteristic of empathy that acts as a double-edged sword for the clinician. It is empathy that sponsors caring work to excise the wounds of the past but also empathy that leaves the care providers vulnerable to the residual wounding inflicted during work that uncovers traumatic material (Landry, 1999). The defensive mechanism of the SR may follow shortly after the revelation of a particularly traumatic client memory.

Secondary traumatic stress disorder (STSD) is used interchangeably with compassion fatigue and is discussed thoroughly in Figley (1995). Compassion fatigue was chosen as a reference term due to its more accessible framing and connotation as opposed to STSD, which possesses a more pathological association. I hypothesize that the silencing response is related to compassion fatigue as a subcomponent. I believe that the SR becomes activated following the onset of compassion fatigue, thus leaving the already burdened caregiver further diminished in terms of efficacy and the trauma survivor further encumbered by the additional weight of shielding others from painful memories (Danieli, 1996). Solomon (1995) incorporated Jay (1991) to present an excellent illustration of the additional burden placed on the trauma survivor:

> He [Jay, 1991] portrays the trauma victim as one who is banished from human society as the bearer of "terrible knowledge": information which others, due to their protective denial tendencies, are unable and unwilling to hear or comprehend. (p. 280)

This tendency is reliably documented on a massive scale in the response of Red Cross personnel to concentration camp prisoners (Eisler, 1997). Miles Lerman, U.S. Holocaust Council chairman, was quoted as saying:

> People, good people, decided to look the other way, including people in the Red Cross. I wouldn't describe them as villains, but as part of the world that found it more convenient to remain silent. (p. A14)

The article by Danieli (1985) outlining the "Conspiracy of Silence" directly influenced this current chapter and my thoughts on the silencing response. Her term referred directly to the tendency of clinicians, family members, friends, colleagues, and acquaintances to limit Holocaust survivors from recounting tales of their own experiences. She wrote:

> Survivors' war accounts were too horrifying for most people to listen to or believe. Additionally, bystanders' guilt led many to regard the survivors as pointing accusing fingers at them. Survivors were also faced with the pervasively held myth that they had actively or passively participated in their own destiny by "going like sheep to the slaughter" and with the suspicion that they had performed immoral acts in order to survive. Reactions such as these ensured the survivors' silence about their Holocaust experiences. (Danieli, 1985, p. 298)

Earlier, Danieli (1984) examined a problematic relationship that developed between a psychotherapist and a Holocaust survivor due to the severe nature of the survivor's experiences. She concluded that therapists often felt unable to cope with the trauma encountered by this client group and that a tendency developed, among mental health care providers, to subtly encourage their patients to leave traumatic experiences out of therapy sessions. This denial of the impact of trauma on current functioning by the therapist became known as the Conspiracy of Silence (Danieli, 1984, p. 23). Danieli recognized that survivors were left with the continued burden of incomplete mourning. The implication of these findings is alarming; unless the therapist is able to approach the issues most salient to the client, there is little possibility of a successful therapeutic outcome (Baranowsky et al., 1998; Rosenman & Handelsman, 1990).

Although the terms compassion fatigue, vicarious traumatization, and the subsequent construct of the silencing response might be seen as related to the psychoanalytic terms *transference* and *countertransference,* I believe these terms do not adequately capture the compassion-fatigued care provider utilizing the silencing response. It is beyond the scope of this chapter to explore the differences between the terms. However, Figley and Kleber (1995) provide further explorations along these lines.

The importance of bringing awareness to the silencing response was stimulated out of the knowledge of Danieli's work (1984, 1985, 1996). The current motivation for this chapter is the evident link between compassion fatigue and the SR, along with a knowledge of the vital ingredient of trauma review in productive therapeutic trauma work (Baranowsky, 2000). PTSD misdiagnosis and subsequent insufficient treatment heightens the necessity of elucidating the SR construct.

MISDIAGNOSIS AND MISTREATMENT OF PTSD

Jim was not HIV-positive but continued to suffer following his close personal brush with life-threatening illness and the impact of bearing witness to the ravages of AIDS on his loved one. Pat knew her client was distressed. Her response was to spend most of the sessions in relaxation training, looking at the bright side, and moving on with life. Pat was a fine therapist, with many years of clinical experience, but she had never felt so helpless in her work. Somewhere deep inside she was cognizant of an old wound that left her feeling similarly helpless and distressed in the face of disease. Pat was not yet ready to face that old wound. She could see Jim's response transform into extreme distress. She herself was becoming increasingly disturbed prior to scheduled sessions with Jim. Regrettably, Jim was not being offered the treatment required, and his distress remained unresolved.

In their time of greatest need, traumatized persons may be inadequately attended to (Ochberg, 1993). A serious deficit exists in both adequate assessment and treatment of (PTSD) and other trauma-based disorders. When traumatic stress is not identified, individual treatment needs will not be met and treatment efficacy minimized (Danieli, 1996). A misdiagnosis scenario might entail a diagnosis of generalized anxiety disorder, social or agoraphobia, dissociative disorder, depression, or schizophrenia, with little recognition of existing PTSD symptomatology. Treatment often relies heavily on those protocols already in effect. These often include psychoeducational groups for stress and anxiety disorder, but they lack a traumatic review treatment component so often essential to symptom resolution (Friedman, 2000).

Numerous researchers have recognized misdiagnosis of PTSD in their study results and treatment reviews (Bende & Philpott, 1994; Domash & Sparr, 1982; Froehlich, 1992; Gayton, Burchstead, & Matthews, 1986). Friedman (1997) reported on two previously published studies that highlight the serious effect of misdiagnosis when a careful trauma history is not initiated.

> [At the extreme end of PTSD] patients may be totally incapacitated by this disorder and may appear to have a chronic mental illness. Such patients may be misdiagnosed . . . unless the clinician has undertaken a careful trauma history and diagnostic assessment. Two reports on psychotic female state hospital inpatients (Beck & Van der Kolk, 1987; Crain, Henson, Colliver, & MacLean, 1988) indicate that those with a history of childhood or adolescent sexual abuse were more likely than non-abused patients to have intrusive, avoidant/numbing and hyperarousal symptoms associated with abuse. In fact, 66% of these previously abused and currently psychotic patients met criteria for PTSD although none had ever received that diagnosis. (Friedman, 1997, p. 3)

Misdiagnosis leads to treatment-fit inadequacies as clients are not being offered validated treatment modalities shown to have clinical efficacy for PTSD (Dietrich et al., 2000).

BULL IN THE CHINA SHOP

If you had a bull in a china shop, there would be little chance you would miss it as items were trampled and damage occurred. Yet, somehow in clinical practice it is possible to miss, ignore, and redirect attention away from the impact of trauma on our clients' lives. It is crucial to recognize that trauma can be missed both passively and actively: actively, by failing to assess trauma and PTSD symptoms despite clear indications and attempts at trauma review by the client; passively, when a clinician recognizes trauma but unconsciously chooses to put attention elsewhere, due to feelings of clinical inadequacy. This can occur even among individuals who have been trained with awareness of PTSD assessment and treatment methodologies.

Missing trauma is most likely to occur when there are several assumptions operating in the clinician that lead to the silencing of the client. The assumptions that follow make up an interconnecting framework that singly or as a group impact on the clinician's ability to attend to recollections of traumatic material.

SILENCING RESPONSE ASSUMPTIONS

1. *I can't do anything about it.* Listening won't help, so I don't want to hear about it.
2. *If we touch on the traumatic event the person will fall apart or be destroyed.* The main notion is that talking about the trauma will only make things worse.

3. *I will be destroyed if I hear about the traumatic event.* The clinician fears knowing about the terror the individual has experienced.
4. *Good things happen to good people*—therefore you must be bad for this to have happened to you.
5. *This is too terrible to be true.*
6. *This violates my assumptive world* (i.e., my neighborhood is safe, therefore this couldn't have happened here).
7. *A strong need on the clinician's part to have the client "Just get over it."*
8. *If it happened to you it could happen to me.* This vulnerability to terrible events might lead the clinician to feel that what happened could be contagious.

There may be other reasons for the selective listening or active avoidance of traumatic memories (Sheldon, 2000; Zimmerman & Weber, 2000). These will become evident with the evolution of the silencing response construct. As these additional factors come to light, it will become clearer that we hold the keys to the obstacles in our path to efficacy as well as our transformation into fine clinicians. It is important to remember that refusal or inability to attend to trauma does not reduce its impact or make it go away. Failing to see, hear, or speak about trauma does not mean that it has not occurred. We cannot expect the signs and symptoms to vanish without appropriate care.

THE SILENCING RESPONSE SCALE

Jim's session was the last of the day, and Pat left her office feeling out of control with grief. Of course it was a serious situation, but why was she unable to function after these sessions, she wondered. She spent that evening alone and quiet. She was drawn to early memories of her mother dying of cancer when she was only 8 years old. Images of the sick room, the smells of acrid medicine, her mother without her lovely hair, tears and explanations about how her mom was going to leave them soon. Why did she have to go? We still wanted her. . . . Couldn't she convince her mom to stay? In the end, her mother died. Everyone was busy with preparations and their own sadness . . . she was alone. Pat was helpless in the face of her mother's cancer, which had taken over and won. Now as an adult she watched her client experience a similar grief, loss, and despair.

In order to make the silencing response more personally relevant, an SR scale was developed. The primary purpose of the scale was to aid clinicians wanting to identify the impact of the SR in their clinical work. The scale can be used in its present state, but remains in the developmental stages.

Based on pilot study data collected from 49 graduate-level Master's of Social Work and Family Therapy students, the scale exhibits internal reliability with an alpha coefficient of .69 and a split-half reliability of .63. The scale has a significant positive correlation with the Compassion Fatigue Scale–Revised at the $p = .002$ level. As Compassion Fatigue scores increase, silencing response scores increase. This suggests that Compassion Fatigue may be an umbrella under which the SR rests. The hypothesis is that when the clinician becomes Compassion-Fatigued, and therefore overwhelmed by work, the silencing response becomes active and further impedes clinical progress.

During the developmental stages of the Accelerated Recovery Program (ARP)[2] for treating compassion fatigue among caregivers, (created[3] by Gentry, Baranowsky, & Dunning, 1997), clinicians appeared to become most vulnerable to the SR when the clients' traumatic memories were reminiscent of unresolved events clinicians had endured (Baranowsky & Gentry, 1999a, 1999b; Gentry & Baranowsky, 1999). This led to the hypothesis that clinicians working with traumatic materials in their practices would continue to rely on the silencing response when dealing with client trauma *until they were able to resolve their own personal issues*. This awareness pointed the program development group toward the Compassion Fatigue–Silencing Response link. As expected, the strong correlation between the two scales offers preliminary support for the hypothesis above (see the Appendix for the complete Silencing Response Scale).

SILENCING RESPONSE SIGNPOSTS

The scale helps us to determine if the silencing response is operating in our work. However, it is also possible to identify the SR by reading through the signpost items listed below.

- Changing the subject
- Avoiding the topic
- Providing pat answers
- Minimizing client distress
- Wishing or suggesting that the client would "just get over it"
- Boredom
- Angry or sarcastic with clients
- Using humor to change or minimize the subject
- Faking interest or listening
- Fearing what the client has to say
- Fearing you will not be able to help
- Blaming clients for their experiences
- Not believing clients

---

2. For more information about this program please contact the author.
3. Under the direction of Dr. Charles Figley, Green Cross Projects Director.

- Feeling numb or avoidant prior to sessions
- Not being able to pay attention to your client
- Constantly being reminded of personal traumatic experiences when working with certain clients

TRAUMA RECOVERY AND REVIEW

Pat recognized her feelings of helplessness in the face of her mother's cancer. Her terror, grief, and loss was a terrible burden for an 8 year old. She was alone and forgotten while those around her dealt with their own pain. She became an expert in what she needed but never got during this sad time in her life. In this realization she recognized what she was not hearing from her client and what was needed. She was helpless to stop the progress of disease . . . she could not protect Jim from losing his loved one ... but she could stand by him with all her clinical wisdom, in support. Pat resolved to offer what was needed to her client.

Treating PTSD with general anxiety disorder groups, or with approaches for depression or schizophrenia, is a hit-or-miss method that frequently fails to offer the direct attention to the traumatic incident experienced by the client. By failing to focus directly on the critical incident, the client often is unable to show marked improvement. Tinnin (1995) wrote that those patients suffering from trauma responses are

Characterized by a failure to respond to the usual remedies and by intense, problematic reactions to therapists. However, a focus on trauma changes all of this [and] promotes a therapeutic alliance with the therapist. (p. 3)

Tinnin (1994), guided by Pierre Janet's (1889) work of over 100 years ago, used a hypnosis technique to aid clients in establishing a trauma narrative coalescing fragmented memories in order to arrive at resolution of the incident. Tinnin (1994) believed that, when memories are coded as images without narrative, they remain unfinished and responsible for recurrent and varied intrusive memories, dreams, and flashbacks. Until the experience is regained and tied to a narrative of a past event, it remains active, so the trauma is constantly recurring (Dietrich et al., 2000).

The trauma narrative process has been found by numerous researchers to be therapeutic for survivors as well as the offspring of trauma survivors (Dietrich et al., 2000; Fried & Waxman, 1988; Krell, 1986; Laub, 1991; Mor, 1990; Rosenbloom, 1988; Rosenman & Handelsman, 1990). Van der Kolk (1994) asserted:

Trauma interferes with declarative memory, i.e., conscious recall of experience, but does not inhibit implicit, or non-declarative memory, the memory system

that controls conditioned emotional responses, skills, and habits, and sensorimo-
tor sensations related to experience. (p. 256)

Thus, the trauma survivor remains riveted to the emotional and physiological
components of his or her experience without a full sense of cohesion that
comes from mastery over a detailed story of the traumatic event (Rothschild,
2000).

Attending to the traumatic incident is the essential "active ingredient" required for improvement, identified in the study of the same name.[4] Each of
the validated trauma treatment methods isolated in the Figley and Carbonell
(1995) study can be linked to ministering to the traumatic memories and working with them until the client's experiences are reframed and integrated in a
new and more adaptive manner. The treatment methods identified in the study
will be discussed briefly in the next section.

SKILLS DEVELOPMENT

When what you are doing in your clinical practice does not seem to end
with the desired results, it is time to reassess clinical strategies in a search for
efficacy. It is at this point that a willingness to change one's approach becomes essential. After investing considerable time working within a specific
approach it is inevitable that we will see change in some of our clients. It is
equally likely that other clients may be resistant to improvement. The clients
who seem to struggle the most and show the least improvement are the ones
who may shift even the most empathetic clinicians toward the SR. It then
becomes our responsibility, to ourselves and to our clients, to learn assessment and treatment methods for dealing with trauma as a means of counter-
acting the silencing response. Fortunately, there are dynamic methods for
dealing with trauma that have demonstrated therapeutic clinical improvement.

In the Figley and Carbonell (1995) study, four approaches to treating PTSD
were nominated following an intensive search of effective methods. Each approach was substantiated by a minimum of 300 clinicians who are practicing
trauma therapists. Gallo (1997) reported that level of distress,[5] four to six
months following treatment, resulted in a stable reduction in SUD ratings on
each of the four "verified" methods. In each method, the requisite element of
treatment involved a review in part (just briefly imagining the stressor) or
whole (a thorough retelling) of the traumatic incident(s). This and other studies reinforce our belief that, effective trauma treatment often relies on the

---

4. Almost all of the "active ingredient" treatment methods focused directly on the
client's trauma.

5.   Measured by self-reported Subjective Units of Distress rating (SUDs), where 1
= no distress and 10 = extreme distress with considerable reductions in ability to
function.

review of traumatic memories (Harvey, Orbuch, Chwalisz, & Garwood, 1991; Tinnin, 1994; Van der Kolk & Fisler, 1995). If the silencing response keeps the trauma story from observation it also likely to keep it from resolution.

Methods that have shown clinical efficacy include *eye movement desensitization and reprocessing* (EMDR; Shapiro, 1995); *visual/kinesthetic dissociation* (Bandler & Grinder, 1979); *traumatic incident reduction* (Gerbode, 1989); and *cognitive-behavioral field therapy* (Blake & Sennenberg, 1998). Acquiring such skills ensure that you have some tools to provide services that do make a difference. Sykes-Wylie (1996b) states that acquiring these sometimes controversial but often verified tools for PTSD therapy "instills in therapists a sense of confidence and mastery in their own capacity to help people, a feeling of hope that even presumably 'hopeless' clients can recover" (p. 37).

Having the skills to address trauma ensures a buffer zone both for compassion fatigue and the silencing response (Dietrich et al., 2000). Clinicians who get positive results when working with trauma survivors are making a difference. They see their clients improve and are therefore less vulnerable to compassion fatigue (Sykes-Wylie, 1996a) and subsequently the SR.

EXTINGUISHING TRAUMA

Recovery of memories is an important component in the integration of past trauma experiences and growth beyond the trauma response. PTSD symptomatology is the response to trauma that imposes long-term suffering on survivors. This suffering becomes exacerbated when previously harmless stimuli become anxiety provoking. In 1927, Pavlov informed us that stimuli–response chains can be paired on primary and secondary levels. This is important in understanding PTSD, as stimuli originally associated with traumatic events can become secondarily paired with innocuous stimuli and lead to the powerful stress reactions we see in PTSD (Rothschild, 2000).

This is illustrated in the following example: A woman is walking on a busy street and someone knocks her on the shoulder. She turns around and is surprised by a mugger who grabs her purse. In the ensuing struggle the woman is injured. The primary attack is re-stimulated when she is at a carnival eating popcorn. Someone taps her on the shoulder while she is walking down the midway. She is startled even though when she turns it is only a friend giving her a gentle pat on the shoulder. Nonetheless, she becomes anxious and panicked by the intrusion. Carnivals and popcorn are now secondarily associated to the primary trauma. This occurs through a simulation of the primary trauma and carnivals and popcorn commence to be feared and avoided stimuli.

In order for the individual to be free of posttraumatic responses (both primary and secondary) there is a need to return to the original trauma in a healthy, safe environment in order to begin the process of extinguishing the negative response links to stimuli. This requires an up-to-date knowledge of appropriate and effective trauma response treatment methods. Utilizing these current PTSD treatment tools increases one's ability to effect positive change.

FROM SILENCE TO DIALOGUE

In clinical work, the desired outcomes are improvement in functioning, a reduction in active symptoms, and a broadening of the client's life appreciation. Anything short of this suggests that treatment is incomplete or insufficient. If one does not address and treat trauma adequately, the outcome is likely to be limited. This will surely impact on the clinician in a negative manner, as without client improvement, one's clinical efficacy will be questioned by both the clinician and others, leaving the clinician susceptible to compassion fatigue (Sykes-Wylie, 1996a). When this is the case, clinician compassion fatigue symptoms may be heightened and include the usage of the silencing response. I believe that clinical skills can be recovered and even enhanced through the acknowledgment, identification, and working through of silencing response issues that arise in clinical work. However, it is important to realize that trauma recovery can occur at various durations, and tolerance for these timelines is essential. There is no one "fix-it" for every posttrauma response.

There are a number of pivotal questions we can ask ourselves as a means of moving toward therapeutic efficacy and away from the silencing response. In short, these questions are a way of keeping ourselves committed to our growth and enhancement as clinicians. Consider the following questions on your road to dialogue:

1. Are there any specific clients whose stories I have difficulty listening to?
2. In what ways do I silence my clients?
3. What am I defending against?
4. Why is this so hard for me to hear?
5. How can I listen to this client without silencing?
6. What do I need to feel safe?
7. What do I need to remain clinically effective?

The main question to ask here is this: If the client is not improving, are we missing the bull in the china shop?

CONCLUSION

Through courageous self-reflection and a dedication to excellence in clinical work, Pat was able to recover from compassion fatigue, move beyond the silencing response, gain necessary skills on the road to dialogue, and offer Jim appropriate treatment.

Compassion fatigue warns us of the danger of becoming overwhelmed by our work. The silencing response occurs when we are most in need of therapeutic proficiency and flexible communication skills. Unfortunately, the silencing response shuts down the therapeutic process and impedes communication. This blocks our clients' need to resolve their traumatic life experiences through memory recollection and investigation. Often, the most important thing we can do for trauma survivors, once they are safe, is to listen. The silencing response violates this process.

Skills development and self-reflection can act as a buffer to compassion fatigue and reduce usage of the silencing response. In this light, the time and expense of skills development and self-reflection far outweigh the cost of misdiagnosis and treatment-fit inadequacies.

It is always important for us to remember that traumatized clientele can be remarkably resilient. After all, they have already survived terrifying events. If clients are suffering from a posttrauma response, what they need is help in reclaiming their mental health equilibrium. By allowing the therapeutic work to commence without silencing, we may become part of the solution to our client's distress. Through reexamining past trauma, they may reclaim their lives.

APPENDIX 8.1
SILENCING RESPONSE SCALE

INSTRUCTIONS: This scale was developed to help caregivers identify specific communication struggles in their work. Choose the number that best reflects your experience (over the last 2 weeks) using the following rating system, where 1 signifies rarely or never and 10 means very often. Answer all items to the best of your ability.

1 = Rarely/Never —2—3—4—5—6—7—8—9— 10 = Always
Sometimes

☐ (1) Are there times when you believe your client(s) is repeating emotional issues you feel were already covered?
☐ (2) Do you get angry with client(s)?
☐ (3) Are there times when you react with sarcasm toward your client(s)?
☐ (4) Are there times when you fake interest?
☐ (5) Do you feel that listening to certain experiences of your client(s) will not help?
☐ (6) Do you feel that letting your clients talk about their trauma will hurt them?
☐ (7) Do you feel that listening to your clients' experiences will hurt you?
☐ (8) Are there times that you blame your clients for the bad things that have happened to them?
☐ (9) Are there times when you are unable to believe what your client is telling you because what they are describing seems overly traumatic?

☐ (10) Are there times when you feel numb, avoidant or apathetic before meeting with certain clients?

☐ (11) Do you consistently support certain clients in avoiding important therapeutic material when time is not a constraint?

☐ (12) Are there times when sessions do not seem to be going well or the client's treatment progress appears to be blocked?

☐ (13) Do you become anxiously aroused when a client is angry with you?

☐ (14) Are there times when you cannot remember what a client has just said?

☐ (15) Are there times when you cannot focus on what a client is saying?

Appendix Scoring

Once all items on the scale are completed, add item scores, then total and review the scoring protocol below. High risk = 95 to 150; moderate risk = 41 to 94; some risk = 21 to 40; minimal risk = 0 to 20. Scoring is based on the data compiled in the pilot study.

REFERENCES

American Psychiatric Association. (1994). *Diagnostic and statistical manual of mental disorders* (4th ed.). Washington, DC: Author.

Bandler, R., & Grinder, J. (1979). *Frogs into princes: Neuro-linguistic programming.* Moab, UT: Real People Press.

Baranowsky, A. B., Young, M., Johnson-Douglas, S., Williams-Keeler, L., & McCarrey, M. (1998). PTSD transmission: A review of secondary traumatization in Holocaust survivor families. *Canadian Psychology, 39,* 247–256.

Baranowsky, A. B., & Gentry, J. E. (1999a). *Compassion satisfaction manual.* Toronto, Canada: Psych Ink Resources. Available http://www.psychink.com

Baranowsky, A. B., & Gentry, J. E. (1999b). Workbook/*journal for a compassion fatigue specialist.* Toronto: Psych Ink Resources. Available http://www.psychink.com

Baranowsky, A. B. (Ed.). (2000). Special issue on neoteric treatment approaches in traumatology. *TraumatologyE* [On-line serial], 5(4). Available http://www.fsu.edu/~trauma/contv5i4.html

Beavan, V., & Stephens, C. (1999). The characteristics of traumatic events experienced by nurses on the accident and emergency ward. *Nursing Praxis in New Zealand, 14,* 12–21.

Beck, J. C., & Van der Kolk, B. (1987). Reports of childhood incest and current behavior of chronically hospitalized psychotic women. *American Journal of Psychiatry, 144,* 1474–1476.

Bende, B. C., & Philpott, R. M. (1994). Persistent post-traumatic stress disorder: Often missed but worth treating. *British Medical Journal, 309,* 526–528.

Blake, D., & Sennenberg, R. (1998). Outcome research on behavioral and cognitive-behavioral treatments for trauma survivors. In V. Follett, J. Ruzek, & F. Abueg (Eds.), *Cognitive-behavioral therapies for trauma* (pp. 16–47). New York: Guilfrod.

Callahan, R. J. (1994, September). *The five minute phobia cure: A reproducible revolutionary experiment in psychology based upon the language of negative emotions.* Paper presented at the International Association for New Science, Fort Collins, CO.

Clemens, L. A. (1999). *Secondary traumatic stress in rape crisis counselors: A descriptive study.* Master's thesis, California State University. Available UMI order No. AAD13–96034.

Crain, L. S., Henson, C. B., Colliver, J. A., & MacLean, D. G. (1988). Prevalence of a history of sexual abuse among female psychiatric patients in a state hospital system. *Hospital and Community Psychiatry, 39,* 300–304.

Danieli, Y. (1984). Psychotherapists' participation in the conspiracy of silence about the Holocaust. *Psychoanalytic Psychology, 1,* 23–42.

Danieli, Y. (1985). The treatment and prevention of long-term effects and intergenerational transmission of victimization: A lesson from holocaust survivors and their children. In C. R. Figley (Ed.), *Trauma and its wake: The study and treatment of post-traumatic stress disorder* (pp. 295–313). New York: Brunner/Mazel.

Danieli, Y. (1996). Who takes care of the caretakers? The emotional consequences of working with children traumatized by war and communal violence. In R. J. Apfel & B. Simon (Eds.), *Minefields in their hearts: The mental health of children in war and communal violence* (pp. 189–205). New Haven, CT: Yale University Press.

Dietrich, A. M., Baranowsky, A. B., Devich-Navarro, M., Gentry, E., Harris, C. J., & Figley, C. R. (2000). A review of alternative approaches to the treatment of post traumatic sequelae. *Traumatology, 6*, 251–271.

Domash, M. D., & Sparr, L. F. (1982). Post-traumatic stress disorder masquerading as paranoid schizophrenia: Case report. *Military Medicine, 147*, 772–774.

Eisler, P. (1997, May 2). Silent witness. *USA Today*, pp. A13–A16.

Figley, C. R. (1995). Compassion fatigue as secondary traumatic stress disorder: An overview. In C. R. Figley (Ed.), *Compassion fatigue: Coping with secondary traumatic stress disorder in those who treat the traumatized* (pp. 1–20). New York: Brunner/Mazel.

Figley, C. R. (1996, December). Integrating the theoretical and clinical components of grief and PTSD. *Trauma & Loss.* Workshop Package #2 presented at the Trauma & Loss Seminar, Toronto, Canada.

Figley, C. R., & Carbonell, J. (1995). *The "active ingredient" project: The systematic clinical demonstration of the most efficient treatments of PTSD. A research plan.* Tallahassee: Florida State University, Psychosocial Stress Research Program and Clinical Laboratory.

Figley, C. R., & Kleber, R. J. (1995). Beyond the "victim": Secondary traumatic stress. In R. J. Kleber, C. R. Figley, & B. P. R. Gersons (Eds.), *Beyond trauma: Cultural and societal dynamics* (pp. 75–98). New York: Plenum.

Fried, H., & Waxman, H. M. (1988). Stockholm's cafe 84: A unique day program for Jewish survivors of concentration camps. *The Gerontological Society of America, 28*, 87–95.

Friedman, M. J. (1997, April). PTSD diagnosis and treatment for mental health clinicians. *National Center for Post-Traumatic Stress Disorder* [On-Line]. Available: http://www.dartmouth.edu/dms/ptsd/clinicians.html

Friedman, M. J. (2000). PTSD diagnosis and treatment for mental health clinicians. In M. Scott & J. Palmer (Eds.), *Trauma and post-traumatic stress disorder* (pp. 1–14). New York: Cassell.

Froehlich, J. (1992). Occupational therapy interventions with survivors of sexual abuse. *Occupational Therapy in Health Care, 8*, 1–25.

Gallo, F. P. (1997, March). Reflections on active ingredients in efficient treatments of PTSD, Part I. *International Electronic Journal of Innovations in the Study of the Traumatization Process and Methods for Reducing or Eliminating Related Human Suffering* [On-line serial]. Available: Traumatology Forum–Green Cross Forum.

Gayton, W. F., Burchstead, G. N., & Matthews, G. R. (1986). An Investigation of the Utility of an MMPI Posttraumatic Stress Disorder Subscale. *Journal of Clinical Psychology, 42*, 916–917.

Gentry, J. E., & Baranowsky, A. B. (1999). *Treatment manual for accelerated recovery from compassion fatigue.* Toronto: Psych Ink Resources. Available http://www.psychink.com

Gentry, E., Baranowsky, A. B., & Dunning, T. (1997, November). *Compassion fatigue: Accelerated recovery program (ARP) for helping professionals.* Paper presented at the meeting of the International Society for Traumatic Stress Studies on Linking Trauma Studies to the Universe of Science and Practice, Montreal, Canada.

Gerbode, F. A. (1989). Handling the effects of past traumatic incidents. *Newsletter of the Institute for Research in Metapsychology, 1*, 1–13.

Harvey, J. H., Orbuch, T. L., Chwalisz, K. D., & Garwood, G. (1991). Coping with sexual assault: The roles of account-making and confiding. *Journal of Traumatic Stress, 4*, 515–531.

Janet, P. (1889). *L'Automatisme psychologique.* Paris: Felix Alcan. Reprint: Societe Pierre Janet, Paris, 1973.

Jay, J. (1991). Terrible knowledge. *Family Therapy Networker, 15,* 18–29.

Krell, R. (1986). Therapeutic value of documenting child survivors. *Annual Progress in Child Psychiatry and Child Development,* 281–288.

Landry, L. P. (1999). *Secondary traumatic stress disorder in the therapists from the Oklahoma City bombing.* Doctoral Dissertation, University of North Texas. Available UMI order No. AAT99-81105.

Laub, D. (1991). Truth and testimony: The process and the struggle. *American Imago, 13,* 267–283.

McCann, I. L., & Pearlman, L. A. (1995). Vicarious traumatization: A contextual model for understanding the effects of trauma on helpers. *Journal of Traumatic Stress, 3,* 131–149.

Mor, N. (1990). Holocaust messages from the past. *Contemporary Family Therapy, 12,* 371–379.

Ochberg, F. M. (1993). Gift from within. Posttraumatic therapy. In J. P. Wilson & B. Raphael (Eds.), *International handbook of traumatic stress syndromes* (pp. 773–783). New York: Plenum.

Pavlov, I. P. (1927). *Conditioned reflexes.* New York: Oxford University Press.

Pearlman, L. A., & Mac Ian, P. S. (1995). Vicarious traumatization: an empirical study of the effects of trauma work on trauma therapists. *Professional Psychology: Research and Practice, 26,* 558–565.

Rosenbloom, M. (1988). Lessons of the holocaust for mental health practice. In R. L. Braham (Ed.), *The Psychological perspectives of the holocaust and its aftermath* (pp. 145–159). New York: Columbia University Press.

Rosenman, S., & Handelsman, I. (1990). The collective past, group psychology and personal narrative: Shaping Jewish identity by memoirs of the Holocaust. *The American Journal of Psychoanalysis, 50,* 151–170.

Rothschild, B. (2000). *The body remembers: The psychophysiology of trauma and trauma treatment.* New York: Norton.

Shapiro, F. (1995). *Eye movement desensitization and reprocessing: Basic principles, protocols, and procedures.* New York: Guilford.

Sheldon, T. (2000, June). The day the world blew up. *Nursing Times, 96,* 12.

Solomon, Z. (1995). Oscillating between denial and recognition of PTSD: Why are lessons learned and forgotten? *Journal of Traumatic Stress, 8,* 271–282.

Sykes-Wylie, M. (1996a). Going for the cure. *The Family Therapy Networker, 20,* 20–25.

Sykes-Wylie, M. (1996b). Under the Microscope. *The Family Therapy Networker, 20,* 25–37.

Tinnin, L. (1994). *Time-limited trauma therapy for dissociative disorders.* Bruceton Mills, WV: Gargoyle Press.

Tinnin, L. (1995). The trauma response. In "Course Notes" from *Essentials of psychiatry: Trauma module* (pp. 1–4). Morgantown, WV: West Virginia University.

van der Kolk, B. (1994). The body keeps the scores: Memory and the evolving psychobiology of post traumatic stress. *Harvard Review of Psychiatry, 15,* 253–265.

van der Kolk, B., & Fisler, R. (1995). Dissociation and the fragmentary nature of traumatic memories: Overview and exploratory study. *Journal of Traumatic Stress, 8,* 505–525.

Zimmerman, G., & Weber, W. (2000). Care for the caregivers: A program for Canadian military chaplains after serving in NATO and United Nations peacekeeping missions in the 1990s. *Military Medicine, 9,* 687–690.

9

*Trauma Treatment Training for Bosnian and Croatian Mental Health Workers**

GEOFFRY D. WHITE

The war (1992–1995) in the former Yugoslavia has brought widespread destruction, displacement, and death to the civilian population, in addition to the usual military casualties of war (*National Geographic,* 1996). For example, the population of Bosnia was approximately 5 million in 1990 (before the war). Since then, 2 million people have become refugees; 250,000 civilians have been killed; and an estimated 30 to 50 thousand women and children have been systematically raped (Post et al., 1993). For the first time in history, the United Nations War Crimes Tribunal included sexual assault as a crime of war (Simons, 1996). Research has chronicled the psychological sequelae of the rape, torture, and traumatization of Bosnian and Croatian women and children (Kozaric-Kovacic, Folnegovic-Smaic, Skrinjaric, Szajnberg, & Marusic, 1995; Simons, 1999; Yule, 2000).

Trauma induced by terrorism has come to refer to the unique destructive effects (Herman, 1992). The term *ethnic cleansing* has come to refer to the unique genocidal intentions by the Serbians aimed primarily at the Bosnian Muslims (Maass, 1996; Simons, 1999). There is little doubt about the perva-

*The trainers for this project were Gerald Puk, Susan Rogers, Steven Silver, and Geoffry White. Thanks to the EMDR institute and Catholic Relief Services for their financial and emotional support for this project.

sive incidence of posttraumatic stress disorder (American Psychiatric Association, 1994; Peterson, Prout, & Schwarz, 1991) among the general population of Croatia, and especially of Bosnia. It has been noted that refugees of war often suffer as much as those who remain (Marsella, Bornemann, Ekblad, & Orley, 1994). It has been estimated that over the course of its three-year siege, Sarajevo experienced the equivalent of 200 Oklahoma City bombings. Of special interest to the current report is the secondary traumatic stress disorder (also known as compassion fatigue; Figley, 1995) and vicarious traumatization (McCann & Pearlman, 1990) experienced by mental health caregivers ministering to the needs of the survivors of the war and ethnic cleansing (genocide).

The literature contains numerous reports evaluating the impact of the war on the civilian population (e.g., Kozaric-Kovacic, Folnegovic-Smalc, & Marusic, 1993; Solvig, 1993; Zivcic, 1993). However, there have been relatively few reports in professional journals of attempts to add effective, empirically tested trauma treatment interventions into the repertoire of indigenous Bosnian, Croatian, or Serbian mental health professionals. The current report describes two trauma treatment training projects that I conceptualized, organized, and carried out in 1995. The projects had three goals:

1. Train indigenous mental health workers in effective trauma treatment methods,
2. Evaluate and treat the secondary PTSD (compassion fatigue) of those mental health workers,
3. Develop regularly scheduled peer supervision/consultation groups so trainees would have regularly scheduled opportunities to discuss and practice their new skills.

The third goal included a supervision component whereby, following each meeting, the trainees' questions and concerns would be immediately faxed or e-mailed to the consultant and trainers. Within a short time, the consultants would respond to these concerns via the same telecommunications systems, thereby creating an efficient international supervision and consultation system.

BACKGROUND

In 1991, I began to follow with interest and concern the breakup and eventual partitioning of the former Yugoslavia (Maass, 1996; Reiff, 1995; Silber & Little, 1995). I witnessed with horror the beginning of the third genocide in Europe this century. As a psychologist with a long-time interest in trauma, I wanted to offer some form of trauma treatment training to mental health professionals in the Balkans. I expected that these caregivers would be especially vulnerable to burnout and compassion fatigue (Figley, 1995), and therefore, these phenomena should be addressed as well. I reviewed and evaluated the current approaches to PTSD and finally settled on a relatively new, but empirically based method known as *eye-movement desensitization and reprocessing* (EMDR; Shapiro, 1996).

THE TRAINING PROGRAM

EMDR is a short-term treatment for trauma-based mental disorders described in detail in a textbook by Francine Shapiro, who developed the technique in the mid-1980s (Shapiro, 1995). The procedure has since been extended to other populations, such as children (Tinker & Wilson, 1999), and the neurobiology of EMDR has been explicated (Bergman, 1998). The initial reports of this method indicated that it reduced the distress associated with traumatic memories with a few treatment sessions. These case reports encouraged the development of methodologically sound, large sample studies. The most rigorous study to date was published in the *Journal of Consulting and Clinical Psychology* (Wilson, Becker, & Tinker, 1995). In this study, 80 subjects suffering from various forms of trauma were treated with three 90-minute EMDR sessions by one of five grained clinicians. EMDR was demonstrated to be effective compared to and untreated, waiting-list control group (which later received treatment). The results were maintained at 90-day followup. A subsequent report verified that the results continued to be upheld at a one-year followup evaluation (Wilson et al., 1995).

I contacted Francine Shapiro in 1993 and asked if she would be interested in supporting an effort to do EMDR training with former Yugoslavian mental health workers. At first I proposed that a group of trainees would be brought to the United States for training. When that proved impossible, it was suggested that a small group of EMDR trainers be sent to Croatia, Bosnia, and eventually Serbia. Dr. Shapiro was very supportive and helpful throughout the project. Indeed, she arranged for three highly skilled EMDR trainers to conduct the workshops. In addition, she covered all travel expenses for the Croatia trip. Catholic Relief Services (CRS) paid all expenses for the trip to Bosnia.

FIRST TRAINING: ZAGREB, CROATIA

Simultaneously with arranging for the EMDR training with Francine Shapiro, I searched for mental health organizations to train in Bosnia and Croatia. Eventually, with the help of the International Red Cross's program in the Balkans, I was introduced to two humanitarian assistance programs: the Society of Psychological Assistance (supported by CRS) and Ruke, another indigenous, nongovernmental organization (NGO). These two groups hosted two three-day training programs, which were conducted in Zagreb, Croatia, in March of 1995. The trainers trained approximately 40 psychologists and psychiatrists, who worked in diverse settings, primarily with refugees but also in hospitals, clinics, day treatment programs, and even a few people in private practice. Over the course of our stay in Croatia, the trainers visited and consulted with the staff of several refugee camps.

A special effort was made to invite mental health professionals form Bosnia to come to the Zagreb program. Two psychiatrists and a psychologist risked their lives on a perilous journey to Zagreb from Sarajevo, the besieged capital of Bosnia, to attend the training program. They were very satisfied with the results of the training and immediately requested a similar program for their colleagues in Sarajevo.

EVALUATION OF THE PROGRAM

Program effectiveness was assessed by means of the standardized anonymous course evaluations used by CRS for all training programs it sponsors. The program received high ratings in terms of overall course evaluation, averaging 4.73 on a 5-point scale.

SARAJEVO

Through a combination of persistence and luck, a second EMDR training program was conducted in Sarajevo in December of 1995. The trainers were there after the frequently broken cease-fire took effect. It was an historic coincidence that our day off was December 14, the day the Dayton Peace Accords were signed in Paris. During our stay in Sarajevo, daily machine gun and mortar fire could be heard in the city. There were more days in Sarajevo without water, electricity, or gas than there were days when basics were available. The day the team arrived a storm dropped a record two feet of snow, paralyzing an already disabled city.

As before, two training programs were conducted, with a day off in between. The first group required translators for a non-English-speaking set of 16 trainees. The second group ($n = 11$) spoke English, which allowed several of the translators to sit in as trainees. The anonymous course evaluations indicated that 75% of the participants rated the training as "very useful" (the highest rating available). The remaining 25% rated the program "useful." No lower ratings were given.

COMPASSION FATIGUE: EVALUATION AND TREATMENT

Compassion fatigue focuses on those individuals who provide therapy to victims of PTSD, who themselves often become victims of secondary traumatic stress disorder as a result of helping or wanting to help traumatized persons (Figley, 1995). It is often the case that health care professionals will not, for various reasons, identify themselves as suffering form compassion fatigue. Although one can admire the courage and determination to help those in need, burned-out caregivers might either incorrectly or harmfully apply therapy techniques with their patients. It is therefor desirable to include a method to evaluate the level of secondary PTSD among trainees. Supervisors and project directors can use this data to identify individuals who need treatment for compassion fatigue. With the help of Charles Figley (1994, personal communication), we had the Compassion Fatigue Self-Test (Figley, 1995) translated into the native language of our trainees in Croatia and Bosnia. This brief inventory was built into the training program as part of the followup consultation groups, the third component of the program.

CONSULTATION/SUPERVISION GROUPS

All too often, training programs do not include a component for an ongoing followup evaluation and remediation of those skills taught during the workshop. I was concerned that this was particularly important for our group of traumatized and depressed mental health workers in the Balkans.

Based on these assumptions, I worked with the indigenous program directors to establish monthly followup consultation/supervision groups, in which trainees could review and practice what they learned during the workshops. These groups, which have met on a frequent (if not monthly) basis have proved invaluable in a number of ways. They allow the trainees to (a) discuss problems implementing the therapy procedures presented during the workshops; (b) practice EMDR with each other, thereby ameliorating some of the burnout they all experience; and (c) evaluate their level of secondary PTSD by completing Figley's Compassion Fatigue Self-Test at the outset of each group meeting basis.

An innovation aspect of these groups is that they are amenable to international supervision via fax and e-mail. That is, at the end of each monthly meeting the trainees' questions and concerns are faxed or e-mailed to the EMDR trainers. Within a short time, they receive responses to their questions. In addition to these advantages, this approach helps maintain their morale and the conviction that the outside world is standing by to help and maintaining an ongoing commitment to them.

CONCLUSIONS

The formal and informal evaluations of the program indicated that the workshop participants were pleased with the training. Results from the ongoing monthly consultation groups show a similar, but less objectively evaluated, level of satisfaction. The supervisors of the followup consultation groups are pleased with the rapid assessment device for evaluation compassion fatigue. It has improved their ability to identify group members who are in distress. It also provides a form of self-monitoring for the trainees, confronting them with their own level of trauma and depression.

The program directors from both settings indicate that approximately 50% of the trainees regularly attend the followup consultation groups. Because these groups were voluntary, this can be taken as an indirect measure of the value trainees placed on the training program. Also, a 50% attendance rate is quite good, considering that many of these mental health professionals must travel long distances over less-than-safe roads to attend the meetings.

As of March 1997, it has been two years since the first training in Zagreb, and 15 months since the Sarajevo workshop. Phone, fax, and e-mail contact with the program staff has been accomplished with little difficulty. With minimal involvement on the part of the trainers, a cost-effective method for international supervision has been implemented. Plans are under way to continue to develop and refine this approach, as it shows promise as an effective way to maintain the results of the trauma treatment training program.

Future plans include refinement of the evaluation and treatment of compassion fatigue. Many caretakers have difficulty admitting to others and to themselves their burnout and emotional distress and then asking for help. Using a rapid assessment device, such as Figley's Compassion Fatigue Self-Test, they now have an expedient way to identify those health care providers in need of help. Charles Figley has offered his assistance in tailoring the assessment and treatment of compassion fatigue to the needs of health care professionals in the Balkans.

Following each program, we received requests for advanced training. It has been suggested that the next workshop consist of a combined group of trainees from Bosnia and Croatia. This is appealing for several reasons. For one, ethnic pluralism was once Bosnia's trademark (Maass, 1996; Reiff, 1995). However, the Dayton Peace Accords partitioned Bosnia into two parts: Bosnian Serbian Republic and the Federation of Bosnia and Herzegovina, a government that unites Bosnian Croatians and Bosnian Muslims (*National Geographic,* 1996). There is concern over whether the parties to the new Bosnian Federation will be able to work together. This is partially because there was a period of time during the war when Bosnian Croats conducted their own ethnic cleansing against the Bosnian Muslims and destroyed many of their historic and cherished buildings, mosques, and bridges (e.g., the famous centuries-old Mostar Bridge; Maass, 1996). Attempts must be made to reconcile these two groups, who lived together peacefully before the war. As Staub (1998) pointed out:

> [H]uman beings tend to create "us"–"them" differentiations and stereotypes. We see our values and way of life as natural and good and easily see others who diverge as bad. . . . Cross-cutting relations among subgroups of society and between nations can overcome these tendencies. To evolve an appreciation of alikeness and a feeling of connectedness, members of subgroups of society must live together, work together, play together, their children must go to school together. (p. 274)

Thus, a followup workshop that would combine our Croatian and Bosnian trainees might contribute something toward peaceful relations, at least between mental health professionals in the new Bosnia. A more complex and controversial plan involves conducting workshops of Serbian mental health professionals. A plan has been under way to do several EMDR programs in Belgrade, the capital of Serbia. An official of the UN protection force expressed interest in a training program in Banja Luka, the likely new capital of the Serbian Republic. The politics of this are complex: On the one hand, our Bosnian colleagues may have a negative reaction to our providing help to people who have been their deadly enemy over the last four years. On the other hand, reducing the overall level of PTSD in the region may help to safeguard the peace. We had an interesting exchange on this issue with the Bosnian psychiatrist who headed one of the NGOs that sponsored the Croatia trip. She posed this question to us: "If asked, would you go to Serbia and do your training program?" "Yes," we impulsively answered. "Good," she said. "The killing will only stop when the pain stops." These issues are currently under discussion.

Finally, concurrent with the program described above, I conducted a photography/essay project. The purpose of this project was to create a vehicle for the children who survive to describe, in words and photographs, their experience of the war.

On both trips, I brought along a few dozen disposable 35-mm cameras. I obtained permission and help from the program staff to have children take photographs of their environment. I also asked the children to write a few pages describing their lives during the previous three years. The results were remarkable. The photographs taken by the children and teenagers are as stark as their writings: bombed-out buildings, a teen mourning at the snowy grave site of a young friend, tanks rolling down city streets, metal dumpsters installed as barricades at street intersections and bearing the words "Shoot Zone, Sniper Danger." There is also optimism and hope contained within the stories and photos: A smiling mother and son pose for a photo in a snow bank; the hopeful face of a teenage girl on the verge of womanhood smiles into the camera lens; an intact stained-glass window shines in the shell of a building that once housed one of the world's most beautiful libraries. I believe that taking the photos and writing the stories was therapeutic for these children. I hope the results will open some eyes and hearts. I have excerpted here some of the stories (Appendix 9.1), which I have come to call *Sarajevo Diary*.

As of February 2000, *Sarajevo Diary* has been on exhibit at the United Nations (December 1999 to February 2000) and at the Museum of Tolerance/ Simon Wiesenthal Center in Los Angeles (November 1998 to February 1999).

APPENDIX 9.1
EXCERPTS FROM CHILDREN'S STORIES

I would like for war to stop so we can go out and play. My house is ruined the same way as my whole country. But I'm alive and when I group up I will defend by Bosnia. (Adnan Husic, 6 years old, born 5/27/90)

What is peace and what does it look like? When the war started, I was 4 years old. One night two shells landed on our roof. My grandmother laid on top of me to protect me with her body. I will never be a soldier because I don't want to kill people. (Rijad Softic, 7 years old, born 3/2/89)

We were a happy family until the war started. We began to hide in basements which were dark and cold. Father told me that two of our neighbors were killed. One shell landed above my window. Soon I adjusted to the shelling. I often sat in the kitchen and just listened. (Alisa Ceric, 11 years old, born 1/22/84)

I tried to imagine what the killer in the hills looks like and if he has children of his own. How does he look in the moment when he launches the shell or when he fires at innocent children? (Vedran Vujovic, 12 years old, born 12/26/83)

God, what have we survived? A beautiful, cultured city in a moment was transformed into a concentration camp. From the surrounding hills, thousands of shells are landing daily. The city is surrounded. For the first weeks, I took it in with curiosity. But later when leaving the basement meant death, when houses around me began to burn, when we began to starve—I understood. (Aleksandra Jelacic, 13 years old, born 11/15/81)

REFERENCES

American Psychiatric Association. (1994). *Diagnostic and statistical manual of mental disorders* (4th ed.), Washington, DC: Author.
Bergmann, U. (1998). Speculations on the neurobiology of EMDR. *Traumatology, 4*(1), 14.
Figley, C. R. (1995). *Compassion fatigue: Coping with secondary traumatic stress disorder in those who treat the traumatized.* New York: Brunner/Mazel.
Herman, J. L. (1992). *Trauma and recovery: The aftermath of violence—from domestic abuse to political terror.* New York: Harper-Collins.

Kozaric-Kovacic, D., Folnegovic-Smalc, V., & Marusic, A. (1993). Psychological disturbances among 47 Croatian prisoners of war tortured in detention camps. *Journal of the American Medical Association, 270,* 575.

Kozaric-Kovacic, D., Folnegovic-Smalc, V., Skrinjaric, J., Szajnberg, N. & Marusic, A. (1995). Rape, torture, and traumatization of Bosnian Croatian women: Psychological sequelae. *The American Journal of Orthopsychiatry, 35,* 428–435.

Maass, P. (1996). *Love thy neighbor: A story of war.* New York: Knopf.

Marsella, A. J., Bornemann, T., Ekblad, S., & Orley, J. (Eds.). (1994). *Admidst peril and pain: The mental health and well-being of the world's refugees.* Washington, DC: American Psychological Association.

McCann I., & Pearlman, L. A. A. (1990). *Psychological trauma and the adult survivor: Theory, therapy and transformation.* New York: Brunner/Mazel.

National Geographic. (1996, June). *In focus: Bosnia.* pp. 48–61.

Peterson, K. C., Prout, J. F., & Schwarz, R. A. (1992). *Post-traumatic stress disorder: A clinician's guide.* New York: Plenum.

Post, T., Stiglmayer, A., Lane, C., Brnad, J., Warner, M. & Sparkman, R. (1993, January 4). A pattern of rape. *Newsweek.*

Reiff, D. (1995). *Slaughterhouse: Bosnia and the failure of the west.* New York: Simon & Schuster.

Shapiro, F. (1995). *Eye movement desensitization and reprocessing: Basic principles, protocols, and procedures.* New York: Guilford.

Shapiro, F. (1996). Eye movement desensitization and reprocessing (EMDR). Evaluation of controlled PTSD research. *Journal of Behavior Therapy and Experimental Psychiatry, 27,* 209–218.

Silber, L., & Little, A. (1995). *The death of Yugoslavia.* London: Penguin Books.

Simons, A. (1999). Making sense of ethnic cleansing. *Studies in Conflict & Terrorism, 22,* 1–20.

Simons, M. (1995, June 28). The first time, court defines rape as war crime. *New York Times.*

Solvig, E. (1993). Psychosocial adaptation of children while housed in a Swedish refugee camp: Aftermath of the collapse of Yugoslavia. *Stress Medicine, 9,* 159–166.

Staub, E. (1989). *The roots of evil: The origins of genocide and other group violence.* New York: Cambridge University Press.

Tinker, R., & Wilson, S. (1999). *Through the eyes of a child: EMDR with children.* New York: Norton.

Wilson, S. A., Becker, L. A., & Tinker, R. H. (1995)). Eye movement desensitization and reprocessing (EMDR) treatment for psychologically traumatized individuals. *Journal of Consulting and Clinical Psychology, 632,* 928–937.

Yule, W. (2000). From pogroms to "ethnic cleansing": Meeting the needs of war affected children. *Journal of Child Psychology & Psychiatry & Allied Disciplines, 41*(6), 695–702.

Zivcic, I. (1993). Emotional reactions of children to war stress in "Croatia." *Journal of the American Academy of child and Adolescent Psychiatry, 32,* 709–713.

10

Strategies for Managing Disaster Mental Health Worker Stress*

DIANE MYERS
DAVID F. WEE

Since the 1970s, professional publications in the field of mental health, emergency services, and disaster management have abounded with reports and studies on the effects of trauma intervention on the responders. During the 1980s and 1990s, much of that literature focused on the psychological effects of trauma exposure among *first responders*—firefighters, police officers, and emergency medical personnel. Simultaneously, as the number of natural and technological disasters was on the rise, studies of the effects of large-scale disaster events on both the victims and the disaster responders increased. Wee and Myers (1998) reviewed some of the literature related to these two populations. In 1995, Figley and his contributing authors provided a groundbreaking exploration and focus on those professionals who provide therapy to victims of trauma: crisis workers, trauma counselors, nurses, physicians, and other caregivers who become victims themselves of secondary traumatic stress disorder (STS) or compassion fatigue. A very small number of studies have further narrowed the focus of research to examine the psycho-

---

*Government publications referenced in this chapter are in the public domain and are not copyrighted. They may be reproduced or copied without permission of the government agency or from the authors. Citation of the source is requested.

181

logical impacts of providing *mental health counseling* to the specialized context of large-scale disasters (Bartone, Ursano, Wright, & Ingraham, 1989; Berah, Jones, & Valent, 1984; Frederick, 1977; Hodgkinson & Shepherd, 1994; Raphael, Singh, Bradbury, & Lambert, 1984; Wee & Meyers, 1997; Winget & Umbenhauer, 1982). Wee and Myers (1998) studied the psychological impact of disaster mental health work on the counselors from Project Heartland, who provided treatment and supportive mental health services to the victims of the Oklahoma City bombing. Most significant among their findings were the following:

- Counselors were psychologically affected by their work, whether or not they personally experienced the bomb blast.
- Of the counselors surveyed, 64.7% exhibited some degree of severity for posttraumatic stress disorder (PTSD) as measured by the Frederick Reaction Index (FRI).
- Additionally, 44.1% of counselors exhibited "caseness" (considered a case or positive risk based on scores at or above the 90th percentile for non-patient norms) on the SCL-90-R Global Severity Index score or two-dimensional T-scores greater than or equal to a T-score of 63.
- Nearly three-quarters (73.5%) of counselors were rated as being at moderate risk (23.5%), high risk (29.4%), or extremely high risk (20.6%) for compassion fatigue, as measured by the Compassion Fatigue Self Test for Psychotherapists (Figley, 1995).
- Also, 76.5% of counselors were rated as being at moderate risk (35.3%), high risk (26.5%), or extremely high risk (14.7%) for burnout, using the same Compassion Fatigue Self Test.
- Over half (52.9%) of the counselors evaluated disaster mental health work as more stressful than other jobs they had experienced.
- Longer duration of work providing counseling services to disaster victims was significantly related to higher mean distress scores.
- Certain categories of counselors had levels of distress higher that their coworkers, including administrators of the counseling program, males, and ethnic groups other than Caucasian.

In their study, Wee and Myers (1997, 1998) found that both the severity of distress and the proportion of distressed workers in this group of counselors were higher than those in most other studies of trauma workers reported in the literature. One other study reporting a high proportion of disaster counselors with some degree of severity for PTSD (60.5%) examined those counselors providing disaster mental health services in Los Angeles's Project Rebound following the 1994 Northridge earthquake.

The counselors studied by Wee and Myers in both the Oklahoma City bombing and the Northridge earthquake constitute a unique group of disaster workers, in that their work is *long-term*. The counselors were employed by local mental health agencies through funding from the Federal Emergency Management Agency (FEMA) Crisis Counseling Program. Similar long-term mental health programs for victims of disasters are often established by local agencies or by university medical centers. The counselors' work usually begins in the first days after the disaster and may extend for a year of more into the recovery period.

Multiple stressors affect these long-term disaster counselors. Myers (Hartsough & Myers, 1985) outlined some of these stressors. Some factors are related to the *individual,* such as health, socioeconomic situation, preexisting stresses, previous trauma and loss, coping skills, identity and self-expectations, culture, spiritual beliefs, and perceptions and interpretations of the event. *Interpersonal factors* include relationships, social supports, and impact of the disaster on the individual and family. *Community factors* include size and nature of the community, degree of social solidarity, prior disaster experience, response of the community to the disaster, and amount of initial and ongoing disruption due to the disaster. Finally, factors related to the *disaster* itself will affect the workers (the presence or absence of a warning, the type of disaster, and scope of the disaster, to name a few). Some of these factors may serve to strengthen and support the worker, whereas other factors may put a worker at risk for compassion fatigue and traumatic stress. All of these factors need to be considered in an assessment of how each individual worker will be affected in the long-term.

Several factors, however, are specific to counselors working in the long-term disaster aftermath in their own community. First, regardless of whether a counselor sustained personal loss in the disaster, he or she will most likely be affected merely by being a part of the affected community:

> A disaster is an awesome event. Simply seeing massive destruction and terrible sights evokes deep feelings. Often, residents of disaster-stricken communities report disturbing feelings of grief, sadness, anxiety, and anger, even when they are not themselves victims. . . . Such strong reactions confuse them when, after all, they were spared any personal loss. These reactions are normal in every way; everyone who *sees* a disaster is, in some sense, a victim. (Hartsough & Myers, 1985, p. 72)

Bolin and Bolton (1996) explained that communities as a complex social whole constitute symbolic objects that provide orientation for residents (Fried, 1963; Hunter, 1974, 1975) and are the basis of residents' "cognitive maps" (Suttles, 1972; Trainer & Bolin, 1976). These mental maps keep the local community safe, familiar, and readily accessible to the residents. Residents identify with their communities and, in doing so, form part of the concept of themselves (Hunter, 1974). In effect, the "wounding" of the community itself can disrupt an individual's sense of self-identity and feeling of safety, regardless of whether the individual suffered personal losses. In short, disaster counselors who reside in the damaged community will inevitably be affected themselves and come to their work bearing personal pain from the event.

In addition to being personally affected by a disaster in their own community, therapists counseling disaster victims face many of the same stressors common to all trauma therapists working with victims beyond the immediate crisis stage. Unlike crisis workers (e.g., psychiatric crisis intervention staff, debriefers, or hotline counselors), whose response is to the immediate effects of a catastrophic event on the survivor, long-term disaster counselors are faced with the prolonged and usually compounded aftermath of the disaster. Counseling victims in the aftermath of disaster involves repeated exposure to the event through the client's recounting and reexperiencing of the event in the counselor's presence. It also involves exposure to the survivor's reactions to the disaster (e.g., intense emotional pain, fear, rage, despair, and hopelessness). In addition, the disaster counselor is exposed to the institutional and other social responses that revictimize the victim, and over which the trauma counselor may have little control (Dutton & Rubinstein, 1995). The process of obtaining temporary housing, replacing belongings, getting permits to rebuild, applying for government assistance, seeking insurance reimbursement, and acquiring help from private or voluntary agencies often is fraught with rules, red tape, hassles, delays, frustrations, and disappointment. Individuals who felt competent and effective before the disaster may experience a serious erosion of self-esteem and confidence, and feelings of helplessness and anger are common, both in the victims and in those who counsel them (Meyers, 1994b). Disaster therapists, like other trauma therapists, become, to some extent, bystanders and helpless (although not silent) witnesses to damaging events (Pearlman & Saakvitne, 1995) and ongoing strife. This helplessness to change what the disaster and its aftermath wreak on the victims challenges the therapist's helper identity (Staub, 1989). In addition, because the disaster counselors task often is quite complex, the results of the therapists' work can be mixed and very slow to appear. Consequently, the worker is exposed to traumatic events repeatedly and over a significant period of time (Dutton & Rubinstein, 1995), often with minimal feelings of efficacy. This helplessness on the part of the therapist to "fix" the situation that causes the intense suffering for the client may be a significant contributor to the disaster therapist's risk for compassion fatigue and STS, as helplessness is one of the key criteria for development of PSTD (Wee & Myers, 2002).

In addition to exposure to the client's experience, another source of trauma for therapists dealing with clients' victimization is the nature of the victimization itself (Danieli, 1985). Through exposure to clients' trauma, therapists not only become aware of their clients' pain but also come to the stark realization that traumatic events can occur; have occurred, perhaps repeatedly; and can occur again (Dutton & Rubinstein, 1995). When trauma therapists enter their clients' worlds, it is no longer possible to deny the potential for trauma in their own lives. The experience of even one surveyor client is an inescapable reminder of the therapist's own personal vulnerability to traumatic loss (Pearlman & Saakvitne, 1995). Having once counseled a flood victim, a therapist never again sees a river as totally benign, and an earthquake counselor forever after eyes bridges with a measure of doubt.

It is for these reasons that therapists working with the trauma of disaster survivors are at such high risk of being traumatized themselves. Because of high risk of compassion fatigue, burnout, and secondary stress disorder, this chapter focuses on what can be done before, during, and after disaster assignments to maintain the psychological health and well-being of these counselors. It will provide recommendations for the prevention of secondary traumatic stress disorder or compassion fatigue based on the research and practice reported in the literature to date with the following groups of workers: therapists providing treatment to trauma victims, emergency service workers (First responders), and disaster workers in general. In addition, it will draw from the author's personal experiences in developing stress management protocols, educational materials, and training programs for mental health counselors in more than a dozen presidentially declared disasters.

The strategies for prevention and treatment of compassion fatigue and STS will be organized into categories of what can be done *predisaster, during disaster,* and *postdisaster assignment.*

PREDISASTER

This section describes actions that can be taken by a mental health agency or group before a disaster strikes to ensure that mental health staff are ready and well prepared should they be required to engage in disaster work. Naturally, many of these strategies will contribute to an efficient and effective disaster mental health response. However, the primary purpose for discussing these actions is to prevent or minimize compassion fatigue, burnout, and STS in workers by providing them with knowledge, skills, tools, and supports they need to perform a difficult and risky job as safely as possible.

Personal Emergency Preparedness

Having a personal and family emergency plan will help any worker who has potential disaster responsibilities, to cope with whatever emergencies may occur while, he or she is at home. All emergency workers should be familiar with hazards and likely emergencies inherent in their local geographic area, and should have contingency plans for themselves and their families. This is important to the safety of families and to the availability of workers for disaster assignment. The more quickly things can be taken care of at home, the more quickly workers can report to work with some worries about their family taken care of. Similarly, if a worker is at work when a disaster occurs, peace of mind and concentration will be enhanced if the family is prepared and able to cope (Myers, 1994b).

Designing an Appropriate Disaster Mental Health Plan

By realistically designing disaster mental health programs based on models known to be effective, mental health planners, administrators, and clinicians can avoid the frustration and potential burnout inherent in misdirected efforts following a disaster.

It is important to base a disaster mental health response on some important key concepts of disaster mental health. Individuals and the community will pass through a variety of phases on the road to recovery, and mental health approaches must be appropriate to the phase of a disaster. A crisis intervention approach and active outreach into the community are essential in the immediate aftermath of the disaster. Community based outreach continues to be a key to reaching victims throughout the long-term recovery process as most disaster victims do not see themselves as needing mental health services following disaster and usually do not seek such services. Community mental health programs provide public information and education about expected stress responses in adults, children, and families, usually framing symptoms as "the normal reactions of normal people to an abnormal situation" and suggesting ways to cope and where to go for help. Direct mental health services to individuals often are more "practical" than "psychological" in nature. Counselors often are most helpful and relevant to survivor needs by assisting survivors with problem solving, decision making, and obtaining resources, rather than providing psychotherapy.

Beyond the immediate crisis stage of the disaster, mental health staff—continuing their active outreach approach and collaboration with other helping agencies—will begin to identify individuals with more serious psychological problems, such as posttraumatic stress reactions, depression, and exacerbation of prior trauma or prior stress. Relationship and marital problems may surface or be exacerbated, including domestic violence. Substance abuse may increase. It is these individuals who likely will require more intensive psychological counseling, and for whom mental health professionals with skill in trauma treatment will be necessary. Myers (1994b) provided a more detailed look at key concepts of disaster psychology as they apply to program design in the various phases of disaster response and recovery.

Selection of Disaster Mental Health Staff

Much of the confusion and stress at the time of disaster impact can be minimized if a mental health agency or professional group has predesignated staff trained as a disaster response team, with call-up deployment procedures in place (Myers, 1994b).

Not all mental health professionals are well-suited for disaster work. Various phases of response and varying tasks require a special "fit" from the worker. In the crisis phase, mental health workers need to use an active outreach approach. They must go out to community sites where survivors are involved in the activities of their daily lives. Such places include affected neighborhoods, schools, disaster shelters, disaster application centers (DACs), meal sites, hospitals, churches, community centers, and the like. The traditional, office-based approach is of little use in these sites. Very few people will come to an office or approach a desk labeled "mental health." However, most will be eager to talk about what happened to them when approached with warmth and genuine interest. The most effective approach is to informally engage survivors in conversation, often dubbed by experienced disaster mental health workers as the "over the cup of coffee" approach. Staff who do well in these roles must be comfortable with an extraverted, outgoing approach. They need to be flexible, able to focus, good at thinking on their feet, and have a commonsense, practical, and often improvisational method of dealing with problems.

Later, as more serious psychological difficulties arise, trauma therapists with treatment skill are needed. However, they must be willing and able to "be with" survivors who are suffering tragedy, concrete losses, and ongoing life disruption without becoming frustrated at not being able to fix the situation of the victim (Myers, 1994b).

Choosing and assigning staff to program areas in which their unique skills are needed, utilized, effective, and appreciated will contribute greatly to prevention of burnout.

Disaster mental health staff also must be selected to match the demographic needs of the population. Counselors with special expertise in working with children, older adults, and particular ethnic groups must be included in the disaster team. Cultural competency is essential for staff working in the postdisaster environment. The primary reason for attending to these issues, of course, is to provide appropriate services to the community.

Predisaster Stress Assessment

A systematic assessment of workers' personal and job stress prior to placing them in disaster mental health assignments can help to screen out those who might be at high risk for compassion fatigue or STS. To measure job-

related stress, Bailey, Steffen, and Grout (1980) developed a stress audit questionnaire to identify "stressors" and "satisfiers" of nurses on intensive care
units (McCammon & Allison, 1995). Similarly, Rosenschweig and Vaslow (1992)
studied FEMA disaster workers and developed a list of top "stress producers"
and "stress reducers." The tools used in both of these studies have potential
for modification into a tool for risk assessment before assigning mental health
staff to disaster work.

Dunning (1998) suggested looking carefully at possible indicators of psychological inquiry, including illness, turnover patterns within a group, requests
for transfer, absenteeism, and impaired job performance. The presence of such
factors could indicate that a work unit or individual workers are at a high level
of risk or are suffering actual burnout. Assigning these workers to disaster
mental health responsibilities might be moving them from the frying pan to
the fire. It also might provide them with much-needed change of pace and
responsibility, but they should be monitored closely and provided with appropriate supervision and support to ensure that cumulative stress from their
prior job and current disaster work does not result in compassion fatigue or
STS.

In addition to predisaster measurement of personal and professional stress
levels, consideration should be given to assessment of compassion fatigue,
burnout, and STS in workers already engaged in trauma intervention before
assigning them to disaster work. Figley's compassion Fatigue Self Test for Psychotherapists (Figley, 1995) is an excellent tool. More research on formal assessment and diagnosis of STS is still needed but a wide range of PTSD
Assessment tools exists that could be used or modified to measure STS.
(Carlson, 1997, offered a comprehensive guide to PTSD assessment tools.)

There will be times when mental health staff themselves have sustained
direct losses from a disaster. There have been many situations in which disaster workers who are also disaster victims have heroically participated in mental health response activities without letting coworkers or supervisors know
of their own losses. Although this is likely a mixture of denial and altruism
commonly occurring after the impact of a disaster, it may put a worker at real
risk if personal, family, and financial needs are not attended to. Every mental
health agency should determine which of its workers have been directly affected in order to support these workers and make appropriate work assignments. The organization can support its own workers by providing formalized
debriefing, counseling services, and support groups for those who were personally affected (Myers, 1994b).

If a disaster mental health counselor does have a personal trauma history,
as a victim either of the disaster at hand or of other trauma, support and
supervision will be important for early identification and intervention with
STS (Pearlman & Maclan, 1995). The question must be asked as to whether
personally affected mental health workers can and should be involved in the
mental health disaster response. They will likely need some time off from

work, both initially and over the long run, to attend to their own personal and family needs. Disaster work assignments should be initially and regularly evaluated with workers to assess how disaster work may affect them on a personal level, and how their personal situations may affect their disaster work. An important factor will be the worker's ability to separate personal coping styles from those of other survivors, and not to impose, consciously or unconsciously his or her own values and methods of coping upon others. The ability to empathize with survivors may be enhanced by the worker's own losses. However, the worker must be able to maintain perspective and avoid the hazards of overidentification with survivors. Taking too much control in a desire to help, playing down others' crises, or avoiding listening to intense feelings because they are too painful for the worker can be potential problems (Myers, 1994b).

Another group of counselors to identify predisaster are new therapists, who may be very vulnerable to compassion fatigue and STS and who could benefit from extra supervision and support. Pearlman & Maclan (1995) found that the newest therapists in trauma work had the most difficulties. This finding is consistent with the burnout literature, which shows that being younger or newer to the work is correlated with the highest levels of burnout (Ackerley, Brunell, Holder, & Kurdek, 1998; Deutsch, 1984) and with the most negative reactions to doing therapy (Rodolfa, Kraft, & Reilley, 1988). Pearlman and MacIan also found that the newest trauma therapists often worked with the most acutely distressed patients, and less than 20% of them received supervision. Their work clearly recommended the need for more supervision and more support for newer therapists working in the trauma field. Identifying these staff at the beginning of a disaster assignment will assure that they can be provided with appropriate supervision and support. Student interns will require similar supervision.

In addition to identifying potentially at risk therapists, Pearlman and Saakvitne (1995) advised that in employment and training settings, those who interview applicants—whether for graduate school, internships, postdoctoral fellowships, or staff positions—should inform potential workers of the risks relating to doing trauma work. They must emphasize the harm that can be done by offering a position to someone who does not have the self-capacities, ego resources, and access to support to do this type of work. This "duty to warn" must be taken seriously by managers and supervisors who hire or assign staff to disaster mental health response teams.

Necessary Supplies for a Disaster Assignment

Once mental health disaster response staff members are selected, they should be provided with official identification that will allow them access into the areas they will be assigned to work. In addition, every worker who might be called out on a disaster assignment is wise to have an emergency bag prepacked. Supplies should be tailored to the nature of the worker's likely assignment. If the assignment will entail any length of time away from home, the bag should include the following:

- Clothes, including sturdy shoes and clothes for inclement weather
- Eye glasses and medications (including over-the-counter remedies for personal stress reactions—antacids, aspirin, antidiarrhea medicine, etc.)
- Personal hygiene supplies
- Flashlight, portable radio, and batteries
- Small first aid kit
- Food and water (one gallon per day) for three days
- Paper, pens, and a clipboard
- Forms or supplies necessary to the worker's disaster assignment
- Sleeping bag
- Cash and change for pay phones (these circuits usually work when other phone lines are out of service)
- Official identification to allow access into restricted areas
- A picture of one's family and at least one comforting item from home
- A good book, a deck of cards, crossword puzzles, and the like

Every worker with the potential for assignment within a disaster-affected area should have up-to-date immunizations for hepatitis B and diphtheria/tetanus (DT). In addition, during the flu season in winter months (November to April), immunization for influenza should be considered for all disaster workers because of the degree of public exposure they experience. Staying healthy and energetic on the job will help to minimize fatigue and burnout.

Education and Training of Disaster Mental Health Staff

Mental health professionals working in any field of trauma must have initial and ongoing specialized training. First, it is essential that graduate and professional schools of social work, psychiatry, psychology, and psychiatric nursing include coursework and supervised practice in the field of trauma assessment and treatment. In addition, conferences, workshops, and other continuing education forums are necessary both to maintain and update knowledge and skills and to provide professional, collegial support.

Specialized training is essential, even for experienced trauma therapists, before working in the field of disaster mental health. Mental health professionals frequently assume that their clinical training and experience are more than sufficient to enable them to respond adequately to a disaster. Unfortunately, traditional mental health training does not address many issues found in disaster-affected population (FEMA, 1988). Although clinical expertise (especially in the field of crisis intervention) is valuable, it is not enough. Mental health personnel need to adopt new procedures and methods for delivering a highly specialized service in disaster situations. Training must be designed to prepare staff for the uniqueness of disaster mental health approaches (Meyers, 1994b). Ideally, graduate and professional programs that train mental health professionals should include coursework specifically on disaster mental health. Most, however, do not.

Because disaster mental health work requires a perceptual shift from traditional mental health service delivery, the acquisition of new skills and information is essential (Myers, 1994b). Effective disaster mental health training will provide participants with certain knowledge, skills, and attitudes that will enhance their effectiveness in the disaster setting. Specialized disaster mental health training is an important, central component of the FEMA Crisis Counseling Program in the aftermath of presidentially declared disasters. It is also an essential component of the American Red Cross Disaster Mental Health Services program. Specialized disaster training is considered mandatory by both programs.

The function of disaster mental health training is to help staff understand the impact of disaster on individuals and community. It provides information about the complex systems and resources in the postdisaster environment. It also helps staff to fine-tune their clinical skills that are relevant and useful in disaster, and aids them in learning effective community-based approaches.

Through videotapes, role play, and other exercises, training allows staff to experience vicariously the emotional climate of disaster relief work. Usually, the experiential expects of the training provide workers with some measure of "emotional inoculation" that will help them to anticipate the emotional aspects of the work. Training also strives to provide staff with awareness of the personal impact of disaster work, and with strategies for stress management and self-care.

A comprehensive disaster mental health training should enable mental health professionals to do the following:

1. Understand human behavior in disaster, including factors affecting individuals' response to disaster, phases of disaster, "at risk" groups, concepts of loss and grief, postdisaster stress, and the disaster recovery process.
2. Intervene effectively with special populations in disaster, including children, older adults, people with disabilities, ethnic and cultural groups indigenous to the area, and the disenfranchised or people living in poverty.
3. Understand the organizational aspects of disaster response and recovery, including key roles, responsibilities, and resources; local, state, federal, and voluntary agency programs; and how to link disaster survivors with appropriate resources and services.
4. Understand the key concepts and principles of disaster mental health,

including how disaster mental health services differ from traditional psychotherapy, the spectrum and design of mental health programs needed
in a disaster, and appropriate sites and activities involved in delivery of
mental health services.

5. Provide appropriate mental health assistance to survivors and workers
   in community settings, with an emphasis on crisis intervention, brief
   treatment, posttraumatic stress strategies, age-appropriate child interventions, debriefing, group counseling, support groups, and stress management techniques.
6. Provide mental health services at the community level with emphasis
   on case finding, outreach, mental health education, public education,
   consultation, community organization, advocacy, and use of the media.
7. Understand the stress inherent in disaster work and recognize and manage that stress for themselves and with other workers (Myers, 1994b).
8. Prepare disaster mental health management staff for unique organizational, clinical, and stress management issues inherent in disaster mental health programs.

An important component of disaster mental health training involves education about potential compassion fatigue, burnout, STS, stress management,
and self-care. Such training helps create a work environment in which secondary stress reactions are to be anticipated and recognized as a common
component of the work, and in which detection and intervention with these
conditions can be facilitated (Dutton & Rubinstein, 1995).

Stress management training developed by Myers (1989a, 1989b, 1992, 1993,
1994a, 1997), Myers and Zunin (1993a, 1993b, 1994a, 1994b), and Wee (1994)
for mental health and other workers in numerous presidentially declared disasters have included the following stress management topics:

- Phases of disaster for workers
- Factors that influence disaster workers' stress reactions (factors related
  to the worker, the role, the setting, the community, and the disaster itself)
- Sources of stress for disaster workers
- Stressors in specific work environments
- Stressors in specific roles (e.g., outreach worker, crisis counselor, treating
  trauma therapist, supervisor, or manager)
- Personal coping strategies for disaster workers before, during, and after
  the disaster assignment
- Stress management techniques
  A) Stress inventory
  B) Breathing
  C) Stretching
  D) Cognitive techniques
  E) Relaxation

F) Meditation
G) Imagination
H) Humor
I)   Creative expression
J)   Time management
K) Conflict resolution
L) Resistance building and "lifestyle" (work schedule, rest, nutrition, exercise, social support, relaxation and recreation

In addition to the above training curriculum, Pearlman and Saakvitne (1995) offered a paradigm of stress prevention strategies for trauma workers that includes personal strategies, professional strategies, organizational strategies, and interventions by helping professionals. Yassen (1995) presented a framework that uses concepts of primary prevention, secondary prevention, and tertiary prevention, and developed a comprehensive, ecological model for the prevention of STS. Munroe et al. (1995) developed a team model for use in prevention of STS. Each of these models could well serve as curriculum for disaster mental health worker stress management training predisaster.

Orientation to the Disaster Assignment

Before disaster mental health staff are deployed to an actual disaster assignment, they should be oriented and briefed as thoroughly as possible about what they will encounter in their disaster assignment location and role. This forewarning can help personnel to anticipate and prepare emotionally for what they may experience in their assignment (Hartsough & Myers, 1985; Myers, 1994b). It also provides them with concrete information that will be essential to them in their work and crucial to their well-being and safety. While preassignment briefings may have to be short and to-the-point because of the urgency of the situation, they should ideally include the following topics (Myers, 1994b):

1. *Status of the disaster:* nature of damages and losses, statistics, predicted weather or condition reports, boundaries of impacted area, hazards, response agencies involved.
2. *Orientation to the impacted communities:* demographics, ethnicity, socioeconomic makeup, pertinent politics, and so forth.
3. *Community and disaster-related resources:* handouts with brief descriptions and phone numbers of human service and disaster-related resources. FEMA or the state Office of Emergency Services (OES) usually provides written fliers describing state and federal disaster resources once disaster application centers (DACs) are opened. If available, provide them to all staff. Provide workers with a supply of mental health

brochures or fliers to give to survivors, outlining normal reactions of adults and children, ways to cope, and where to call for help. For volunteers or mental health personnel who have come from another locale to help, provide a brief description of the sponsoring mental health agency.

4. *Logistics:* arrangements for official identification cards, workers' food, housing, obtaining messages, medical care, and so on.

5. *Communications:* how, when, and what to report through mental health chain of command; orientation to use of cellular phone, two-way radios, or amateur radio volunteers, if used.

6. *Transportation:* clarify mode of transportation to field assignment; if workers are using personal vehicles, provide maps, delineate open and closed routes, indicate hazard areas.

7. *Health and safety in a disaster area:* outline potential hazards and safety strategies (e.g., protective action in earthquake aftershocks, flooded areas, etc.). Discuss possible sources of injury and prevention. Discuss pertinent health issues such as safety of food and drinking water, personal hygiene, communicable disease control, disposal of waste, and exposure to the elements. Inform of first aid/medical resources in the field.

8. *Field assignments:* Outline sites where workers will be deployed (shelters, meal sites, etc.). Provide a brief description of the setup and organization of the site and the name of the person in charge. Provide a brief review or appropriate interventions at the site.

9. *Policies and procedures:* Briefly outline policies regarding length of shifts, breaks, staff meetings, required reporting of statistics, logs of contacts, and so on. Give staff all necessary forms.

10. *Self-care and stress management:* Encourage the use of a team approach or "buddy system" to monitor stress and needs. Remind staff of the importance of regular breaks, good nutrition, adequate sleep, exercise, deep breathing, positive self-talk, appropriate use of humor, and "defusing" or talking about the experience after the shift is over. Inform workers of debriefing to be provided at the end of the tour of duty.

DURING DISASTER

This section outlines strategies that can be taken by the mental health agency, by supervisors, and by disaster mental health workers themselves to prevent compassion fatigue during the actual disaster mental health assignment. Suggested approaches include briefing of disaster mental health staff before deployment; supervision of staff; consultation; continuing education and training; psychotherapy; organizational support and workplace strategies; defusing and debriefing; working as a team; mental health worker professional strategies; and mental health worker personal strategies.

Briefing of Disaster Mental Health Staff

Several approaches to stress prevention and management during disaster have already been discussed in the "predisaster section." The first is to continue to brief workers before they begin any new assignment. During ongoing disaster recovery, if work sites, roles, or responsibilities change, briefing the worker on the new situation can reduce anxiety and ease the transition into the new assignment.

Supervision of Staff

The importance of supervision for disaster workers was discussed in the predisaster section. During the immediate postimpact phase of disaster, workers respond with enthusiasm and often heroism to the immediate needs of the situation. It is the rule, rather than the exception, that mental health staff, like other disaster responders, tend to overextend themselves in their efforts. Disaster workers usually are not the best judges of their level of functioning, and often underestimate the effects of stress and fatigue on their health and performance. Thus, good on-scene supervision is helpful. The following suggestions may be helpful to supervisors dealing with disaster-related stress among mental health workers (Myers, 1994b):

1. Remember that *early identification and intervention* with stress reactions is the way to preventing worker burnout. Review stress symptoms with workers before they go into the field. Provide handouts for workers regarding stress management and self-care.
2. Assess workers' appearance and level of functioning regularly. It is not uncommon for workers to deny their own level of stress and fatigue. For example, they may say they are doing fine, but exhibit multiple stress symptoms and appear very fatigued.
3. Try to rotate workers among low-stress, moderate-stress, and high-stress tasks. Limit workers' time in high-stress assignments (such as working with families identifying the deceased at the morgue) to an hour or so at a time, if possible. Provide breaks and personal support to staff in such positions.
4. If possible, limit the length of shifts to 12 hours *maximum*. A 12-hour shift should be followed by 12 hours off-duty.

5. Ask workers to take breaks if their effectiveness is diminishing; order them to do so if necessary. Point out that their ability to function is diminished due to fatigue, and that they are needed functioning at full potential to help with the operation. Allow workers to return to work if they rest and functioning improves.

6. On breaks, try to provide workers with the following:
   - bathroom facilities;
   - a place to sit or lie down away from the scene; quiet time alone;
   - food and beverages; and
   - an opportunity to talk with a supervisor or coworkers if they wish.

Supervision is important not only on-scene in the immediate disaster aftermath. Its importance continues and magnifies as staff move into long-term recovery work with the community and with clients. Cerney (1995) noted that much secondary trauma can be avoided or its effects ameliorated if therapists use regular supervision or consultation. Within the process of supervision, blind spots can be detected, overidentification can be corrected, alternative treatment approaches can be discussed and evaluated, and (especially important in prevention of compassion fatigue) the therapist's overextension or overinvolvement can be analyzed and understood. Pearlman and MacIan (1995) emphasized the special importance of good supervision for those therapists with a trauma history and those who are newer therapists. It is important to continue to monitor the needs of those disaster mental health staff who are also disaster victims. Appropriate supervision, consultation, and support can help ensure that they do not become overwhelmed, and that their personal needs and professional roles do not become blurred. Supervision should not only include clinical guidance and oversight but also ensure that treatment and supportive approaches are appropriate to the phase of disaster, meet the goals and objectives of the disaster mental health program, and are culturally and ethnically fitting.

Consultation

In addition to providing staff with supervision, many postdisaster mental health projects have employed consultants and trainers specifically to provide stress management services and education to mental health personnel (Varblow, 1994; Wee & Myers, 2002). Consultants with prior experience from other disasters and other mental health projects can offer refreshing insights and concrete ideas that can help staff in reaching their goals. More importantly, consultants can suggest approaches to stress management and STS prevention that have been used elsewhere in the field and proven helpful.

Continuing Education and Training

Hand in hand with the importance of good supervision is the necessity for continuing education and training throughout the duration of the disaster mental health program. Goals and topics of an initial disaster training program were discussed in the predisaster section. In ongoing disaster mental health programs, staff may need in-depth training on a subject covered only briefly in the comprehensive training, or they may find that topics not covered at all in the initial training are needed. Some common training needs and interests seem to occur regularly in long-term mental health recovery programs. Examples include the following, although specifics will vary, depending on the goals and approaches of the specific mental health program (Myers, 1994b; Wee, 1994):

- Treatment of PTSD, anxiety, and depression
- Treatment of PTSD and alcohol abuse or dependence
- Interventions with complicated bereavement
- Disaster and family issues
- Approaches and interventions with domestic violence
- Cultural competency
- Intensive training on special populations (e.g., children, older adults, people with disabilities, or specific cultural or ethnic groups)
- Group dynamics and techniques for use in disaster
- Expressive therapies (art, music, writing) for use with adults and children
- Stress management interventions for survivors and workers
- Long-term recovery issues and interventions
- Outreach techniques for long-term recovery
- Holidays and the anniversary of the disaster, including reactions and community recovery events
- Community organizing at the neighborhood level
- Specialized topics important to understanding and helping survivors (e.g., insurance issues, the city or county permit process, and working with architects and contractors)
- Specialized topics pertinent to the local disaster (e.g., floodplain management, seismic safety, and hurricane warning systems)
- Resources available to disaster survivors
- Public education, consultation, and advocacy approach to disaster
- Unique needs of disaster mental health management and supervisory staff, including compressed time frames, meeting program goals and objectives, supervision of staff, funding issues and constraints, and personal and professional stress management
- Preparing for termination of the disaster mental health project, includ-

ing termination of relationships with clients, referral of clients to appropriate resources, notification of community regarding ending of services, closure issues and interventions for staff, recognition of staff

It is helpful for staff to complete written evaluation of training sessions as they occur. Evaluations provide information to managers and trainers about the perceived usefulness of training (Meyers, 1994b). In addition, they give the message to staff that their training needs are taken seriously and that every effort is being made to make training relevant and of top quality. It gives the even more important message to staff that they are valued and that the organization appreciates their professional skill and contributions. Both training and consultation provide rewards for staff that have tangible positive effects on morale (Myers, 1994b).

Psychotherapy

In addition to supervision and training, personal psychotherapy can be important in preventing compassion fatigue and intervening with STS in disaster mental health staff. Dutton and Rubinstein (1995) emphasized that trauma workers with personal histories of traumatization are likely to require deliberate personal attention to their own healing process in order to manage more effectively the difficult task of coping with their own STS reactions. In emphasizing the helpfulness of personal psychotherapy for the trauma therapist, Pearlman and Saakvitne (1995) pointed out that, among other things, it provides a regular opportunity to focus on oneself, one's own needs, and the origins of one's responses to the work. They also underscored the explicit acknowledgment that psychotherapy provides: that one is deserving of care and one's personal needs are valid and important.

Individual expressive therapy—such as art, music, or movement—can help therapists to become and remain centered and to reclaim their emotional lives in the chaotic postdisaster environment. Group therapy and support groups also can be of help to disaster mental health workers, providing a safe space both for healing and for exploring the interaction of a therapist's past with his or her current work with survivors (Pearlman & Saakvitne, 1995). Group therapy and support groups for disaster mental health workers are particularly effective in dealing with the unique aspects of disaster work, which other trauma therapists have not encountered and may have a hard time understanding.

Organizational Support and Workplace Strategies

In addressing organizational approaches to prevention of.STS, Pearlman and Saakvitne (1995) emphasized the importance of creating an atmosphere of respect for both clients and employees. This is important in the early phases of disaster, in which mental health staff may be working with survivors in chaotic, field-based situations, as well as in long-term recovery work, where staff may work with clients in both field and office settings. Organizational support and respect are conveyed to staff by providing assistance with concrete, disaster-related needs (e.g., time off and on-site childcare); adequate briefing of workers; work-related supplies; official identification; well-designed procedures for management of telephone calls, communications, and paperwork; transportation; food and housing on disaster assignment, if necessary; policies regarding maximum duration of shifts (no longer than 12 hours) and frequency of breaks (every 2 to 4 hours); and excellent training, supervision, consultation, support, and recognition of staff efforts (Myers, 1994b). Pearlman and Saakvitne (1995) also underscored that mental health staff should have adequate employee benefits, such as health insurance with provision for mental health care and time off for vacations, in order not to endanger themselves with compassion fatigue and STS.

Yassen (1995) described the symbolic as well as actual value of such physical things as having an office, good lighting, privacy, environmental safety and security, employee amenities (e.g., access to food and fluids, office supplies, places to take breaks), and availability of colleagues. She also outlined the important, but less tangible, aspects of the work environment, related to the values, expectations, and culture of the setting. Harvey (1985), for example, identified the importance of a clear philosophical value base as being a key element in comparing rape crisis centers. Workers must understand the organization's implicit as well as explicit demands on them, and Yassen (1995) listed important aspects for the organization to clarify to its personnel:

- *Value system*
- *Tasks:* job descriptions, philosophy, expectations, task variety, adequacy of supervision, in-service and career opportunities, training and orientation, job security, and pay
- *Managerial:* lines of authority, accessibility of leaders who are open to feedback, role models, accountability, and ability to motivate and build morale
- *Interpersonal:* personnel guidelines, respect for differences, value of social support and mutual aid, trust among staff, and sensitivity to the needs of individuals (e.g., personal days, stress management training)

Dutton and Rubinstein (1995) suggested other workplace strategies for preventing and responding to STS. They advised adjusting workers' caseloads to include a diversity of clients, thus reducing their amount of contact with severely traumatized clients, and diversifying work-related activities beyond direct contact with victims (e.g., teaching, supervision, research, and consultation).

Defusing and Debriefing

Defusing is an effective and frequently employed intervention for workers in highly stressful disaster mental health assignments. It is a shortened version of critical incident stress debriefing (CISD), a technique developed in the early 1980s to assist emergency workers in managing the traumatic stress associated with their jobs (Mitchell, 1983). A defusing consists of a meeting with a small number of staff, led by a disaster mental health practitioner with specialized training. It is usually done at the end of a shift, before leaving work for the day. A defusing usually lasts 20 to 45 minutes and allows workers an opportunity to talk about their work and their reactions. The goals include mitigation of the impact of the day's work, reduction of stress symptoms, education about coping strategies, group support, and assessment of the need for other interventions (Mitchell & Everly, 1995).

CISD involves a longer, more in-depth group intervention to assist workers with processing their exposure to trauma. In immediate postdisaster response, a formal CISD usually is not recommended *during* a worker's disaster assignment. It can take workers "too far and too deep" into their feelings about the nature of the work, leaving them feeling undefended and vulnerable at a time when they must go back into the face of disaster the next day. Thus, a briefer form, the defusing, is more appropriate. The exception to this rule is when disaster mental health workers are involved in long-term disaster recovery counseling, which may take them many months or even years into the postdisaster time-frame. In long-term work, regularly scheduled debriefings—at weekly, bi-weekly, or monthly intervals—can be very helpful as a structured, supportive intervention for staff. Slight modifications to Mitchell's basic CISD model often are used for this long-term support purpose (Myers & Zunin, 1994b).

Working as a Team

Building a team approach to disaster mental health work can provide both prevention and active intervention with secondary traumatization (Munroe et al., 1995). Social support is a known source of significant psychological benefit for trauma survivors (Keane, Scott, Chavoya, Lamparski, & Fairbank, 1985; Solomon, 1986). A strong team approach can provide the same social support for trauma mental health professionals (Munroe et al., 1995). Stress management training materials for disaster workers (Hartsough & Meyers, 1985; Myers, 1989a, 1989b–1997, 1994b; National Institute of Mental Health, 1987a, 1987b) have long emphasized the importance of working in a buddy system in a disaster, utilizing teams of at least two workers to ensure that staff can serve as a check-and -balance for each other and monitor each others' stress level while providing support and encouragement.

Mental Health Worker Professional Strategies

A multitude of publications have offered suggestions for disaster worker self-care during the immediate response phase of disaster (Hartsough & Myers, 1985; Myers, 1989a, 1988b–1997, 1994b; National Institute of Mental Health, 1987a, 1987b; Wee, 1994). The following are suggestions for mental health staff, summarized from these publications, for management of stress while working on a disaster operation:

1. *Request a briefing at the beginning of each shift* to update yourself and your coworkers on the status of things since your last shift. This can help you gear up for what you may be encountering during your shift.
2. *Develop a buddy system with a coworker.* Agree to keep an eye on each other's functioning, fatigue level, and stress symptoms. Tell the buddy how to know when you are getting stressed ("If I start doing so-and-so, tell me to take a break"). Make a pact with your buddy to take a break when he or she suggests it, if the situation allows.
3. *Encourage and support coworkers.* Listen to each other's feelings. Don't take anger too personally. Hold criticism unless it is essential. Tell each other "You're doing great" and "Good job." Give coworkers a pat on the back. Bring each other a snack or something to drink.
4. *Try to get some activity and exercise.* Even something as simple as using the stairs instead of the elevator can provide exercise during a busy workday. Gently stretch out muscles that have become tense.
5. *Eat regularly.* If you are not hungry, eat frequently, in small quantities. Try to avoid excessive sugar, fats, and caffeine. Drink plenty of liquids.
6. *Use humor to break the tension and provide relief.* Use it with care, however. People are highly suggestible in disaster situations, and survivors or coworkers can take things personally and be hurt if they feel they are the brunt of "disaster humor."
7. *Use positive self-talk,* such as "I'm doing fine" and "I'm using the skills I've been trained to use."
8. *Take deep breaths, hold them, then blow out forcefully.*
9. *Take breaks if your effectiveness is diminishing,* or if asked to do so by your supervisor. At a minimum, take a break every four hours.
10. *Use a clipboard or notebook to jot things down.* This will help compensate for the memory problems that are common in stressful situations.
11. *Try to keep noise to a minimum in the worksite.* Gently remind others to do the same.
12. *Try to avoid unnecessarily interrupting coworkers* when they are in the middle of a task. Think twice before interrupting.
13. *Let yourself defuse at the end of each shift* by taking a few minutes with coworkers to talk about your thoughts and feelings about the day.
14. *When you are off duty, enjoy some recreation that takes your mind off the*

disaster. Draw on supports that nurture you. These may include friends,
meditation, reading, or religion.

15. *Pamper yourself during time off.* Treat yourself to a special meal, get a
    massage, or take a long bath.

16. *If needed, give yourself permission to spend time alone after work.* However, do not totally withdraw form social interaction.

17. *Get adequate sleep.* Learn relaxation techniques that can help you fall
    asleep.

18. *On long disaster assignments, attend periodic debriefing or worker support
    groups* to talk about the emotional impact on yourself and on coworkers. Use stress management programs if they are available. If such programs are not offered, try to get them organized.

19. *On disaster assignments away from home, remember the following:*
    • Try to make your living accommodations as personal, comfortable,
      and homey as possible. Unpack bags and put out pictures of loved
      ones.
    • Bring familiar foods and snacks from home that may not be available
      on your disaster assignment.
    • Make new friends. Let off steam with coworkers.
    • Find local recreation opportunities and make use of them.
    • Remember things that are relaxing at home and try to do them now:
      For example, take a hot bath or shower, read a good book, go for a
      run, or listen to music.
    • Stay in touch with people at home. Write or call often. Send pictures.
      Have family visit if possible and appropriate.
    • Avoid excessive use of alcohol and caffeine.
    • Keep a journal.

Yassen (1995) emphasized the importance of balance and boundaries for
the prevention of professional STS. Disaster mental health workers need to
have balance in both the quantity and quality of tasks in their work life, paying close attention to the proportion of their work that involves direct trauma
treatment and balancing it with other professional responsibilities. Finding a
satisfactory and healthy balance between professional and personal life also is
important. Setting time boundaries, professional boundaries, and personal
boundaries is essential. Cerney (1995) wrote that to maintain boundaries necessary for good health, disaster mental health staff may need to prioritize
their commitments and even terminate some of them. She also noted the importance of therapeutic realism, emphasizing that mental health personnel
must not allow themselves to fall into the belief that they must be able to
handle every kind of patient or an unlimited number of patients. Studies continuously find that many mental health staff hold the irrational belief that
they must operate at peak efficiency and competence at all times with all people

(Deutsch, 1984; Forney, Wallace-Schutzman, & Wiggers, 1982), which can be a key contributing factor for STS in disaster mental health workers.

Mental Health Worker Personal Strategies

Personal strategies include lifestyle choices such as exercise, a healthy diet, and a balance between work, play, and rest (Myers, 1994b). Also important are creative expression, meditation and spiritual replenishment, self-aware-ness, and humor (Yassen, 1995). Other informal strategies—such as maintain-ing strong personal support networks of family and friends, developing diverse interests, limiting trauma exposure and media coverage of the disaster out-side work hours, and seeking positive experiences outside of (disaster) work—can be helpful (Dutton & Rubenstein, 1995; Edelwich & Brodsky, 1980). Other activities that contribute to disaster mental health worker self-care and health promotion include being willing to talk about events and feelings; practicing yoga or meditation; practicing deep breathing and other relaxation techniques; praying; using self-talk and positive self-encouragement; maintaining mean-ingful practices and rituals; reading; keeping a journal; engaging in creative pursuits such as art and writing, making music, or dancing; getting a mas-sage; taking a warm bath or shower; attending the theater or movies; going out to dinner; spending time with family, children, friends, pets, and nature; traveling; and pursuing hobbies (Hartsough & Myers, 1985; Myers, 1994b; Myers & Zunin, 1994b; Pearlman & Saakvitne, 1995; Wee & Myers, 2002).

POSTDISASTER

Postdisaster strategies for mitigating stress for workers include planning for the ending of their assignment, program closure activities, critique of the project, debriefing of staff, follow-up, and recognition of staff.

Planning for the Ending

There is a certain amount of work to be done in ending what has been a long-term but time-limited disaster mental health program. Typically, such programs last from one to two years following the disaster. Staff should re-ceive consultation and training and hold planning sessions about how they will end the program. Whether staff were involved for short-term (a few weeks or months) or long-term (months to years) commitments, they usually experi-ence a mixture of emotions at the end of the work: relief that it is over and the sadness or guilt at leaving it behind. In addition, there is often a sense of "letdown" and some difficulty in transitioning back to regular job and family responsibilities. Mental health personnel working in disasters can be helped to anticipate these mixed emotions through education and training about common reactions and coping strategies that can help with the changes.

Program Closure Activities

Ending the services of a well-accepted, effective disaster mental health recovery program requires time and planning. Both community and staff must be prepared for it. Terminating the program in a thoughtful, professional, and responsible manner will help staff to feel pride in their accomplishments rather than feeling guilt at "abandoning" the survivors. The following suggestions can be helpful (Myers, 1989b–2001):

- *Plan a timeline for phase-down activities,* starting at least 3 months before the program will end.
- *Conduct case reviews* to identify individuals or families who will need continuing assistance; plan appropriate referrals.
- *Develop a resource list* of ongoing services and distribute the list to clients.
- *Provide training to mental health staff about common reactions* of disaster staff at termination of their work assignments (e.g., guilt, sadness, depression, fatigue, disillusionment, boredom, detachment, anxiety, and need for closure).
- *Provide consultation and support for staff* who will be unemployed at the end of the project.
- *Critique and review achievements of the project.*
- *Inform the public of the project termination date* and plan a public closure activity, if any.
- *Consider a conference, symposium, or workshop* where professional staff can present lessons learned from the program and implications for future practice or research.
- *Thank the community for its support of the program.*
- *Write final reports and program evaluations.*
- *Debrief staff.*
- *Provide recognition for staff.*
- *Develop follow-up protocols and resources* for staff experiencing compassion fatigue or STS in the aftermath of the project.

Critique of the Project

A critique can be helpful to staff by bringing closure to a disaster mental health project. A critique is a critical evaluation of the project, its difficulties, and its successes. It is different and separate from a debriefing, which attends to the psychological and emotional impact of the work personnel. A critique can result in positive changes in the disaster plan, policies, and procedures to improve a mental health team's approach in the next situation (Myers, 1994b). A critique also can help staff to take pride and feel a sense of ownership in the project. It helps them to see the positive effect of their efforts in the disaster recovery.

Debriefing of Staff

The purpose of a formal debriefing is to address the emotional and psychological impact the disaster assignment has had on the workers. McCammon and Allison outlined the conceptual and components of a variety of posttrauma debriefing models (1995). Important to all of the models is the empathy, understanding, and peer support generated when the debriefing is conducted for a group of people who have worked together. The debriefing should be run by a mental health facilitator with experience in disaster and specialized training in debriefing techniques. This allows staff to identify and talk about the feelings associated with the disaster project, provides "normalization" of their responses, and lends peer support as the project comes to a close. Debriefing serves an educational purpose, informing workers of the common stress and grief reactions and transition issues to expect when the project is over. Resources to assist workers with transitional issues, compassion fatigue, or STS in the aftermath of their assignments should be discussed.

In long-term disaster assignments, debriefings may be used on a regular basis to assist staff with the feelings and stresses involved in their work. These debriefings, as well as a final or exit debriefing at the end of a long project, will require modification of Mitchell's debriefing model used in circumscribed critical incidents (Mitchell, 1983). Mitchell and Everly (1995) presented a variation of CISD called the "mass disaster/community response CISD" that encourages participants to explore the most negative impacts of the entire experience, while also exploring with participants any lessons learned and anything positive they will take away from the experience. The multiple stressor debriefing model developed by Armstrong, O'Callahan, and Marmar (1991) and the disaster worker debriefing model developed by Myers and Zunin (1994b) also work well for the purpose of intermittent stress management and exit debriefing. Both of these models, although based on the prototype of Mitchell's model, include the added dimension of encouraging participants to discuss any of a large number of incidents they might have experienced in the weeks or months of their disaster work. In these models, questions are framed to encourage discussion of incidents that were "challenging" or "difficult," with participants discussing the events themselves as well as the thoughts, feelings, stress reactions, and coping approaches associated with the events.

In addition, Myers and Zunin invited debriefing participants to share not only a positive experience they had during the disaster, but one that had a meaningful or profound effect on them. This inquiry is based on the belief that disaster work is not only traumatic but also profoundly meaningful and often very touching for workers. Debriefing staff about only the negative and stressful aspects does not allow them to fully process the many facets of what the disaster meant to them. Brian Flynn, Ed.D., chief of the Emergency Services and Disaster Relief Branch, Center for Mental Health Services (U.S. Department of Health and Human Services), is a 20-year veteran of disaster mental health. Following his work in the aftermath of the Oklahoma City bombing, he wrote:

> What I witnessed and experienced in Oklahoma City deeply moved me. Many people assume that the experience traumatized me and, to some extent, it did. However, in many ways, it was one of the most profoundly positive experiences in my personal and work life. I am so deeply moved by the experience that, even now, tears sometimes accompany my attempts to tell the story. . . . When I received a psychological debriefing on leaving Oklahoma City, I was asked to identify the single most positive event of my experience there. This is the story I told.
>
> I did not enter the highly secure site of the bombing until all of the rescue and body recovery work was complete. A chain link fence was surrounding several city blocks outside which people gathered to stand vigil and leave mementos (flowers, notes, religious icons, teddy bears). Inside the perimeter, in the medical supply area, I talked with several workers who were in the process of dismantling that operation. When they became aware of my mental health role, one woman to whom I had been speaking said, "Wait here, I want you to see something. I'll be right back." She returned carrying a rather worn and limp brown teddy bear. The bear had on a silly yellow hat on which was written "Hug Specialist." Around its neck was a stethoscope and it wore a hospital wristband stating to whom it should be returned if lost.
>
> This woman explained to me that one of her roles was to have workers inside the perimeter hug the bear. She then took the bear outside the fence where people from the community hugged it. And she repeated the process. The bear thus became the link between those inside who were involved in some of the most difficult work imaginable and those who stood vigil outside, wanting so much to help. It was the *bearer* of their connection, their affection, their hope. Who could have thought of such a simple, but moving, way to connect people necessarily separated by role, steel, and troops yet connected by their common hopes and persistence? Symbols. Rituals. Although I have received much recognition in my 25-year federal career and it means a great deal to me, none means more to me than when she asked me that morning to hug the bear. (Flynn, 1995)

The accomplishments of disaster mental health counseling are less visible and tangible than the physical rebuilding of bridges and buildings. Mental health staff often feel frustration at the slow pace of their work, question the efficacy of their efforts, and feel there is little to show for the long months of their work. Specially designed small group exercises can augment debriefing by helping staff to recognize and appreciate their contribution to the community's healing, to understand the personal meaning of their experiences, and to begin the transition to other endeavors. Two examples follow (Myers, 1989b–2001).

As the Project Ends

In small groups, staff discuss the following questions, then report some of their key points back to the larger group.

1. How has this disaster mental health assignment been different from other jobs you have had?
2. What have been the most challenging aspects of the work?
3. What have been the special rewards of the work?
4. How have you been changed by the work? What are some things you will be taking with you from this job?
5. Describe a meaningful, profound, or touching incident that happened to you during your work.
6. What do you anticipate your transition will be like as you heave the disaster project and move on? What will help you with this transition?

Legacy Exercise

In small groups, staff discuss the following questions, recording their answers on flip charts (the charts will later help in writing a final report of the project's accomplishments). When they are done, they report their key points back to the larger group.

Despite your knowledge that the community healing process is not over, and will go on long after this project has ended, what is the legacy you have left behind?

1. What has the project given to individual survivors?
2. How has the project helped our community in the healing process?
3. What will the project leave behind in the community?

Follow-up

Knowing what we know about the risks of compassion fatigue and STS in trauma intervention workers, it would be both prudent and compassionate to provide followup to disaster mental health workers after the completion of their disaster assignments. Although resources for any problems that develop or continue from their disaster work should be discussed during worker debriefing, a formalized followup in the form of a questionnaire or stress assessment should be considered. The Compassion Fatigue Self Test for Psychotherapists or a PTSD assessment scale can be used at the end of the assignment and at periodic intervals in the first year following disaster work. If the same tests were used to evaluate worker stress predisaster, they will provide an interesting analysis of the impact of the work. For the individual workers, however, the assessments can indicate the need for additional debriefing, support, or psychotherapy to treat compassion fatigue or STS resulting from the assignment. Support and treatment services should be offered as a matter of course to workers whose test results indicate a significant level of distress.

Recognition of Staff

Recognizing the efforts and accomplishments of mental health staff will assist in bringing closure to their disaster experience and in validating the value of their work. A plaque, a letter of appreciation, a declaration from local or state government, or a souvenir such as an official disaster photograph will have much meaning for personnel.

Those outside the field of mental health may not recognize the risks inherent in psychological trauma intervention. However, disaster mental health staff routinely place themselves in positions of risk for compassion fatigue and STS in order to assist the community in its recovery. A small thank-you goes a long way.

SUMMARY

The research and literature focusing on the impact of trauma on first responders, disaster workers, and trauma counselors indicates that these personnel are at risk for PTSD, compassion fatigue, burnout, and STS. Wee and Myers's research (1997, 2002) with disaster mental health workers following the Oklahoma City bombing and the Northridge earthquake clearly indicated that disaster mental health workers, a highly specialized group of trauma workers, are at high risk for compassion fatigue and STS in the course of their work with disaster victims. This chapter has outlined strategies and interventions that can be used predisaster, during a disaster, and after a disaster to mitigate and intervene with compassion fatigue and STS.

REFERENCES

Ackerley, G. D., Burnell, J., Holder, D. C., & Kurdek, L. A. (1998). Burnout among licensed psychologists. *Professional Psychology: Research and Practice, 19,* 624–631.

Armstrong, K., O'Callahan, W. T., & Marmar, C. R. (1991). Debriefing Red Cross disaster personnel: The multiple stressor debriefing model. *Journal of Traumatic Stress, 4,* 581–593.

Bailey, J. T., Steffen, S. M., & Grout J. W. (1980). The stress audit: Identifying the stressors of IC nursing. *Journal of Nursing Education, 19,* 15–25.

Bartone, P., Ursano, R., Wright, K., & Ingraham, L. (1989). Impact of a military air disaster. *Journal of Nervous and Mental Disease, 177,* 317–328.

Berah, E., Jones, H., & Valent, P. (1984). The experience of a mental health team involved in the early phase of a disaster. *Australia and New Zealand journal of Psychiatry, 18,* 354–358.

Bolin, R., & Bolton, P. (1986). Race, religion, and ethnicity in disaster recovery. *University of Colorado, Program on Environment and Behavior, 42.*

Carlson, E. B. (1997). *Trauma assessments: A clinician's guide.* New York: Guilford.

Cerney, M. S. (1995). Treating the 'heroic theaters.' In C. R. Figley (Ed.), *Compassion fatigue: Coping with secondary traumatic stress disorder in those who threat the traumatized* (pp. 131–149). New York: Brunner/Mazel.

Danieli, Y. (1985). The treatment and prevention of long-term effects and intergenerational transmission of victimization: A lesson from Holocaust survivors and their children. In C. R. Figley (Ed.), *Trauma and its wake: The study and treatment of post-traumatic stress disorder* (pp. 295–313). New York: Brunner/Mazel.

Deutsch, C. J. (1984). Self-reported sources of stress among psychotherapists. *Professional Psychology: Research and Practice, 15,* 833–845.

Dunning, C. (1988). Intervention strategies for emergency workers. In M. Lystad (Ed.), *Mental health response to mass emergencies* (pp. 284–307). New York Brunner/Mazel.

Dutton, M. A., & Rubinstein, F. L. (1995). Working with people with PTSD: Research implications. In C. R. Figley (Ed.), *Compassion fatigue: Coping with secondary traumatic stress disorder in those who treat the traumatized* (pp. 82–100). New York: Brunner/Mazel.

Edelwich, J., & Brodsky, A. (1980). *Burn-out: Stages of disillusionment in the helping professions.* New York: Human Sciences Press.

Federal Emergency Management Agency. (1998). *Disaster assistance programs: Crisis counseling programs: A handbook for grant applications* (DAP-9). Washington, DC: Author.

Figley, C. R. (Ed.). (1995). *Compassion fatigue: Coping with secondary traumatic stress disorder in those who treat the traumatized.* New York: Brunner/Mazel.

Flynn, B. (1995). Thoughts and reflections after the bombing of the Alfred P. Murrah Federal Building in Oklahoma City. *Journal of the America Psychiatric Nurses Association. 1,* 166–170.

Forney, D. S., Wallace-Schutzman, F., & Wiggers, T. T. (1982). Burnout among career development professionals: Preliminary findings and implications. *Personnel and Guidance Journal, 60,* 435–439.

Frederick, C. J. (1997). Current thinking about crisis or psychological interventions in United States disasters. *Mass Emergencies, 2,* 43–49.

Fried, M. (1963). Grieving for a lost home. In J. Duhl (Ed.), *The urban condition: People and policy in the metropolis* (pp. 151–171). New York: Basic Books.

Hartsough, D., & Myers, D. (1985). *Disaster work and mental health: Prevention and control of stress among workers.* Rockville, MD: National Institute of Mental Health.

Harvey, M. R. (1985). *Exemplary rape crisis centers: A cross-site analysis and case studies.* Rockville, MD: National Institute of Mental Health.

Hodgkinson, P. E., & Shepherd, M. A. (1994). The impact of disaster support work. *Journal of Traumatic Stress, 7,* 587–600.

Hunter, A. (1974). *Symbolic communities.* Chicago: University of Chicago Press.

Hunter, A. (1975). The loss of community: An empirical test through replication. *American Sociological review, 40,* 537–552.

Keane, T. M., Scott, W. O., Chavoya, G. A., Lamparski, D. M., & Fairbank, J. A. (1985). Social support in Vietnam veterans with post-traumatic stress disorder: A comparative analysis. *Journal of Consulting and Clinical Psychology, 53*(1), 95–102.

McCammon, S. L., & Allison, E. J. (1995) Debriefing and treating emergency workers. In C. R. Figley (Ed.), *Compassion fatigue: Coping with secondary traumatic stress disorder in those who treat the traumatized* (pp. 115–130). New York: Brunner/Mazel.

Mitchell, J. T. (1983). When disaster strikes . . . the critical incident stress debriefing process. *Journal of Emergency Medical Services, 8,* 36–39.

Mitchell, J. T., & Everly, G. S. (1995). *Critical incident stress debriefing: The basic course workbook.* Ellicott City, MD: Critical Incident Stress Foundation.

Munroe, J. F., Shay, J., Fisher, L., Makary, C., Rapperport, K., & Zimering, R. (1995). Preventing compassion fatigue: A team treatment model. In C. R. Figley (Ed.), *Compassion fatigue: Coping with secondary traumatic stress disorder in those who treat the traumatized* (pp. 209–213). New York: Brunner/Mazel.

Myers, D. (1989a). *Training manual: Disaster mental health.* Sacramento, CA: California Department of Mental Health.

Myers, D. (1989b–2001). Unpublished training materials.

Myers, D. (1992). *Hurricane Andrew disaster field office stress management program after action report.* Miami, FL: Federal Emergency Management Agency.

Myers, D. (1993). *Disaster worker stress management: Planning and training issues.* Washington, DC: Federal Emergency Management Agency and Center for Mental Health Services.

Myers, D. (1994a). *A stress management program for FEMA disaster workers: Program description, operational guidelines, and training plan.* Washington, DC: Federal Emergency Management Agency and Center for Mental Health Services.

Myers D. (1994b). *Disaster response and recovery: A handbook for mental health professionals.* Rockville, MD: Center for Mental Health Services.

Myers, D., & Zunin, L. M. (1993a). *After action report: 1993 Florida wither storms disaster field office stress management program.* Tampa, FL: Federal Emergency Management Agency.

Myers, D., & Zunin, L. M. (1993b). *After action report: 1993 Midwest Floods stress Management Program.* Kansas City, MO: Federal Emergency Management Agency.

Myers, D., & Zunin, L. M. (1994a). *Stress management program after action report: 1994 Northridge earthquake.* Pasadena, CA: Federal Emergency Management Agency and California Governor's Office of Emergency Services.

Myers, D., & Zunin, L. M. (1994b). *Stress management program for disaster workers: A national cadre of stress management personnel: Training manual.* Atlanta, GA: Federal Emergency Management Agency.

National Institute of Mental Health. (1987a). *Prevention and control of stress among emergency workers: A pamphlet for managers.* Rockville, MD: Author.

National Institute of Mental Health. (1987b). *Prevention and control of stress among emergency workers: a pamphlet for workers.* Rockville, MD: Author.

Pearlman, L. A., & MacIan, P. S. (1995). Vicarious traumatization: An empirical study of the effects of trauma work on trauma therapists. *Professional Psychology: Research and Practice, 26,* 558–565.

Pearlman, L. A., & Saakvitne, K. W. (1995). Treating therapists with vicarious traumatization and secondary traumatic stress disorders. In C. R. Figley (Ed.), *Compassion fatigue: Coping with secondary traumatic stress disorder in those who treat the traumatized* (pp. 150–177). New York: Brunner/Mazel.

Raphael, B., Singh, B., Bradbury, B., & Lambert, F. (1984). Who helps the helpers? The effects of a disaster on the rescue workers. *Omega, 14,* 9–20.

Rodolfa, E. R., Kraft, W. A., & Reilley, R. R. (1988). Stressors of professionals and trainees at

APA-approved counseling and VA medical center internship sites. *Professional Psychology: Research and Practice, 19,* 43–49.

Rosenschweig, M. A., & Vaslow, P. K. (1992). Recommendations for reduction of stress among FEMA disaster workers. Rockville, MD: National Institute of Mental Health.

Solomon, S. D. (1986). Enhancing social support for disaster victims. In B. J. Sowder & M. Lystad (Eds.), *Disaster and mental health: Contemporary perspectives and innovations in services to disaster victims* (pp. 115–129). Washington, DC: American Psychiatric Press.

Staub, E. (1989). *The roots of evil: The origins of genocide and other group violence.* Cambridge, U.K.: Cambridge University Press.

Suttles, G. (1972). *Social construction of communities.* Chicago: University of Chicago Press.

Trainer, P., & Bolin, R. (1976). Persistent effects of disasters on daily activities: A cross-cultural comparison. *Mass Emergencies, 1,* 279–290.

Varblow, P. (1994). Stress management. In *Project rebound: 2nd quarterly report.* Los Angeles: Los Angeles County Department of Mental Health.

Wee, D. (1994). *Disaster training for crisis counselors.* Unpublished training Materials.

Wee, D., Johnson, K., & Myers, D. (1997). Disaster mental health: Impact on workers. In *Trauma in the lives of children* (pp. 257–263). Alameda, CA: Hunter House Press.

Wee, D., & Myers, D. (2002). Response of mental health workers following disaster: The Oklahoma City bombing. In C. R. Figley (Ed.), *Treating compassion fatigue* (Vol. II; pp. x–x); New York: Brunner/Mazel.

Winget, C. N., & Umbenhauer, S. L. (1982). Disaster planning: The mental health worker as 'victim-by-proxy." *Journal of Health and Human Resources Administration, 4,* 363–373.

Yassen, J. (1995). Preventing secondary traumatic stress disorder. In C. R. Figley (Ed.), *Compassion fatigue: Coping with secondary Traumatic stress disorder in those who threat the traumatized* (pp. 178–208). New York: Brunner/Mazel.

Epilogue

CHARLES R. FIGLEY

In this final section of the book, I will review the suggestions made for *doing something* about compassion fatigue, along with my own. Because the book is devoted to treating compassion fatigue, we presented the theoretical and empirical justification for doing so in the first section. That section also includes the first step in doing something about the problem: taking the self-test for helpers. This test helps us determine the degree to which we are at risk of developing burnout and developing compassion fatigue, and the degree to which we derive satisfaction from our compassionate efforts.

STRATEGIES FOR TREATMENT

Contributors to the book present dozens of treatment innovations, starting with the comprehensive, and systematic Accelerated Recovery Program noted in Chapter 6. This program, although not the chapter, incorporates most of the content in the chapters that follow it. This program of treatment has been tested now with dozens of professionals. The Employee Assistance Program of the U.S. Federal Bureau of Investigation and numerous other public and private offices have used it. One of the reasons for its success is that it is both eclectic and flexible. If one self-soothing method does not work, another is tried. If one method for reviewing and processing the traumatic event is not effective, others will be tried until one best suited for the professional works.

Fundamental to all efforts to help us survive the sadness and depression of working with the suffering is humor. It should be quite clear after reading Chapter 7 that humor has both an immediate and a long-term effect when working with the suffering. As Moran notes in that chapter, humor is the universal cure-all in that it is considered by many as encouraging emotional expression at a time when it is vital to do so. Humor enhances social support because it is more fun to be around funny people. Humor allows sad, discouraging, and generally distressing situations to be reframed in a more acceptable way. Certainly humor lowers stress and provides ways of handling difficult situations. Indeed, developing our capacity for humor is a way of preparing for adversity.

White (Chapter 9) notes the requirements for self-care when away from home and especially in a violent environment. Baranowsky shows us how we sometimes attend to our own needs by silencing the very person we are devoted to helping. These approaches to noticing and helping ourselves while delivering traumatology services suggests the major importance of preparedness and prevention.

STRATEGIES FOR PREVENTION

Most chapters in this book discussed the implications for avoiding or preventing compassion fatigue, such as developing our humor capacity. The final chapter, however, is especially systematic about planning and preparing for disaster work—especially large–scale disasters. Indeed, this chapter is so systematic that the Green Cross Projects organization has adopted it as part of its resource book for members preparing to be deployed to a disaster.

Institutional Policies and Procedures

Although the authors note briefly, an area that receives little attention herein is institutional attention to preventing compassion fatigue. Recently, for example, Maslach and Leiter (1998) suggested that policies and procedures should take into account all that causes distress and all that takes it away. They argue for a work-sensitive approach that ensures employees' personal needs are considered in providing health care, vacation and leave policies, strategies for mental health promotion, and other effective strategies. They are the latest in a series of experts on burnout promoting a more friendly and sensitive workplace. Unfortunately, Maslach and Leiter do not know about the wide variety of agencies and offices that deploy professionals in helping the suffering. The secret world of law enforcement, for example, is often the last to admit and do something about compassion fatigue, although that situation is changing (Figley, 1999).

Building on what is discussed throughout this volume, I offer the following suggestions to departments managing professionals who may be at risk of compassion fatigue:

1. *Awareness of risks and costs of working with the suffering and workers' families.* Among other things, there is a recognition that good workers hurt sometimes and that good families hurt with them and somehow enable them to return to work in better spirits.
2. *Commitment to lower the risks and costs.* There is a constant source of support of the troops in showing that the department is attempting to lower the risks of compassion fatigue and family burnout (Figley, 1997). Moreover, when workers and families are affected, the department dispatches the best support possible to help them recover as quickly as possible.
3. *Adequate applicant screening for resilience and awareness.* Those most at risk are those without resiliency—both as individuals and as families. Moreover, those who thrive in this work are especially aware of the affect the work has on them and on their families. As a result, there is faster corrective action and more acceptance of the duty-related stress and the actions necessary to deal with it.
4. *Adequate policies and procedures to educate and protect workers.* Every orientation for new workers and every postincident debriefing should include information about critical incident stress and compassion fatigue. There should be sufficient education and effective and informed procedures for handling stress and its cumulative effects.
5. *Work group attitudes and action plans.* When considering the work group, partners on patrol should also be knowledgeable about and effective in handling critical incident stress, compassion fatigue, and family burnout. There appear to be seven axioms in operation in this area:
   a. *The 5:1 ratio rule.* For every three hours of discussing a case that is traumatic, there should be one hour devoted to personal processing. This may take the form of non-work conversation over a beer off duty, it may be a formal postincident debriefing or humor regarding the nature of the work, or it may entail other activities that result in attention to the self.
   b. *CISD/M plans and actions.* Critical incident stress debriefings and stress management are now part of every modern emergency response department in most developed countries or in the leading departments everywhere. It is recognized today as the single most popular crisis intervention following highly stressful events. The theory is that if workers are able to discuss freely with fellow workers or others the event, they will avoid the predictable acute stress and more troubling posttraumatic stress disorder or compassion fatigue. Workers are urged to first summarize the facts and just the facts of the critical incident. Next they are urged to discuss their thoughts and reactions during and following the incident and the traumatic stress symptoms they cause. Each team should have at least one person trained in debriefing and defusing methods. Ideally, everyone would be trained

and work with any other group that needs help.

c. *Humor and other stress reduction methods.* Gallows humor is common throughout the world among groups dealing with stressful work. As noted earlier and in Chapter 7, humor plays a major role in reducing stress because it causes a release of endorphins in the brain. These hormones are associated with the class pleasure response and frequently override fear, depression, and inaction. In sufficient dosages, they even enhance the immune system, thus keeping us healthier. Work groups should recognize those activities that result in a reduction of stress and laugh more frequently. Most often, however, it is necessary for the group to adopt additional methods such as team sports, card playing, going to sporting events, and (if acceptable) forms of prayer or other spiritual and meditative activities that lower stress levels.

d. *Low tolerance for substance abuse.* "Friends don't let friends who drink drive." Neither should fellow workers. We must recognize that abuse of any substance may be a replacement for more effective stress-reduction methods. Team members need to speak up, take chances, and be honest with fellow workers.

e. *Facilitation of coworker health and self-care.* Similarly, fellow team members should be like siblings and promote health, healthy living, and self-care. This takes many forms, including serving as a role model to younger workers.

f. *Individual actions.* In addition to actions that should be taken by departments and teams to prevent compassion fatigue and their causes, each individual worker should take action on his or her own behalf.

g. *Letting go of work.* Workers need to become more effective in strategies for disengaging from work. Many helpers' lives are shaped by their work. It can be all-consuming. Yet, in order to build a firewall between ourselves and potential career-killing stress, boundaries should be built. "Leave the office at the office and the ranch at the ranch." The worker may need help from her or his family to keep with this useful tenet.

Some workers at a recent workshop shared their strategies:

"When I get in my car and say to myself, 'this is my car and not the squad car.'" By doing so he recalls the fact that he is not being paid now, there will be plenty of bad guys when he returns to work.

"The photo does it." Another takes out or imagines that he takes out and looks at a photo of his family. It reminds him of what is important in life and to not dirty his home with the trash from work.

"It's the family, stupid" is a statement one worker says to herself to remind her of her priorities.

Strategies for Gaining a Sense of Achievement and Satisfaction

Another major factor in reducing compassion stress, especially at the end of the workday, is acquiring a sense of achievement and satisfaction. Workers do this in a variety of ways. One way is to establish achievable standards of work performance so that if setbacks happen, workers can view their work in a larger context than a single incident. Allowing and welcoming support from others is also important. Most often our colleagues offer reassurance not just to be nice but in return for similar reassurances when it will be needed in the future.

Again, a recent workshop produced these strategies that help reduce compassion stress and retain a sense of job satisfaction:

I say "I am only one person" to remind others or myself that it takes many people many days to achieve a difficult goal. (Experienced critical care nurse)

My instincts are to be very self-critical and get stuck there. I force myself to go to my file with copies of my achievements and commendations. It's made me cry at times, the relief it's brought me. (Recently retired school counselor)

I put my self in the hands of Jesus. I ask for direction and relax until that happens. Most often it's the next day at work. (Police captain)

Strategies for Acquiring Adequate Rest and Relaxation

There are many books written about the importance of a solid night's deep sleep, the need for regular exercise, good nutrition such as a low fat diet, and adequate time off to enjoy life's joys. Yet so many workers and their families believe they have insufficient time. They need to develop a schedule that includes these activities. Much time is wasted on strategies for lowering stress when these measures increase our tolerance for it.

The Perfect Stress Reduction Methods

Everyone must find the perfect methods. These are fast, reliable, discrete, and manageable. Any bookstore includes a large number of books on stress reduction. Workers and their adult family members should shop for the best method for them.

FINAL POINT

Some will see the title of this book and think that they do not need it. They have fooled themselves into believing that either the compassion stress they feel is inevitable and can not be managed effectively or they have learned ways to detach themselves. In his moving and passionate testimonial about the real-life emotional challenges of being a physician, Hilfiker (1985) noted the shortcuts to avoiding what we now call Compassion Fatigue. He observed those who kid themselves into believing that they can avoid it by using any one or a combination of strategies. Clinical detachment is one strategy. Efficiency and productivity is another distraction away from the humanity of the patient. And of course, focusing on the job byproducts of prestige, authority, hierarchy, and wealth in the role of healer, gives the false sense that we can also be compassionate.

REFERENCES

Figley, C. R. (1997). *Burnout in families: The systemic costs of caring.* Boca Raton, FL: CRC Press.

Figley, C. R. (1999). Police compassion fatigue (PCF): Theory, research, assessment, treatment, and prevention. In J. Violanti (Ed.), *Police trauma: Psychological aftermath of civilian combat,* pp. 38–51. Springfield, IL: Charles C. Thomas.

Gallo, F. (1998). *Energy psychology: Explorations at the interface of energy, cognition, behavior, and health.* Boca Raton, FL: CRC Press.

Hilfiker, D. (1985). *Healing the wounds: A physician looks at his work.* New York: Pantheon.

Index